LIFE OF TOM HORN

THE WESTERN FRONTIER LIBRARY

LIFE OF
TOM HORN

*Government Scout
and Interpreter*

WRITTEN BY HIMSELF

TOGETHER WITH HIS LETTERS
AND STATEMENTS BY HIS FRIENDS

A Vindication

With an Introduction
by **Dean Krakel**

UNIVERSITY OF OKLAHOMA PRESS
Norman

Life of Tom Horn is Volume 26 in the Western Frontier Library.

Library of Congress Catalog Card Number: 64-20758

ISBN 978-0-8061-1044-8 (paper)

15   16   17   18   19

INTRODUCTION
BY DEAN KRAKEL

I WAS BORN and grew to young manhood in northern Colorado. East of Ault, where we lived, there is a high grass-covered plain. It had been buffalo range at one time—a vast treeless expanse edged with miles and miles of nothing but blue horizon. This country is filled with remnants of days gone by: dried buffalo horns, crumbling homesteads, windmill towers, stretches of barbed wire, parts of wagons strewn about, and a maze of trails—yesterday's symbols of fighting today's elements.

Then too, there were Indian campsites with tell-tale tipi rings, fire holes, pieces of flint, and broken stone implements. Poking about as a boy, I could always muster up visions of the Indian and his free way of living.

Ault is located in a richly irrigated district, fed by snow water from the towering Front Range of the Rockies. These mountains begin down around Pikes Peak and run north through the country, then west to the Medicine Bows and Laramie Plains. The sweep of this range is one of the most thrilling panoramas in the world: a chain of giants, blue-white and translucent, telescoped by the crispness of high altitude. It was a wonderful country to have lived in—rich in history, natural beauty, and strong people.

Having been a huge cattle range at one time, this area was well known to Tom Horn, who had a brother, Charles, living in Boulder and a sister in Briggsdale (twenty miles east of Ault). The business of being a stock detective meant trips to Denver and Cheyenne, so he was around quite often.

Tom was born in Missouri and grew up in the post–

Civil War violence of the Middle West. He was impressive in appearance, being well over six feet tall, with sharp, clean facial features. His eyes however, were small and penetrating. In reminiscing about the gunman, one cowboy recalled, "Tom could stare a hole straight through you." He was meticulous about his dress and everything he owned, especially his horse. Tom read widely, but most of all he enjoyed seeing an ornery bronc and a good rider tangle in the sagebrush. He was an admirer of Theodore Roosevelt. T.R.'s philosophy of walking softly and carrying a big stick apparently appealed to him. Physically Horn was lean and muscular; he sat well in the saddle and was an excellent calf roper. I have known old-timers around Ault who said they rode with Horn and shared the same pot of beans with him. One claimed to possess his rifle. Most of them declared emphatically that he hadn't "hung" in Cheyenne, on that dismal November day back in '03; it had all been faked.

Since Dad's brother lived in Cheyenne, quite often we drove the forty miles in our model "A." I can still see Cheyenne as it appeared then. Once we had crossed the state line and topped the last hill, "there she was," scattered along bottomland and shrouded in layers of gray smoke. Seeing the place always gave me a pleasant sensation. The name itself was magic. It had personality. The wind was always blowing and a freight train or two was to be heard wailing in the distance, building up steam for the struggle up cantankerous Sherman Hill. The store windows were filled with saddles, horse blankets, boots, and bright Western clothing. A trip to Cheyenne wouldn't have been complete without a tour through the old majestic-looking Union Pacific Depot and a long nostalgic look at the Deadwood Stage Coach encased there.

No city was quite like Cheyenne during Frontier Days.

Introduction

As a boy, I suspected that during the last week of July all the cowboys, Indians, and cavalrymen in the world were assembled for this annual extravaganza. In those days of the 1930's, the U.S. Cavalry was on its last leg, but you wouldn't have known it from the number of companies there. Each year the parade had a float portraying the hanging of Tom Horn, and generally riding close by was T. Joe Cahill. Joe had been Horn's hangman. The old lawman always wore a big grin and waved his Stetson as he pranced his horse up and down the street, nodding to acquaintances.

Years later I got to know T. Joe, and he, more than anyone else, whetted my interest in the life of Tom Horn. While archivist and assistant professor in the Western History Department at the University of Wyoming Library (1952–56), I would come to Cheyenne and spend hours with Joe at the Elks' Club. He talked, and I listened. One of the most dramatic Western accounts ever told, in my opinion, was his recollection of the hanging. Tom Horn had requested that T. Joe be his executioner. Among Westerners at that time, no tribute could have been higher. A printed version of the story appeared in the *Denver Post's* "Empire Magazine."

There were others involved in the final episode of Horn's life: Judge T. Blake Kennedy, attorney Clyde Watts, newspaperman Charley Thompson, Dr. George Johnston, Governor Fenimore Chatterton, all of Cheyenne, and rancher Andrew Ross of Pierce, Colorado. I had the privilege of interviewing all of them, but none had the spirit and sincerity of T. Joe Cahill.

I felt that I knew the Tom Horn case as well as anyone could, five decades removed; yet when my book *The Saga of Tom Horn* appeared in 1954, I found myself caught in undercurrents of controversy. The *Saga* was primarily a compilation of source materials arranged chronologically. One thing I had hoped to do was set the record straight, since a farrago of Tom Horn misinformation existed.

My book caused anxiety and trouble. The fact that the biggest newspaper in the Rocky Mountain region had been sued for doing exactly what I had done put me in hot water, so several pages were cut out and new pages tipped in.

In my research of the case I found gaps. Undoubtedly Tom Horn had killed four men, two in Colorado, two in Wyoming. Yet the important question remained unanswered: "Did he kill fourteen-year-old Willie Nickell, near the Nickell ranch at Iron Mountain, Wyoming, on the morning of July 18, 1901?" Horn was a stock detective schooled by the Pinkertons. He had fought the Apaches as a government scout and served in Cuba during the Spanish-American War. He was a professional assassin capable of the most brutal killing, yet for the greater part of his life he was quiet and mannerly. When he drank too much, he became loud, caroused the red-light districts, and was filled with quarrelsome braggadocio. Tom apparently was never completely attuned to the changing times—he really didn't like the world in which he lived.

It is my belief that whoever killed little Willie did so mistakenly. Tom Horn was too experienced a bounty man to have committed such a fatal error. Yet, it appears that facts of the long trial over the killing held in Cheyenne's Laramie County Court House might have been stacked against him from the outset. Obviously he knew a great deal. Too many key witnesses weren't heard from in a satisfactory manner. Among them was Tom's occasional girl friend, Glendolene Kimmell, the school teacher from the Iron Mountain District. John C. Coble, a wealthy rancher and admirer of Horn, was another. Coble had become embroiled with Kels Nickell, Willie's father, and they had had a gut-cutting feud. Neighbors throughout the country frequently had open disputes with one another, and tradition says that Willie and some of his classmates at the Iron Mountain School were anything but chums. These attitudes obviously mirrored family moods. There are other things, tragic as they may be, that could be discussed; to boil them all down, the motive for the crime was never clearly established.

The Joe LeFors–Charles Ohnhause so-called "Confession of Tom Horn" was a fiasco. LeFors, a deputy U.S. marshal, had baited Horn into making loose, barroom-like conversation, while Ohnhause, a stenographer, hid in an adjacent room and listened. Leslie Snow, a Cheyenne officer, joined Ohnhause in placing his ear to the door. In spite of Tom Horn's having been somewhat boozed up, what the stenographer wrote down, and LeFors and Snow swore was the absolute truth, put him behind bars. I doubt that such a ruse would be accepted in today's courts. Certainly Joe LeFors' jurisdiction in the case would be hotly contested.

Tom's own testimony was strong, and he parried well and openly with the prosecution. His ability to recall names, places, and dates was full evidence of his intelligence. Cowboy friends brought to the stand by his attorneys unintentionally hurt his chances with the jury. In the case of Otto Plaga, testifying to Horn's whereabouts on July 18, the prosecution cleverly tied the witness in knots. In the end, Plaga's veracity was disputed.

I question the pre-trial counseling Horn obviously received, especially regarding statements made to LeFors. This was jurisprudence quicksand, and, once in, there was no getting out. The defense attorneys retained by Tom Horn's backers were to have been the most brilliant battery of attorneys ever assembled in the Frontier State. Yet Walter Stoll and Associates, for the prosecution, out-talked, out-maneuvered them, won the case, and heard the death sentence pronounced.

There were other important factors that were against Horn: The jury was, by occupation if for no other reason, hostile to the well-heeled interests Horn was accused of representing. Then, too, this was the heyday for throwing darts at big capital in any form, not excluding owners of baronial-like livestock empires. The press, which was tainted with the yellow journalism of the period, gave the man on trial the business by rooting out details that were irrelevant but none the less damning. By the time the final saga of Horn's life was well under way, the Denver and Cheyenne presses, booming in circulation, had molded public opinion into a gigantic mountain of negativism. Politically, a new trial was out of the question.

I have always believed (and it is not my idea singly) that Tom was "handled" for reasons other than his own salvation. Yet not once during a long confinement did he crack or hint of telling tales. One supporter of Tom Horn who lived on the Laramie Plains was so cynical about it that he even suspected that the jail break after Horn had been sentenced was nothing but a desperate frontal hoax. After all, Horn could have gotten killed.

When November 20, the day Tom Horn was to die, finally arrived, Cheyenne took on a carnival atmosphere. Saloons did a land-office trade and a lot of card-table money was bet that he wouldn't swing. Hundreds jammed the streets and, as the hour for the execution drew near, pressed around Laramie County Courthouse. Cordons of special police were summoned to keep the onlookers at a distance. A machine-gun was mounted on top of the county building—just in case. A few blocks away, in the Capitol Building, the governor pondered the magnanimity of a stay of execution.

A high board fence had been hastily erected to veil the gallows and scaffolding from public view. Shortly before the announced time of execution, newspapermen, law officers, and friends of Horn who had been invited to witness the grim event quietly filed into the arena. There were delays which must have been exasperating; a northerly wind blowing over a skift of frozen snow added to the misery of the hour.

At last all was set. When Tom Horn was escorted from his cell, he was handcuffed and showed no signs of being distraught. During his last minutes of life he joshed, heard a mournful railroad ballad sung by two dear friends, and then listened intently as a churchman droned a message asking for eternal forgiveness. From down below, where knees were beginning to buckle, there came muffled sounds of sobbing. As the hangman readied the black hood to slip over his head and another fumbled with the noose, Tom Horn, surveying the witnesses, said icily: ". . . that's the sickest-looking lot of damned sheriffs I ever saw."

The *Life of Tom Horn, Government Scout and Interpreter, A Vindication,* by Himself, was published in 1904 by John C. Coble. The book is not really a vindication. It is none the less excellent biography. While the appendix is spiked with interesting letters, testimonials, and transcripts, they don't really add up to anything in the way of an explanation of what happened in Wyoming. The only person who could have written that story was Tom Horn, and he was "hanged by the neck until dead."

PREFACE

IN PREPARING this autobiography for publication, there has been no attempt to make it literature. No sentence has been added; and no alterations have been made, save to avoid ambiguity, and to promote clearness and strength. All changes have been kept strictly in harmony with the style of the author. For the convenience of the reader the manuscript has been broken into chapters; and of course the chapter headings were not original with Horn.

For obvious reasons, the Westernisms, and even the slang, have been retained. Horn was thoroughly Western. Born and reared in the West—if, indeed, it can be correctly said that he was "reared"—he passed his entire life here, with the exception of the period of his service to his country during the war with Spain; and, being Western, his conversation was replete with local expressions, not always elegant, yet rarely profane and never vulgar.

I wish to repeat this: *Tom Horn was seldom profane.* And this association will be sustained by those who really knew him—a fact which alone serves to disprove that so-called famous "confession," the language of which smacks very much more of the talk of those who edited the "notes taken on the spot."

But, as I have suggested, there have been no additions made to this autobiography, and such alterations as have been made do not alter the text in any material manner. Rather, it has been the object, in editing the manuscript, to present the writer's life-story in his own pleasing style, with his own strong personality gleaming through the whole.

Note his unerring memory, even to minute details; the objects of his hero-worship and the sort of men they were; his unconsciously expressed forgiveness for injuries; his untiring faithfulness to duty under the most trying circumstances; his strong sense of justice; and note particularly that although his manuscript was written to hurry lagging time, and for the private perusal of his friends only, it contains not the slightest strain of vulgarity. No expurgation has been necessary.

This autobiography is now given in book form for general circulation, in response to an insistent public demand. The fact that such a "Life" had been written had no sooner become known than I was besieged by his personal friends and acquaintances and by interested readers of the published reports of the trial, for the publication of the autobiography prepared by Tom Horn. Letters reached me by every mail from almost every state and territory of the Union; and I may be permitted here to state that there was scarcely a letter among them all which did not declare a belief in the innocence of Horn, "after carefully considering the details of the case."

Telegrams and letters reached me, also, from daily newspapers, monthly magazines and publishing houses, making propositions for "exclusive publishing rights."

And so I have yielded. In your hands is the book. For it, is asked a reading without prejudice. For its writer, is asked that which, during his closing years, was denied him—*fair play*.

JOHN C. COBLE

Iron Mountain Ranch, Bosler, Wyoming
March 1, 1904

CONTENTS

LIFE OF TOM HORN

CHAPTER ONE

Horn's Boyhood — His Dog "Shed," — Bennie, the Model Boy —
Horn Leaves Home for the West

I WAS BORN near Memphis, Scotland County, Missouri, November 21, 1860—a troublesome time, to be sure; and anyone born in Missouri is bound to see trouble—so says Bill Nye.

Up to the time I left home I suppose I had more trouble than any man or boy in Missouri. We had Sunday schools and church, and as my mother was a good old-fashioned Campbellite, I was supposed to go to church and Sunday school, as did most of the boys and girls in the neighborhood. I had three brothers and four sisters, and there was not one of them but acted as though he really liked to go to those places. I had nothing particular against going, if it had not been for the 'coon, turkey, quail, rabbits, prairie chickens, 'possums, skunks, and other game of that kind, with once in a season a fat, corn-fed deer; and they were all neglected to such an extent by the rest of the family, that it kept me busy most every Sunday, and many nights through the week, to do what I considered right in trying to keep on proper terms with the game.

I would steal out the gun and take the dog and hunt all day Sunday and many a night through the week, knowing full well that whenever I did show up at home I would get a whipping or a scolding from my mother or a regular thumping from father.

My mother was a tall, powerful woman, and she would

3

whip me and cry, and tell me how much good she was trying to do me by breaking me of my Indian ways, so she called them (though I had never seen an Indian, and did not know what their ways were). Then if a skunk or 'coon or fox came along and carried off one of her chickens during the night, at daylight she would wake me and give me the gun, and tell me to take old "Shedrick," the dog, and go and follow up the varmint and kill it.

For a kid, I must have been a very successful hunter, for when our neighbors would complain of losing a chicken (and that was a serious loss to them), mother would tell them that whenever any varmint bothered her hen-roost, she just sent out Tom and "Shed," and when they came back they always brought the pelt of the varmint with them.

To this day, I believe mother thought the dog was of more importance against varmints than I was. But "Shedrick" and I both understood that I was the better, for I could climb any tree in Missouri, and dig frozen ground with a pick, and follow cold tracks in the mud or snow, and knew more than the dog in a good many ways. Still, I think, even yet, that there never was a better dog. I always thought "Shed" could whip any dog in Missouri (and at that time I did not know there was any other place than Missouri, except, perhaps, Iowa. I knew of Iowa, because one of our neighbors came from there). But I had many a hard fight myself to keep up the reputation of old "Shed," for as he began to get old and wise, I do believe he thought I would always help him. Once in a while Dad would go to an election or public sale or horse race or something, and "Shed" would go with him and sometimes the dog would get whipped. When he did get whipped, he always came home looking pretty badly used up, and after an occurrence of that kind, "Shed" would not leave me for days.

4

I recollect a family of boys named Griggs who had what they always claimed was the best 'coon dog and the best fighter in the world (Missouri or our neighborhood was the world to them), and now I think he must have been a good dog and no mistake; but at that time I did certainly hate him. Whenever the Griggs boys and I ran together, we had a dog fight, and the termination of the meeting was always a fight between Sam Griggs and myself. I also distinctly recollect that on nearly every occasion "Shed" and I both went home pretty badly used up. Sam Griggs always said I helped "Shed" and he would try to keep me from doing so; then Sam and I would mix. I guess we fought a hundred times and he always quit when he "had his satisfy" for I never did nor could lick him.

The Griggs dog was named "Sandy" (because he was yellow, I suppose), and my argument always was that my dog "Shed" knew more than "Sandy." To illustrate, once Sam Griggs was up in a tree to shake off a 'coon for "Sandy" to kill. A limb of the tree broke and down came Sam, and "Sandy" jumped on him and bit his ear and bit him in the arm and shoulder and used Sam up pretty badly before he could get "Sandy" to understand that he was not a 'coon or a wild cat. I always claimed that "Shed" would have had more sense than to jump on me if I had been fool enough to fall out of a tree.

My mother was always anxious to have all the children go to school during the winter months, and I always had to go, or to start anyway; but all the natural influences of the country were against my acquiring much of an education. During the summer we had to work on the farm, and work hard and long hours putting in crops and tending to them. Thus I had little legitimate time to fish and hunt bee trees. So when winter came and the work was all done and the

5

crops all in, I wanted to go and look after the game, but as I was ordered to go to school, I had to go.

The first natural influence of any importance was that the school house was a mile from the house we lived in, and there was always more or less snow on the ground in winter, and on the trail to school I would always be finding fresh rabbit or 'coon or cat tracks crossing the trail to school. I never could cross a fresh track, for I would see one and the rest of the children would pay no attention to it, so, I would follow it a little ways just to see which way it went, and then I would go on a little farther, and then I would say to myself, "I will be late for school and get licked." Then an overpowering desire to get that rabbit or 'coon or wild cat, as it happened to be, would overcome me, and I would go back in the orchard behind the house, call the dog, and as he would come running to me, the stuff for school was all off, and "Shed" and I would go hunting. So you see, had the school house been nearer, I could have gotten there a good deal oftener than I did.

I could never keep my mind on my books when I was at school, for if it happened to commence to snow I could not help thinking about how fine it would be to trail 'coon on the morrow, and I would speculate a good deal more on the skins of the varmints I could catch, and could see far more advantage in having a good string of pelts than in learning to read, write, and cipher.

Things were beginning to get rather binding on me about this time anyway, as a cousin named Ben Markley came to live with us. He was a son of my mother's sister, and I guess he was the best boy in the world. Oh, how many hundred times I was whipped or scolded and asked by father, or mother or school teacher, why I did not do as Bennie did.

Ben never forgot to wash or comb his hair. He never

swore. He could walk to school and not get his boots muddy. One pair of boots would last him as long as four pairs would me. He never whispered in school; never used tobacco. He never went hunting nor fishing on Sunday, and never wanted to. He never had any fights and he would talk of an evening about what the lesson would be in Sunday school next Sunday. Those were some of his good points, but not all, for he was held up as a model of perfection by everybody. Of course my opinion of him was different.

I knew he could not shoot. He could not climb a tree. He did not know a 'coon track from a cow track. He was afraid of bees when a bee tree was to be robbed. He said 'coon skins were nasty, and skunks he could not go at all. He did not know how to bait a hook to fish. He could not swim, was afraid of horses, and once he struck old "Shedrick" with a piece of hoop pole. I had known a long time before this that he was a failure, so far as I estimated boys, so when he struck the sharer of my joys and sorrows, I jumped onto him. I was about thirteen and he was about seventeen, but I had him whipped before my mother and the rest of the family could get me off him. Dad was there but he did not try to help the women pull me off, for I do think Ben was a little too good for him.

Well, after that, "Shed" and I left him alone and he put in a good deal of his spare time leaving us alone. That row with Bennie made me no favorite with the women folks, something that was of little importance to me.

The climax of my home life came the next spring. Some emigrants were going along the road, and behind the wagons were two boys on one horse, bareheaded, and one of them had an old, single-barreled shot gun. They met "Shed" and me on the road and stopped to talk to us. I remarked that a man who shot game with a shot gun was no good. The oldest one of the boys asked me if I called myself a man, and the answer that I made him caused them both to get off their old mare and tie her to the fence. The younger and smaller of the two held the gun and the big one and I started to scrap. Things were looking so unfavorable to the boy I was fighting with that the smaller boy laid his gun down on the ground and was going to help his brother. He gave me a kick in the jaw as a preliminary, but he never smiled again. Old "Shed" sprang and caught him and threw him down and bit him in the arm and shoulder in doing it. That stopped the fight between the other boy and me, as I had to let the big one go to take care that "Shed" did not hurt the small one too much.

Well, I took the dog off and told them they had better get on their old mare and go and get the rest of the family if they wanted to win a fight, and then the big one picked up the gun and helped the small boy on the mare, and he raised the gun and shot poor, old "Shed." "Shed" whined and I could scarcely believe such a thing had been done. The big boy then got on the mare with the other one and they went off at a gallop. I carried "Shed" home, which was about a quarter of a mile away, and he died that night.

I believe that was the first and only real sorrow of my life.

Dad got on his horse and went and overtook the emigrant train that night, and I guess there was "something doin" for he came home that night before "Shed" died and he was pretty badly done up himself. Dad was called the hardest man to whip in Northwest Missouri, but when he came home that night he looked to me like a man who had had at least what I would have called enough.

I was about fourteen years old by this time and I wanted to go somewhere. I had heard of California and thought that would be a good place to go. Dad and I had a disagreement one day, and he had the trace of a single buggy harness in his hand, and he struck at me with it. I grabbed it and then the fight was on.

Well I tried to do something, but the old man was too much for me. When I saw I was in for a daisy, I told him to just help himself, as it was his last time, for I was going to leave home.

He helped himself, and when he got through, he said: "Now, if you are going to leave home, go! and just remember that the last time the old man whipped you, he gave you a good one. Go," he said, "but ask your mother for a lunch to take with you. You will be back by night if you start in the morning, and if you take a lunch with you, you won't miss your dinner."

This happened at the barn. I lay down on the hay and lay there all night. Next morning, mother and the girls carried me to the house and put me in bed where I lay for a week. Dad had done his work well.

As soon as I could get around, I sold my rifle for $11.00, kissed my mother for the last time in my life, went out and took a look at old "Shedrick's" grave, got a lunch, and started West.

CHAPTER TWO

Horn Becomes Overland Mail and Stage Driver — Night-Rider,
Boss of Quartermaster's Herd, Government Interpreter—Sieber Kills
Chugadeslona — Sieber and Horn Visit Pedro, Chief
of Friendly Apaches

I HAD, of course, heard of the West, California, Texas, and
Kansas also, but from all the geography I had picked up
at school I could not form any idea as to the location or
character of these places. I had not the faintest idea, except
that I supposed they were West.

There was no railroad there, and as I had no horse nor
team, I started on foot. I headed West, and walked and
walked day after day, stopping at farm houses to get my
grub; and many a good woman would give me a lunch to
take with me. I never went hungry, and as it was in July
and August, I could sleep anywhere. One woman, named
Mrs. Peters, made me stay all day at her house and wear
some of her son's clothes while she washed mine, and
started me out into the world again as clean as a new dollar.

When I got to Kansas City, I spent the first cent since
I left home.

I stayed in Kansas City for two days and then hired to
an employment agency to go to Newton, Kansas, to work
on the Santa Fe railroad.

I worked on the railroad at Newton about twenty-six days
and got $21.00 for it, and then went with a man named
Blades with his two teams on toward Santa Fe. Traveling
in this way and with freighters, I finally reached Santa Fe
in the latter part of 1874, just about Christmas time, in

10

fact. Up to the time I left home I had never been five miles away but once, and that was when I went to the county seat of our county—Memphis—a town of perhaps seven thousand.

By the time I got to Santa Fe I was a different boy from what I was when I left home. I was getting wisdom—and gray-backs. In January, 1875, I hired out to Mr. Murray, superintendent of the Overland Mail Route, that ran from Santa Fe to Prescott, Arizona.

I drove from Santa Fe to Los Pinos for a couple of months for $50.00 a month, and was furnished a rifle to guard the mail and protect the passengers and keep up appearances, I guess. Then I was sent on to drive from Los Pinos to Bacon Springs or Crane's Ranch. I drove a couple of months there, and in May I was called in to Santa Fe by Mr. Murray, and sent with another man to the Beaver Head Station, close to the Verde River, in Arizona, to take mules to replace some stolen by the Indians.

So within a year from the time I left home I was on the Beaver Head Creek, in the heart of the Indian country, and could speak Mexican fairly well.

My feelings were so different and my life was so different from what it was at home that it seemed to me then as though I had been all my life on a stage line.

I left Beaver Head and went down the river to Camp Verde, a government post, but I was not traveling on foot any more, for I had a good horse, saddle, bridle, and a Winchester rifle. That fall I went to work for George Hansen, herding oxen at night for the men hauling wood into Camp Verde. I got $75.00 a month for three months, and five years ago, George Hansen told me I was the best night herder he ever saw. Nearly all the teamsters and choppers were Mexicans, and at Christmas when I left there and

11

went to Prescott, I could speak Mexican as well as a native could. It had taken me just about a year to get from Santa Fe to Prescott, but I had learned more in that year than in all my previous life.

The cavalry horses for the Department of Arizona all came overland from California at that time, and they came in big bunches of about four hundred each, so I hired out to the Quartermaster to herd these horses till the different posts sent and got their allowance, Fort Whipple, right at Prescott, being the Department Headquarters. There were three of us to do the work, and as the other two were Mexicans and I was an American, although only sixteen years old, I was made boss of the Quartermaster's herd.

When all the cavalry horses were issued to the different troops of the Fifth Cavalry, I was out of a job, and Al Sieber, chief of scouts, came into Whipple from Tonto Basin and stayed a couple of weeks, and when he was getting ready to go back south he asked me how I would like to go with him as Mexican interpreter at $75.00 a month. He told me I would be with him all the time, and I was tickled to get a chance to go, so in July of '76 we set out for San Carlos Agency, where we arrived in about ten days.

My work, as I found out, was nothing at all. Sieber just wanted me because I was young and active and could travel with him all day and herd the horses at night, and do the cooking and tend to the packs and clean his gun every night; and all of this was fun for me.

The San Carlos, or Apache, Reservation was 60 miles wide and 120 miles long, and Sieber and I, with a few Indian scouts and police, were on the go all the balance of the year around on the Reservation. Sieber was keeping an eye on the peace and conduct of the Indians. Sieber spoke Apache and Mexican both, and as there were always Indians with us, I began to learn the language very rapidly.

That was a glorious time for me, as I could hunt deer and turkey to my heart's content, and if I would leave camp and be gone all night to some Indian camp, Sieber never said a word against it; in fact, he encouraged it, as he saw I was getting onto the Indians' ways and language very fast.

Sieber was one of the grandest men in the world in my eyes, and although old and white-headed and a cripple for life now, he is still a nobleman. Up to some time after this I had never seen Sieber's "mad" on in an Indian fight, and he was always, during our many years of association, as kind as a school ma'am to me, but oh, what a terror he was when he arose in his wrath! You bet there were things doin' then.

The first time I ever saw him right mad was when we went to where an Indian was making *tis-win* (Indian whisky). The Indian was an old offender, and Sieber began to talk to him in Mexican, which Sieber said the Indian understood perfectly. The Indian, whose name was Chu-ga-de-slon-a (which means "centipede" in Missouri), spoke to Sieber in Apache, and told him that he was always watching around like an old meddlesome squaw. Sieber said: "Yes, I am always watching such men as you, that make devil's drink." Chu-ga-de-slon-a said: "I have a notion to kill you, Jon-a-chay," and that was what made Sieber mad. "Jon-a-chay" in Apache means "meddler."

Well, the Indian picked up his gun as he said this, and Sieber sprang toward him, and I guess must have pulled his knife as he did so, for he caught that Indian by the hair and made one swipe at him with his knife and nearly cut his head off.

The Indian had been fermenting his stuff in a big earthenware pot. Sieber slung this Indian to the ground, looked at

13

him for a minute, then picked him up and threw him partly into this big pot. The pot would not hold the Indian, or he certainly would have put him entirely in. I am pretty sure that I was scared; anyhow I had a very queer feeling.

Sieber turned to some squaws who were helping make this tis-win and told them to get their horses, get away from there and go back where the rest of the Indians were on White River and tell the rest of the Indians that they had better leave off making that stuff, as he, Sieber, calculated to stop the biggest part of the making of it somehow. And when he caught a man at it the first time he would put him in the calaboose; but when he caught a man at it like the one he had just killed, who was always making tis-win, that he would just slay him, so he could make no more trouble among the other Indians by making and selling them tis-win.

We then went into camp close by and stayed a couple of days, and I don't think Sieber slept a wink for those two days and nights; also he had very little to say and he looked awfully stern and determined. I was very uneasy, myself, as were the Indians with us, but I asked no questions of Sieber and he said nothing to me more than to keep the mules and horses close to camp and never lay my gun down for one minute.

At the end of two days we broke camp and went over on White River, and camped right in the forks of White and Black Rivers. Our Indians stayed in camp, and Sieber and I went up the river about a mile to the camp of a chief named Pedro, and we had a long talk with the old chief, who spoke Spanish perfectly.

Pedro had always been tolerably friendly towards Sieber, and Sieber told the old chief what he was trying to do.

Pedro said he did not want his men either to make or to drink whisky, and that he would help Sieber at all times. He also told Sieber that all Indians were not bad, but that some of them were as good as any man the Great Spirit put on earth, but that he had six hundred warriors, and some of them were as bad as a bad Apache could be, and that he could not do anything with them. He said that the bad ones never got killed, and they never got good nor old and disabled, but just remained and were always in any and all trouble that came up.

"You see, they are part Devil," said Pedro, "or they would get old or get killed some time."

Pedro ordered his women to feed us, which they did, giving us roast venison straight, but it was well roasted, and we ate heartily. Pedro asked Sieber where he got me, and if I was not a Mexican half-breed, but Sieber said I was a pure American. Pedro said: "Well, I hear him speaking Mexican to my men and boys and that is the reason I thought he was a half-breed." Sieber said: "He is learning Apache very fast, too."

Pedro then commenced to talk to me in Apache. I was very much embarrassed at first, for Pedro, the great Chief Warrior, Friend of the Whites, Counsellor, and Orator, was to me a great personage; but when once I got to talking Apache to him, he made me feel at home. Pedro asked me to stay and visit with him a few days and go hunting with his young men, and I told him I would like to do so but that I had to go away when Sieber went. Sieber was away at some distance talking to some old women and Pedro and I walked over, and Pedro asked Sieber to let me stay and visit with him for a while. He asked Sieber also to stay but Sieber said it was not convenient for him to do so.

While we were talking of this visit, some soldiers came into the forks, and Indian runners came running and told us of it. It caused some little excitement, which Pedro immediately proceeded to quiet.

CHAPTER THREE

Micky Free, Scout and Guide—Horn Begins Life Among the
Apaches — "The Talking Boy" a Full-Fledged Indian —
A Lodge and Housekeeper

IT PROVED TO BE Lieutenant Wheeler, of the Fifth Cavalry,
with about twenty men. A rumor had gone into San Carlos
to the effect that we were held by the Indians, and Wheeler
had come out to see.

Wheeler was led by the famous Micky Free. I will here
give a little sketch of the pedigree and disposition of this
still noted character. Micky Free was born in 1855, on the
Sonoita River, close to the Mexican and Arizona line. His
father was an Irishman named Hughes, and his mother was
a Mexican woman. His father and mother were killed in
1862 by the Indians, and he and his sister were carried off
into captivity. Micky was then about seven and his sister
about nine years old. He now spoke both Mexican and
Apache like a professor, and was the wildest dare-devil in
the world at this time. He had long, fiery red hair and one
blue eye, the other having been hooked out by a wounded
deer when he was twelve years old. He had a small, red
mustache, and a "mug" that looked like the original map
of Ireland.

He was about twenty-one or twenty-two years old at
the time of which I am writing, and had been working for
the government for several years. Always considered an in-
valuable man by the government, he was thoroughly quali-
fied for a typical scout and guide in every sense, except the
fact that he never had any regard for his own life, and

17

would, with a smile on his face, have led Wheeler and his handful of men against old Pedro and his 600 warriors, knowing that Pedro could be reinforced by 1,000 more men in four hours, and by 2,500 in ten hours. Such was Micky Free. He is now living on the White Mountain part of the Reservation, and has a large Indian family, and is wealthy in "horses, cattle, squaws, and dogs," as he himself puts it.

Well, to resume: Sieber and I went back down to the forks and met Wheeler, and Sieber and he had a long talk. They then sent a squad of soldiers back to San Carlos to report everything O.K., and Sieber and his party safe and sound.

Micky Free had a sweetheart in Pedro's band, and as soon as Wheeler made camp and Sieber and I showed up all right, Micky went off with his girl, and we did not see anything more of him until midnight, when I heard him challenged by the soldier guard, and shortly after I heard a hum of voices in the dark and I knew Micky and Sieber and Lieutenant Wheeler were holding a council of some kind. I could hear Wheeler and Sieber talk to Micky in Spanish, and then I could hear them talk to one another in English, and I knew there was something in the wind. I knew, also, when Wheeler and Sieber talked English, they did so because they did not want Micky to understand them. I could not hear what they were talking about, and neither could I go to sleep.

Presently a voice said to me, in Apache: "Are you the 'Talking Boy?' " I was scared for an instant, for I was fully awake, though I had heard no one move. There sat Micky by the head of my bed.

Micky saw me start when he spoke to me, and he gave a low laugh as though he were tickled.

I told him I was the "Talking Boy" (as the Apaches

called me), and he said that the Soldier Captain and Sieber would speak with me, and that they awaited me. I got up and took my gun and went over to where Sieber and Wheeler were. They asked me how I would like to live there with Chief Pedro for a while by myself—that is, with no other soldiers or scouts. When it came to the question of living there for a while, I felt a little timid; and then old Sieber gave me a long, fatherly talk. He said, in substance: "Tom, do you like this kind of life, and do you calculate to follow it? That is what I want to know first." I told him I did like it, and calculated to follow it if I was made of the right kind of stuff.

"Now," said he, "I want you to do what I am going to tell you. In the morning take your horses (I had three head) and go up and live with Pedro. Pedro is a good man, and he has taken a fancy to you, and you are picking up the Apache language very fast; in six months you will speak the language like a native. You are naturally born for a life of this kind, and are just the right age to begin. You are an excellent shot, a good hunter, and after a few years of this kind of life you will become a good and valuable man in the Indian wars which will continue for many years to come. Now, I will take you up to Pedro's camp in the morning and leave you there, for Pedro sent Micky down here to ask for you, as he likes you personally, and wants very much to have a government representative in his camp."

I told Sieber I would try it, and we then made arrangements about my pay and grub, and the next morning Sieber, Wheeler, Micky, and I went up to Pedro's camp, and I turned my extra horses loose with the old chief's band that were herded and looked after by the Indian boys and girls, and I saw Sieber, Wheeler, and Micky ride down the river without me.

19

I was watching them, and wondering where I would get off at, when old Pedro said: "Well, my son, you are an Apache, now." Pedro then gave me a lot of good advice, and called his son (or one of them, for he had about forty children); but he called one named Ramon, and told me there was a brother for me, and for me always to call him Chi-kis-in (brother). He told Ramon to treat me as a brother.

"And now," ended Pedro, "my camp is your camp, and my lodge will be your lodge till you set up one for yourself. There are many fine girls here, and I know several that are waiting now to get a chance to throw a stick at you." (The custom of Apache girls is to throw a stick to you if she likes you. You can then court her after their fashion.)

So, here I was, in the latter part of '76, a full-fledged Indian, living in Pedro's camp as a government agent, though receiving $75.00 a month as interpreter. I got along well, considering everything; hunted to my heart's content, and game was plentiful.

I made frequent trips to San Carlos and Fort Apache. On one of my trips to San Carlos we met a herd of horses that had just come up from Sonora to be sold to the Indians; stolen in Mexico, so Sieber said. They were selling at from $12.00 to $20.00 a head, and I bought eight head of them; also bought two fine Mexican saddles and bridles for $80.00. I gave four of the horses and a saddle and bridle to my new Indian brother, and we went back to Pedro's camp rich and respectable. I also gave one of the Mexicans $5.00 for a fine Mexican blanket, which I gave to Chief Pedro, and I do believe he thought more of that blanket than he did of any squaw he had; and he was sure rich in squaws.

This was only a short time before Christmas of '76.

The following morning, after my new brother and I got back to Pedro's camp, we were summoned before the chief, and he made us a long, fatherly talk, and told us how well fixed we were, and said it was time we had a lodge of our own, as it would look as though we could not make our own way, living so long as we were in one of his lodges. We were advised to buy each of us a wife and set up a house of our own. This was given to us in the privacy of his council lodge. We were then dismissed.

That day my brother and I took a long ride; in fact, we went to Fort Apache to show off our new saddles and bridles. At Fort Apache my brother (whom I will call Chi-kis-in from now on) met one of his sisters, or rather a half-sister, and she had just lost her buck; another Indian had killed him, and she was going to Pedro's camp to live. She had four horses and three kids, the oldest about nine years and the youngest about six years old, and she had also five dogs. It was ration day in Fort Apache, and hundreds of Indians were there drawing their rations, which every Indian drew once a week (every Friday). Well, Chi-kis-in and I concluded this was the chance to get a housekeeper, for it was a sure thing Pedro wanted us to have a lodge of our own. A word of advice, I may add, was the same as a command from Pedro.

This woman, who was called Sawn, said she would be our housekeeper if we would keep grub in camp. Keeping house in an Indian camp meant to do our washing, cooking, to tan our buckskins, make our moccasins, herd our horses, and, in fact, do everything there was to be done. In those days an Apache buck did nothing but hunt.

In a week's time we had a fine lodge and were the proudest "Injins" in camp.

CHAPTER FOUR

Major Chaffee and First Military Indian Agency — Pedro's "Medicine" for Bad Indians — Horn Out of a Job — Goes Prospecting — Tombstone, and Why so Called — Indian Troubles — Interprets Once More — First Appointment with Geronimo

SHORTLY AFTER THIS, which was early in '77, I was called to San Carlos by Major Chaffee, (who is now General Chaffee of world-wide fame).

Major Chaffee had come to Arizona in the fall of '76, and early in '77 was selected by the government as Indian agent. The first military Indian agency was thus established at San Carlos; all previous agents had been civilian agents. Indians, newspapers, and merchants all over the country said the civilian agents could, would, and did sell grub, such as flour, sugar, coffee, soap, baking powder, and beans, a great deal cheaper than the merchants could afford to. I, myself, have seen grub by the twelve-mule-team-load hauled away. Rations were supposed to be issued to twelve thousand Indians every week, and for years not more than five thousand of them would come in for their rations; and it was claimed that the civilian agents sold the extra grub, issued the rations on paper for all the twelve thousand Indians, and did a big business in competition with the local merchants.

Major Chaffee called Chief Pedro and myself down to explain to Pedro the change in affairs, and to get Pedro to use his influence to have all the Indians do as he, Pedro, was doing, that is, come in and draw their rations once a week and be counted, and to stop, if it could be done, all the raiding, stealing, and killing around in the country.

The council and big talk lasted for several days and nothing much came of it. Pedro said he could and did control his band of close to six hundred warriors and their families, but that there were hundreds of Indians no one could control. He advised Major Chaffee to take his soldiers and go and kill off all the bad, turbulent Indians, and he offered Major Chaffee two hundred good warriors to help him do it. Major Chaffee then asked Pedro how it would do to send me out to talk to the bad Indians and to live with them; maybe they could be controlled in that way.

Pedro was a grand and very impressive orator for an Indian, and he always stood up while talking, and when Major Chaffee proposed to send me to the Cibicu country, where the bad Indians lived (and of which I will write later), to try to pacify them, the old Chief said, "No, he must not and shall not go unless you allow me to send at least one hundred warriors with him. Soldier Captain, you know soldiers. I am an Indian chief, as was my father and my father's father, and I have more influence with the Indians than any man on earth, and I know the Apaches as you know your soldiers. But the day you send this boy to the Cibicu country alone, will be the day he dies, for to you, I, Chief Pedro, do say no white man can go among them and return. They will burn him at the stake and send an old Indian woman in and tell you to keep your flour and sugar and send on some more warriors for them to burn."

Of course, when Major Chaffee saw the old Chief talk so long and earnestly and passionately, and after I had told him what the old Chief said, then, and for the first time, did Major Chaffee understand what kind of people he had to deal with, and I was not sent to the Cibicu country.

Pedro told Major Chaffee that the Agua Caliente and Chiricahuas were even worse than the Cibicus, as they lived in Mexico and raided up into Arizona and then went back across the Mexico line, and the American troops could not follow them; that so long as there was Agua Caliente and Chiricahua Indians, just so long would there be Indian wars. The old man knew what he was talking about, for the war with those Indians continued for exactly ten years longer.

There were many different branches of the Apache tribe, named as follows: Tonto Apaches, San Carlos Apaches, White Mountain Apaches, Cibicus, Agua Caliente (or Warm Spring), and last and worst of all, the Chiricahuas. These Indians all spoke the same language, but were divided according to their dispositions. Thus a bad Tonto would leave the Tontos and go to the Cibicus or to the Chiricahuas, and a timid Chiricahua would go to the Tontos, so at the time of which I am writing you could find a good Indian or a bad one by knowing to what tribe he belonged. They all wore their hair different, and to one accustomed to them, they could be told apart as far as you could see them.

Well, at the end of this talk which lasted several days, we all went back to the White Mountains and I stayed there till the middle of May and was then sent for to go to San Carlos, and there I was told by the Quartermaster that there was no more money in the Department to pay me so I would have to be discharged until another appropriation was made. All the rest of the scouts and packers were in the same fix.

We were consequently discharged, and Major Chaffee told us that he had understood there had been a good many irregularities around the Agency and that one of the strictest requirements of the Interior Department was that no white man not in the employ of the government would be allowed to live on the Reservation, and we were given to understand that we must "git up and git out."

I went back to the Indian camp and told the old Chief all about the whole business, and that I must go. We had a big feast and dance that night and my friends each gave me a present of some kind, consisting principally of hair ropes, raw-hide ropes, hackamores, moccasins, buckskin bags and all kinds of stuff such as Indians make. The Apache women and some of the bucks were very skillful in making raw-hide and hair work of all kinds, and I had, during my residence with them, picked up a good deal of the work, but it is something that takes years of practice to become perfect in. Before I left the Apache and Mexican country, I, myself, had become an expert in all work of that kind, as I learned all that the Indians and Mexicans both knew. And many an hour and day and week have I passed here in jail making raw-hide ropes, hair ropes, hackamores, bridles, and quirts.

Well, the work was over for most of us and we had to drift; and as Tucson was the Mecca of every border-man in that country, to Tucson we went.

I had seven or eight good horses and a fine outfit, as did others of the scouts. Sieber was our leader, of course, then there were Archie McIntosh, Sam Bowman, Frank Monic, Charley Mitchell, Long Jim Cook (six feet, eight inches in height), Frank Leslie, Frank Bennett, Sage, Merijilda Grijole, Jose Maria Yescus, and Big Ed Clark, scout. All of these were scouts or interpreters, and then there were a good many packers. I think there were twenty-one of us in the bunch.

We stayed around Tucson for a while that summer till Ed Scheflin came in from California and was getting an outfit at Tucson to go to where he had found some rich mineral a few years before that time. Scheflin and Sieber were well acquainted, and they had a talk. So we all concluded we would go to this place as we had nothing else to do. Most all of the packers had gone to work "skinning" mules for some of the freighters, so that when we did finally pull out with Scheflin, there were only about five or six of our original crowd. Scheflin described the country to Sieber, and Sieber told me it was the "Cochise" country, as Sieber and I called it, for Cochise, a Chiricahua chief of great fame, had been born there, and two of his grandsons, Chihuahua and Natchez, still lived there a good deal of the time. Scheflin's party were all well armed, but they were like all pioneer miners, seemed to care not in the least when Sieber told them, when we were ready to start, that we were going into the very heart of the country where the worst Indians in the world lived; that we would have to fight and fight hard if the Indians happened to be in there, and that there never was a time when there were not Indians there; that we would not be there long till every hostile Indian in the South would know of it.

"Scheflin assures us that there is mineral there, and lots of it," said one big prospector, "and if there are any bad Indians there they will have to look out for themselves." Sieber said, "Come on boys!" and we pulled out.

There were about sixty men in the party, and as I was talking to Sieber that night at Pantano, he told me about those prospectors, of whom I knew very little. Scheflin had found silver there, and was run out by the Indians and one of his partners had been killed and he had gone to California and got these men, and every one of them was a frontiersman, a miner, and a warrior, and no Indians could keep them out of that country now that they were sure there was mineral there, for nothing has ever yet stopped people of that kind. If they found the mineral there as Scheflin assured them, it would be as that big fellow had said in Tucson. The Indians would have to look out for themselves.

Six days after we left Tucson we camped on the ground were Tombstone now stands, and after we made camp, Ed Scheflin said, "Boys, we have arrived; for right here is where I was camped when Lenox was killed, and now come on and I will show you where I was digging."

We all followed him up in the hills about a mile, and sure enough there was a hole twenty-three feet deep, just as Scheflin had said there would be. The entire exposure was all ore and good ore at that, and those miners went as crazy as bats over it. Scheflin had this claim all staked out, and all the men had made some kind of a contract with Scheflin before he brought them there. Scheflin told all of them to go back to camp and that he would hold a council that night.

That night all these prospectors got together and Scheflin made them a talk, and reminded them of some agreement entered into before they left California and Nevada, which, as I afterwards understood, was for Scheflin to get a quarter-interest in all claims staked by the party; but Scheflin did not say in this talk what their agreement was. He told them there were millions of dollars there to be had for the digging, and he made a motion to call the camp Tombstone, as the initial monument of his claim was right at the grave of Lenox, who had been killed by the Indians on the first trip to that country.

"Tombstone shall be the name of the new camp," said every one, and then the meeting broke up.

Next morning by daylight every man was ready to go to look for mines. Sieber and I went way up toward the divide and staked out a claim that day. And I will say here, that though the claim was not worth a dollar, we sold out that fall for $2,800.00.

Scheflin's claim, that he had previously worked, turned out to be a bonanza, and was known as the "Grand Central." Scheflin left the camp in three years, a very rich man. Many others of the party also made fortunes there, as Tombstone turned out to be one of the big silver camps of the Southwest.

I made plenty of money by hunting, as I could get $2.50 apiece for deer, and I kept the camp pretty well supplied. The news went broadcast that a new mining camp was struck, and by October there were fifteen hundred men there and plenty of stores and saloons.

Such was the starting of Tombstone, that in one year had a population of seven thousand souls.

In October of that year a detachment of soldiers, with Micky Free as guide, came to the new camp, or Tombstone, as we will now call it, and made inquiry for Sieber and myself. Sieber and I were up in the middle pass after deer when the soldiers came in. Lieutenant Von Shroder was with them, and had a letter from General Wilcox, Department commander, wanting Sieber and me to go to Fort Whipple at once, and to consider ourselves under pay and orders from the time we received the communication.

When we got back to Tombstone, Von Shroder was waiting for us. So, as we both had enough of mines and mining, we hunted up a man named Charley Leach, and he gave us $2,800.00 for our claim, and on the sixteenth day of October we pulled out for Fort Whipple.

General Wilcox told us, when we got to Whipple, that

28

everything was in bad shape and that the Indians were "raising Cain," and he wanted Sieber to take up his work where he had left off early in the summer, and see if something could not be done to quiet the Indians. Some of the Indians were making whisky; all of them were drinking it, and they were robbing and raiding and killing, and the soldiers could never come up with them.

The Sixth Cavalry had come into Arizona the year before and relieved the Fifth Cavalry. The Sixth had never been in the mountains, and while General Wilcox said the Sixth was one of the best regiments in the army, they could never get at the Indians.

Under Sieber's directions, a scouting force was again organized, Sieber as chief of scouts and I as interpreter. I was now to get $100.00 per month; but it did not take an old hand to see that we were going to have trouble, and a lot of it.

San Carlos, of course, was to be our headquarters, and it was very little of the time that we were to put in there. Sieber himself was a tireless worker, and anyone to hold a job under him, when there was work to do, had to go day and night; for in a case of emergency Sieber would entirely forget to sleep, and he could live on what a hungry wolf would leave.

I was sent to old Pedro's camp to get some Indians Sieber wanted as scouts and police, and as it took a week to get the ones I was sent after, I had a good visit with my old friends. Many of the young bucks of about twenty years of age wanted to go and fight their own people, but Sieber and Pedro were of one mind about them, for it was the work of able and experienced warriors to get the Indians back where they were eight months before. The tamest and best of the Indians needed a strong hand to control them, like Pedro,

29

for instance, and the wild and bad ones were as Pedro had previously said to Major Chaffee—uncontrollable.

"You will have years of hard work, and many and many of them will have to be killed," said the old counselor, proud that he did, indeed, know the Apaches.

Nana at this time (spring '78) sent in word by an old squaw that he and Geronimo, who were living in Mexico, wanted to come and live on the Reservation, and that he wanted to see Sieber and have a talk with him. He sent word that he did not know any of the officers in the Department, and he said they didn't know anything about what an Indian wanted, anyhow, and for Sieber to come to the Terras Mountains and make certain signs, and some of Geronimo's men would come to him. We were to be at a certain place at the full of the May moon. That was just what Sieber wanted; so he sent the old squaw back to tell these two chiefs that Seiber, Merijilda, and I would be there. (Merijilda Grijola was a Mexican captive raised by the Nana and Geronimo bands of Chiricahuas.)

We started from San Carlos so as to reach the designated place by the full of the moon. We followed the San Bernardino Creek from its head down to where it runs into the Bavispe River, in Mexico. Just as we were crossing the Bavispe River, we saw an Indian coming down a ridge on foot towards the Terras Mountains. While our horses and mules were drinking in the river, the Indian came and stood on the bank and leaned on his gun and looked at us, but did not speak a word till our animals were through drinking, and we rode out on the side he was on. Sieber and Merijilda spoke to him, and I did the same. He said to me: "Who are you? I know these two men, but I never saw you before."

Merijilda told him who I was, and told me, also, who the Indian was. In talking to an Apache, you may never

30

ask his name, for no Apache buck ever pronounces his own name, and when once you know the custom, you will never ask his name. You may ask who he is, and he will tell you what band he belongs to, but his own name he never speaks.

Well, this man turned out to be the one sent by Nana and Geronimo to meet us, and his name was Hal-zay. He was the first hostile Indian I had ever seen, and he sure looked the brave that he was. Tall, slender, and smiling, he stood there looking as unconcerned as you please. He was dressed in a low-cut breech clout and a handsome pair of moccasins. For ornaments he wore a belt full of cartridges, with a long Mexican knife. Sieber said he was a half-brother to Natchez, and that he was one of the worst Indians there was in the entire tribe. As he appeared then, now smiling good-naturedly and now laughing, he did not seem to be the bad man Sieber said he was. I will write later on of his death at the hands of an old man in Pedro's band.

Hal-zay said Nana and Geronimo were waiting for us up on the top of the Terras Mountains, and he told Meri-jilda to go to a place in the Terras Mountains called by the Indians Tu-Slaw. We asked him if he were not going back with us, and he said no. We then started on to where he had directed us to go. Sieber and Merijilda said that this fellow would watch to see that no soldiers were following us to trap the rest of the hostiles.

CHAPTER FIVE

Arrival at the Hostile Camp — The Council — Geronimo in the
Height of His Power, the "Biggest Chief, the Best Talker, and the
Biggest Liar" — Horn Interprets at the Big Talk — "Not Scared,
but a Little Shaky" — The Apaches' Grievances — Sieber's
Reply to Geronimo

IT WAS ABOUT 10:00 A.M. when we saw the first Indian,
and it was night when we got up on top of the mountain to
the main Indian camp. There must have been one thousand
or twelve hundred Indians in camp. Camp fires were burning everywhere. Just when we got to the edge of the camp,
an Indian boy about ten or twelve years old spoke to us,
and told us to follow him and he would take us to a camp-
ing place. We followed him to the place he indicated, then
made camp and turned our animals loose, and the boy said
he would take care of them. We got to work and straightened things around a little, and four or five women came
with wood and built a fire for us, bringing cooked meat.
We had some bread, and as we were very hungry we enjoyed a good meal.

When we were through eating, an Indian buck came up
and began to talk to us, and asked us did we want anything more to eat, and we told him we had had enough.
He said we would be looked for at the council at sunup the
next morning, and we told him we would be there. The
old squaw came up then, the one that had come to San
Carlos with the message that took us to the place we then
were. Quite a lot of squaws had gathered around by this
time, and were laughing and talking to us as if we belonged
to them.

Merijilda had been raised with these Indians, and he asked Sieber if he might go and visit around a while, and Sieber said yes, that he might, and that I might go, also, if I wanted to. Sieber spoke to Merijilda in Spanish, and many of the Indian women understood what he said, and we were invited by the women to go with any and all of them. I went one way and Merijilda another, for the camp was very large. Merijilda didn't get back to camp that night, and it was nearly morning when I got back. I did not see half a dozen men that night, but there were women and children by the hundreds.

The old woman who had brought the message to us at San Carlos wanted me to stay at her lodge all the time I was in the Indian camp, but I excused myself by saying I had to stay where my chief could find me any time. This old woman gave me a good send-off among the Indians by telling them how well I had treated her, and had given her all she could eat, fed her mule, and given her a lot of flour and sugar and meat when she left. Of course, she did not know that I did this because Sieber and Major Chaffee ordered me to do so, and I would not spoil a good thing by telling her!

At daylight the women were at camp to give us some more meat, I made some coffee, and we had breakfast. Just as it was ready, Merijilda came in, and after we got through, he led the way to the council. The sun was just coming up. Now all the women and kids were out of sight, and only warriors were around the place selected for the council. Then Geronimo got up out of a crowd of Indians and came over and shook hands with Sieber, and for the first time in my life I saw this man of whom I had heard so much from both Indians and white men.

Certainly a grand-looking war chief he was that morning

33

as he stood there talking to Sieber; six feet high and magnificently proportioned, and his motions as easy and graceful as a panther's. He had an intelligent-looking face, but when he turned and looked at a person, his eyes were so sharp and piercing that they seemed fairly to stick into him. Anyhow, that was how they looked to me; but I was a little shaky, anyhow.

"How are you, young man?" said he to me in Apache.

I told him I was all right. I might as well have told him I was a little shaky, for he knew it anyhow. He asked us to come over into the center of the circle, where we had the talk, and then he said to Sieber: "Who will interpret for you?" Sieber told him I would do it.

While Sieber could talk Apache very well and understand it very well, still he could not talk anyways near well enough to take in all that a man like Geronimo said. Geronimo then said to me: "I speak very fast, sometimes. Can you undertake to interpret as fast as I talk?"

I told him he had but one mouth and tongue, that I could see, and for him to let loose. "Well spoken!" said he; and then he asked Sieber what he had come down there for, and Sieber said to hear what he (Geronimo) had to say. "I want to hear you talk," said Sieber.

Well, the big talk was on; and how that old renegade did talk! Of the wrongs done him by the agent, and by the soldiers, and by the White Mountain Apaches, and by the Mexicans and settlers, and he had more grievances than a railroad switchman, and he wanted to go back to live on the Reservation. He wanted to be allowed to have a couple of Mexicans to make mescal for him, and he wanted the government to give him new guns and all the ammunition he could use. He wanted calico for the women, and shoes for the children when there was snow on the ground, and any

34

and everything he ever saw or heard of he wanted. Geronimo was the biggest chief, the best talker, and the biggest liar in the world, I guess, and no one knew this better than Sieber.

Geronimo must have talked an hour or two, and Sieber never said a word in reply. At last Geronimo stopped talking, for he had asked for everything he could think of, and he was a natural born genius at thinking of things.

Sieber sat perfectly still for some time, and then arose and looked around him, and it was sure a beautiful spot we were camped, and Sieber looked around as though he was admiring the view and the camp.

"Tom, tell Geronimo just what I say, no more and no less," said he. "You have asked for everything that I know anything about," continued Sieber, "except to have these mountains moved up into the American country for you to live in, and I will give you till sundown to talk to your people and see if you don't want these mountains moved up there to live in. If you are entitled, by your former conduct, to what you have asked for, then you should have these mountains too." That was all. Sieber turned and walked out of the council.

Not an Indian stirred nor spoke for a long time, and then Geronimo arose and said: "Anybody's business that is in that man's hands will be handled as he says, or it won't be handled at all. We will meet here again at sundown."

Everybody then went his own way. I went back to our camp and Sieber was lying down on his back on his blankets looking up at the sky, and he did not move for a long time. At last he got up and said to me: "Tom, did you ever know of another such a man as Geronimo?" Of course I never did, and I told him so.

"Well, go on away now, for I want to think today of all

35

the mean things I can say to that old wolf tonight. Come about noon and make me some coffee, and tell those women that feed us to bring me some meat then, and tell them to keep away from me today."

I went away and visited and got acquainted during the day, and was welcomed in every camp. Sieber had bought some calico and a few presents for the women that he knew from former experience would have to wait on us, and he told me to give them to the women who seemed to have the business in charge. I did so, and they were received by the women with great apparent joy. And then I learned that it was considered quite a privilege to be allowed to cook for us, as those who did so were sure to get nice presents in the shape of calico, beads, needles, thread, and pearl buttons.

When sundown came, Sieber and I again went to the place where the council was held, and saw a good big fire had been built, and there was a lot of dry wood piled up, and two women were there to keep the fire in proper shape. I guess there must have been three or four hundred warriors there, and most of them had on a blanket of some kind or other.

Sieber stood and looked all over the crowd, and then said to Geronimo:

"This morning you asked for many things, and you knew I could not give you many of the things you asked for, and I do think that you asked for the most of them because you love to talk, and not because I could or would do as you asked me. Anthing I do promise, you know full well you will get, for you have ever found me as I said I would be. I am not the fluent orator that you are, neither do I put in my time asking for or trying to get that which I know I can never obtain.

"Now, this I do say to you: Go to the Reservation, and do as you will be advised to do by the government, and you will get all that the government can give you. You know what the government can give you, for you have lived there and drawn your rations, as many Indians are doing now. You will also be given a blanket for each of you, and other things just as you have before received; but I can promise you no more, for it is spoken by my government that you shall get no more.

"Geronimo, I have no idea you will do as I say, for you do not love peace. You are a man of war and battle, else you would not be war chief of the Chiricahua tribe. You could go to the Reservation and stay maybe one season, and maybe only one moon. But within this camp may be some who do really want to come up and settle down to a peaceful life. Any and all such I will take back safely, and most of your people know what you will get. Twice already have I taken you there, and twice have you become uneasy and left. Never did a complaint come to the government that you were not fed. Never did you complain of not having clothing and blankets enough. But there would be a row between this tribe and some of the other tribes, or someone would sell you a lot of whisky and you would all, or a great many of you, get drunk and away you would go; and until now you have not complained of not getting what the government promised you.

"This thing cannot last. The white men are as the leaves upon the trees. There are hundreds and hundreds of white men to every Apache. It is true many and many of the white men can not protect themselves from such warriors as there are here, for it is my opinion in the world there are none better. Still, all the Chiricahua and Agua Caliente in existence, or nearly all, are within hearing of the words I am

37

saying now, and they cannot stay on the war path and not be exterminated. Slowly of course, but one by one you will be killed or captured, and how will you ever replace them?

"True, you can say the Americans cannot and will not be allowed to come armed and in force into this, a Mexican country, to fight you.

"Such have been the conditions so far, and I know that you have no fear of the Mexican soldiers, and many a time have I heard your women say they could whip the Mexican army, and that the Mexicans were poorer than the Apaches. And to that I will say that within a short time, a year or two, or maybe three, that a peace talk will be held by the Mexican and American governments, and arrangements will be made to allow American soldiers and scouts to enter these mountains in force and in pursuit of you, and then you will be doomed to capture, or will be all exterminated; for, as I said before, the American troops are without number. I have ever spoken words of advice to you in council. Never have I told you one lie, and not a warrior here now will say he thinks I talk two ways.

"Consider well what I have said to you. I leave in four days for San Carlos." Sieber then turned and went back to our camp.

His talk had, as I could see, made a deep impression on the Indians. Merijilda was left there with me. Presently Geronimo spoke to one of the sub-chiefs, and he came over to where we were standing, and said that the Apaches would be alone; or, in other words, for us to leave the council. We left, of course, and went back to camp. All night long did the council fire burn, and at daylight, when I got up and looked around, I could see bucks returning to their camps. They had talked among themselves all night!

38

DURING THE REST OF OUR STAY a good many Indians came and told us they were going back with us.

There was a camp or troop of soldiers at old Fort Tony Rucky, not far from where we would cross the Mexican line going back, and we knew we could get rations there for the Indians that returned to the Reservation with us.

I traded two fine Mexican blankets for two good horses and two mules. They were all splendid animals. The blankets cost me $12.00 in Tucson; so I made a good trade. The Indian I traded with did well, also, for he of course stole the stock from the Mexicans!

There was no more council, for Sieber had said his say. When we were ready to start to San Carlos, at the time set by Sieber, sixty-two Indians were ready to go with us, among them being the chiefs Nana and old Loco, a once famous chief, but at this time he must have been eighty years old, or maybe more.

Geronimo came to us when all was ready to start, and said he was glad that these Indians were going back, as they were mostly widows (whose men had been killed) and children, and a few very old bucks. Geronimo told me to come to his camp at any time that I had any word to bring him from the government officials, and not to be afraid, as I would always be well treated and perfectly safe. "You are a young man," he said, "and will always be at war with me and mine; but war is one thing and talking business is another; and I will be just as pleased to meet you in battle as in council."

We then pulled out for San Carlos Agency.

At night, after we had camped on the Bavispe River, Merijilda left us to go on ahead with dispatches to General Wilcox and Major Chaffee. We had to have troops to escort us as soon as we crossed the Mexican line into the United States. When we got up close to the line, we swung off toward the Bonito Cañon to wait for this escort, which arrived in a few days, and we then proceeded toward San Carlos.

We finally got to the Agency all right with our Indians and made them camp in the forks of the San Carlos and Gila rivers.

We had not been back a great while till another squaw came in and told us more of the same Indians we had the talk with in Mexico were ready to come to the Reservation. Sieber was then laid up with the rheumatism, so I was ordered to go with some troops and escort them in. I then saw what their game was—that is, to raid and kill in Mexico and bring the stock to San Carlos.

There were about fifty, or, to be accurate, forty-nine in this second bunch, and they had about five hundred head of horses and mules. Trouble was sure just beginning for us! There was a duty on horses and mules coming from Mexico into the United States, and at San Bernardino, on the line, was a bunch of custom horse men from El Paso, Texas, to collect duty on this stock. Not a soul of us knew what to do. We could not pay this duty, and these officers would not let us bring in this stock without it, and the Indians told us that the Mexican troops were following them and would perhaps overtake them in a day or two.

The renegades, of course, could not and would not understand the condition of affairs. There were about fifty warriors with this last bunch of Indians, but they had not shown up to us. They were in the rear to head off the Mexicans.

Luckily, the Mexicans turned back after getting within about twenty miles of the line. The custom house men counted the horses and mules and finally let us go on; the officer in charge of our escort promising to do what was required by the Custom Department later on.

All that year I was going back and forth between the Mexican line and San Carlos bringing in bunches of Indians and big bunches of stock.

The Mexican government was just "raising Cain" because we were doing as we did. There was no mistake but that it was wrong, and very wrong; but we were powerless, and it did look to the Mexicans as though our troops were upholding the Apaches and protecting them in their raiding.

We had about two thousand head of horses and mules taken from the Mexicans and several delegations of Mexican rancheros came to San Carlos and proved their property, but they all went back empty handed. The Indians would not give up the stock voluntarily, and our agent would not take them by force; so Mr. Mexican had to go back as poor as he came. Mad! Well, you should have seen them!

There was a Mexican newspaper at Tucson called *El Fronterizo,* and it did sure write some warm articles on the subject. Don Carlos Valasquez, the editor of this paper, came to San Carlos personally to see what could be done. But nothing was ever done. The Indians made their play stick, and we had to protect them in it.

Along in the spring of '79 a good many warriors came

41

in and all of them made a big talk and said they were going to remain on the Reservation and draw their rations, and be good and go out on the war path no more. There were still a lot of renegades in Mexico under Geronimo and Ju (called "Who"), but they were hopeless as far as getting them to come in was concerned.

In June of '79, we scouts and interpreters were again all discharged and fired off the Reservation. Appropriation had run out and the Quartermaster had no money to pay us. Of course we all went to Tucson.

Tuly Ochoa & Co. had the contract to furnish the beef to the Indians at San Carlos from July, '79, for one year, and they employed me to handle the San Carlos end of it, and gave me $150.00 a month. It took, on an average, 225 beeves a week, all issued on foot.

Loco was still camped in the San Carlos and his band by this time numbered about 650 Indians. They must have had close to five thousand head of horses and mules. The grass was fine, and their horses were all fat, and the bucks were running the whole country. In August, '79, I turned loose two thousand head of steers about six miles above the Agency and the Chiricahua bucks did have a good time with them. Every day, when they wanted meat, they would just round up and kill what they wanted. Of course, I complained to the agent, and the best he could do was to have me keep count of the ones killed by them, and that suited me all right, for I did well with my counting. I could not get any cowboys to stay at the camp to look after the cattle, so they were soon all killed off by the Indians. The Chiricahuas were not the only ones doing the killing. The San Carlos and White Mountain Indians all helped themselves.

It did not take a very wise man to see that the Indians were running the mill to suit themselves. Major Chaffee had been relieved and sent to Fort McDowell and a man named Tiffany, a civilian, was agent. There were no troops at the Agency and things looked a good deal more like a hostile Indian camp than did the camp of Geronimo when we had gone to have a talk with him the year before in Mexico.

A man named Stirling was chief of police at the Agency and he had eleven police to keep the peace of the Agency. They worked for the Interior Department and not for the War Department.

Stirling was absolutely without fear and an able and intelligent scout, but what could he do toward handling five thousand or six thousand wild or half-wild Indians with but eleven police? These police were Indians, and would have been splendid men had they had any show; but as things were, they were disgusted.

Tiffany, the agent, was so busy selling the Indians' rations to freighters, prospectors, and merchants in Globe and Mc-Milenville that Indian troubles did not bother him in the least. Major Chaffee had accumulated a large amount of rations during his time as agent, and all the storehouses were full of rations when Tiffany took charge. Tiffany was a very industrious and business-like politician, and immediately commenced to disburse that grub at the rate of $5.00 for a hundred pounds of flour, and $10.00 a hundred for sugar. That was dirt cheap in that country at that time, but Mr. Tiffany soon found himself arrested and taken before the United States Court at Tucson, and I think was charged with not being able to account for $54,000.00 worth of rations. This all happened in six or eight months. Nothing was ever done to him that I remember of, though he was in the courts for several years with this business.

CHAPTER SEVEN

An Indian Outbreak — Death of Stirling — Horn Carries News of
Outbreak to Camp Thomas — Pursuing the Renegades — "Six Men
Killed in One Minute" — Horn's knowledge of Apache Language
Saves the Command

SUCH WAS THE CONDITION of affairs at the Agency itself,
so it was small wonder that in the spring of '80, Ju came
up from the renegades in Mexico and brought one hundred
men with him to take Loco and his band back to Mexico.
I was living five miles above the Agency and the Chiricahua
camp was halfway between me and the Agency. I think it
was May 5, 1880, that this outbreak occurred.

There were supposed to be about seven hundred Indians
belonging to Loco's camp, but no one knew the exact number. The settlers in the country said there was a continuous
string of Indians going and coming from Mexico to San
Carlos, and I think such was the case. Personally I do not
know, for I was at San Carlos all the time.

At daylight, or a very little after, I heard a lot of firing
at the Chiricahua camp. There were Indians camped all
around me, and they began to arm themselves and in about
ten minutes word came in that the Chiricahuas were leaving for the war path. There were "things doin'" then for
sure. In a few minutes all the Indians around my camp were
ready. Of course we did not want to fight, as the Bronks (as
we called the Chiricahua) far outnumbered us. Across the
Gila Valley rose a big spire of iron ore, or rather a good
many of them, making an ideal fortification, and there we
all went. It was a fine fort, its prominence giving us an

excellent view of the country, and as the Bronks had to pass along directly under us, it gave us such a view as even few Indian scouts have a chance to see.

Just as the sun came up, here they came. Great droves of horses and mules were strung out for about a mile and a half. There must have been five thousand head of them. Squaws and Indian children everywhere, driving the stock. Of course they had their camp outfits. The squaws were all yelling at the children, and the children yelling at the loose stock. A small bunch of perhaps twenty warriors was in front, and behind was the main band of warriors.

Stirling had heard the outbreak just at daylight, as I had. He was at the Agency. He jumped on his horse, and with one Indian policeman, a captive called Navajo Bill, he rode right into the Chiricahua camp. He "never smiled again," as he was killed just as he came up to the bank of the San Carlos River. A squaw cut his head off. He was shot about seventy-five or one hundred times. Navajo Bill escaped, but how, one can scarcely tell, for he was right with Stirling.

Navajo Bill swung back toward the Agency and the rest of the police came to him, and again they rode at the Chiricahuas, and one more policeman was killed. There were at least two hundred Chiricahua warriors, and these police, (there were only seven of them when they came up to where I was) kept right up with the Broncos, and killed one of them just below and in plain sight of myself and the party with me.

After this Chiricahua was killed, the rest of them seemed to think that something must be done, so they threw out several little bunches of men, about five or six in a bunch, and they dropped into gulches and in the grass and willows. The police saw this and went to high ground and stopped.

The Chiricahua were about half an hour passing the

45

point where I was located. Some of the warriors in the rear guard stopped and looked at us for a minute or two, but I could not hear what they were saying. They were not more than three hundred yards from us. We on our part made no attempt to fire on them, and for my part I was glad to see them leave us alone. They could not have hurt us much where we were, as we had a fine place, and there were fourteen men with me, all of whom said there was no danger of the Indians firing on us.

As soon as the Bronks had passed and gone, I went to the Agency and found a very confused state of affairs. There were no troops. Stirling, the chief of police and main-stay of the Agency, was killed. The Indians had cut the telegraph wire running into the Agency, and the chief clerk in charge of the Agency was only a tenderfoot, and he thought all the Indians on the Reservation had gone on the war path. There were lots of guns and ammunition at the Agency, and the chief clerk was giving a rifle and ammunition to every Indian buck who wanted one. The Indians at the Agency and below the Agency knew that it was only an outbreak of the Chiricahuas, but they were taking all the guns and ammunition they could get. The chief clerk kept no account of the guns, and did not know to whom he had given them, and very few of them did he ever get back.

We could get no news from anywhere, and it was necessary to inform the troops as soon as possible, so I started up to Camp Thomas, thirty-two miles up the river and in the direction in which the Bronco Indians had gone. I got up there by ten o'clock, for I rode fast. The commanding officer at Camp Thomas had gotten the news that there was something wrong, but he could get no news from San Carlos, and when I got into Camp Thomas there was a squad of soldiers all ready to start toward San Carlos to see if they could learn what the trouble was. These men were at the Adjutant's office all ready to go when I rode into the post.

Sieber was there talking to some Indians, and all those Indians knew was that the Indians down the river had signalled that there was trouble from the Chiricahuas. Apaches can signal for a long ways when there is trouble, but they cannot give details by their signals.

There were only two troops of Cavalry at Camp Thomas, but their telegraph was all right, and troops all over the Department were soon notified. The Gila River was swollen, and I had to swim it to get to Camp Thomas, but I swam it at San Carlos, (San Carlos and Fort Thomas—now abandoned—are both on the Gila River).

It was a sure thing the renegades would have to keep east toward the upper Gila, as the river was so high they would not attempt to cross it unless forced to by the troops.

Sieber made arrangements for the troops to come toward Ash Creek, and he and I again swam the river, and struck out toward that part of the country he thought they would come through. We thought that I was before them, and so I proved to be.

On Ash Flats, about twelve miles from Camp Thomas and about twenty-five miles from San Carlos, we could see the dust they raised. There were so many of them they could not travel fast. They were handicapped by the hundreds of extra horses they had. We got on top of what was called Green's Hill, and watched the big dust which was, maybe, two and a half miles away. Sieber said they would all scatter that night and go in small bunches toward Mexico and all come together again close to the line.

While we were looking at the dust, (they were in a swale, so we could not see the Indians themselves) to our left, we saw six Indians coming straight toward us, about five hundred yards away. They were coming to get on Green's Hill themselves, apparently, but they saw us just as we saw them.

They turned around and rode into a gulch that led off toward the main band of Indians. They were videttes, for a large body of renegades when they are traveling keep out guards on all sides and before and behind.

All that Sieber and I could do was to watch them. Sieber had told the troops at Thomas how to come on the Eagle Creek trail, and that we would find them that night. The way the troops were directed to go, they would be about twenty miles from where we were then some time during the night; so Sieber said we would go and join the troops, but that we would have to wait till the Indians split up, for all the troops in Camp Thomas could not stop that bunch of Indians and that it would be several days before any more troops could join us.

We pulled out for where our troops were to come. They were guided by Micky Free, and he was so reckless and loved to fight so well that he would have led those two troops right into any kind of a trap. Micky knew he could get the troops into any kind of a trap and come out all right himself, for the fellow seemed to bear a charmed life.

We struck the troops as we expected, that night, and Sieber told the officer in command how things were. Gatewood (that was his name) said that if we could strike them the next day he would "try them a lick." He said, "We may not be able to lick them, but we will try it if we can find them."

So we did. We struck them and got six men killed in a minute. Sieber told Gatewood that the warriors we were trying to whip were better men than his soldiers in any place

48

that we could strike them. We buried our dead men and made arrangements to send the wounded back to Camp Thomas, and we had only thirty-six soldiers left. Gatewood was shot in the shoulder, but he would not go back.

By the time we started again it was getting late in the day, so, as the Indians were some distance ahead by this time, Sieber, Micky Free, and I started on and left the troops to come more leisurely. We three got over on the head of Eagle Creek late that night, and the next morning we found that the Indians had broken up into small bands and they left about a thousand head of stock on the head of Eagle Creek. They did not abandon them because they had to do so, but because they did not care for them. I forgot to say that we got about two hundred head of horses where we struck them the day before. From that time on they left a string of horses behind them. Most of the animals were played out.

Gatewood took these horses and turned back. It took all his men to handle the stock. Sieber, Micky, and I went on after the Indians, knowing that more troops would come in to try to join us from Fort Baird and the New Mexico country.

By the middle of the afternoon we were again in sight of the Indians as they crossed the divide onto Blue River. So we kept along and passed the Indians that night, at least, the bunch of them that we were following. We went over toward Clifton that night and next day rode into the town and found that they knew the Indians were out and that everybody in the country had come into the little towns around. We decided we would go on over to the Stein's Peak Mountains, as we knew the Indians were sure to come that way. We heard that some soldiers had gone toward

Ash Springs, so Sieber told me to go and get them and camp them at Cottonwood and Indian Springs, and at a place called Horse Camp.

I started and found the troops at Ash Springs, but they were pretty well worn out and they wanted to rest their horses a while. I had gotten a couple of good horses at the Rail N Ranch and was pretty well fixed for a mount. We did not leave Ash Springs till night, and it was morning as we pulled into Whitlock's. As we were watering our horses, I noticed that the cattle were running up above us, and there were the Indians.

They were just coming around a point, and as I saw them they saw the soldiers. The soldiers started to deploy skirmishers on foot, and the Indians turned and ran up on a rocky point and gave us a good big stand-off.

I had told this officer (I do not recollect his name) of how we got whipped over on the other side of the Gila, and he said all he wanted me to do was to show him Indians.

This lieutenant had run behind the ruins of an old adobe house, and was directing his men to get the horses out of range of the Indians. I saw the Indians separating into bunches, and I heard one of them directing the others how to go and get a position on high ground, and drive us away, so their outfit could get into water. I told the officer what the Indians were saying, and what they were going to do, and he said: "Damn 'em! If they want this water they can have it, for it is strong alkali and warm to boot." So we all mounted and rode down into the flat and let the Indians come in to water. Had we not left, the Indians would have gotten the whole works of us.

(This is just the commencing of the regular Indian war.)

The Indians, after about an hour, came down towards us for a ways with their entire outfit, and then swung up the San Simon Valley, and the bucks dropped behind so as to keep between us and the squaws. They were headed towards Doubtful Cañon, and so I told the officer in charge of the troops.

That poor fellow did not know what to do. The Indians outnumbered us and could whip us, and I told him so; and I had previously told him of the way Gatewood made his fight with no show to win, and got six men killed and eleven wounded. So, as we could not do anything to the Indians after they had gone, we struck out in the same direction, keeping them or their dust in sight. I knew that there were plenty of soldiers out after the Indians, and that there would be one or more troops of cavalry after each band of Indians, and I thought all the rest of them would be in the same fix as ourselves. This I told the lieutenant; so we then wanted to find more soldiers.

Things proved to be exactly as I had an idea they would be. When we got up to Indian Springs, in the Stein's Mountains, the Indians had turned from the open valley directly into the Stein's Mountains towards the head of Doubtful Cañon.

Hostile Indians from the upper Gila country would nearly always come through that section of the country, as it was decidedly an Indian rendezvous, and from Stein's Mountains to the Mexico line there were neither settlements nor forts.

As the Indians turned into the mountains, we saw there was quite a commotion among them, and shortly after we heard firing over on the east side of the mountains.

Our Indians had heard it first, as they were a couple of miles closer than we were to the firing. It proved to be Sieber and Micky Free, with three small bunches of soldiers they had picked up and got together, and they were on

51

trail of, and had come up with, two more bunches of these Indians that had separated upon the head of Eagle Creek.

The firing continued for about an hour. The Indians we were following went directly towards the firing and we did the same. We were not more than a mile from our band, and some of the guard for the Indians were not over half a mile from us. When we got to the top of the divide, we could see there was a fight on between the troops and the Indians on the other side, so we went as fast as we could to join them.

It was getting late, and was just about sundown when we got to the part of the troop where there were two dead soldiers and five wounded ones. The main command was just drawing off, and as it was night, and all of the cavalry horses were about played out, or at least well jaded, camp was made there in what was called Cottonwood.

We were all tired and hungry, and the first thing we did was to get something to eat. Micky Free and I lay down and went to sleep as soon as we got something to eat.

CHAPTER EIGHT

Wanted: More Soldiers — Sieber's "Growl" — Apparent Misman-
agement of Indian Affairs — A Scout's Duty — Major Tupper Wants
"to Get a Lick at the Indians" — Forty Soldiers and Twenty-five
Scouts Against Three Hundred Chiricahua Braves — Over the Line
into Mexico — Sieber Locates Hostile Camp

ABOUT ELEVEN OR TWELVE o'clock Sieber came and woke
us up, and told us to get our horses and be ready to go
with him on after the Indians. I asked Sieber what was the
use of monkeying along after those Indians by ourselves
when all the soldiers could not handle them. Sieber spoke
to me in a language that was more liable to be called forcible
than elegant, and told me that the action or scarcity of soldiers was no concern of mine; that if they could not whip the
Indians, that did not concern me or him; that I was a government scout and he was my chief, and that he could not
command the Department and get sufficient troops on hand
to whip the Indians. "But," said he, "I can and will keep
up with the Indians, and you and Micky must come." Sieber
was mad, and anyone that knew him and worked under him
would soon come to do as he said and ask no questions.
I was tired and sleepy, but here was this old, gray-headed,
iron-hearted man who had been at work while I was asleep;
for, during the time that we drew away and made camp and
got something to eat, he had gone on foot and noted which
way the Indians went. Then he had come back and gotten
something to eat, and woke Micky and me to go on. Sieber
at this time was fifty-five years old; but, as I said once before, in a case of this kind he never seemed to want to sleep,
and he did not get a chance to eat afterward.

53

We rode all night across and up the San Simon Valley, and Sieber said the Indians would strike the Chiricahua Mountains at Turkey Creek, or maybe go on up as far as Cane Creek.

At sunup we were not more than ten miles behind the Indians, for they had gone just as Sieber said they would. Where the Turkey Creek comes out of the Chiricahua Mountains the ground is higher than it is out in the valley where we were, and we could see the Indians going in on Turkey Creek. They made a terrific dust, and it was seen plainly by the soldiers we had left in the night, a distance of thirty-five or forty miles.

The Indians went into camp on Turkey Creek and stayed there all day. They had out guards on all sides. We (Sieber, Micky Free, and I) camped on a little gulch that ran into Turkey Creek. There was a spring at the head of this gulch on a mesa, and we could see for quite a good distance around us. The Indian camp was about two miles above us. Some of the Indian pickets were in sight of us most of the time. Sieber said they would not molest us if we did not go right up to their camp, and this we had no idea of doing.

By ten o'clock that morning we could distinctly see the dust of our troops coming across the San Simon Valley. The dust sprang into sight all at once, and the Broncos saw it at the same time that our party did. We heard a great yell up at the hostile camp when this big dust was first sighted. It was still about twenty-five miles off. After we saw this dust, Sieber told Micky and me to keep awake and on the lookout, for he was going to take a little sleep.

We did keep a good eye open, but we were not molested. Our horses were very tired, but each of us had two horses, and that gave us a great advantage over the troops.

54

Somewhere about four o'clock in the evening the troops pulled in and went into camp about three miles below the Indians, on Turkey Creek. The cavalry horses were very tired and warm, and it took some time to get them watered. A consultation was held by all the officers and scouts. Pat Kehoe had come up with the soldiers, having overtaken them during the day. Pat said there were only bucks in the party, with the exception of a few squaws to tend camp. Sieber, Micky, and I had not seen any of the camps made by them since they split up on Eagle Creek, and I saw only bucks at Whitlock's, and as the bunch that had come together did not have the least fear of us, we thought that we were following the warriors, and that they were making a play to keep all the troops after them; that the most of the women and children and a few of the best warriors had kept a little behind, and calculated to drop in behind the troops, and so get into Mexico unmolested.

The Indians were swarming on the hills above us, but did not act as though they were going to attack. Sieber said they were breaking camp and pulling out again to travel all night, and that the Indians in sight just wanted to take a look at us before they left. By six o'clock they had all gone, and Sieber told Micky and me to get ready to follow them.

After dark we pulled out for a place called Cloverdale, as Sieber said that would be the next stopping place of the Indians. Sieber was mad, and would not talk for a long time. We were crossing the head of the San Simon Valley and swinging well east again.

Along about midnight we stopped to change horses. Sieber then commenced to talk to me, and Micky asked him to talk in Spanish so he, too, could understand. Sieber had his roasting talk on.

"What is the use," he said, "for us to be monkeying along

here after these Indians. There never will be soldiers enough to catch up with us to whip them, for there are at least two hundred of them; this division of the party are no doubt led by Natchez and Chihuahua, and man for man in the rough country they can easily whip any troop in the world, for they will never come into an engagement unless they have far the best of the ground; and if it comes to a pinch they can abandon everything and go on foot, and then no one could do anything with them. I have reported to the Department commander a half-dozen times during the winter that these Indians would break out as soon as spring came, and I have pointed out to him that he had no transportation for his troops, and that there was no preparation made to pursue them when they did go. Now, you see how it is. There are those soldiers we just left. They have no grain for their horses, and very little or no rations for themselves. And here we are 'piking' along after these fellows just as though we were doing some good.

"Boys," went on Sieber, "this outbreak means a long war, and there will come a time when there will be some kind of organization for the soldiers in the field. They must have transportation in the shape of wagons and pack trains, and camps must be established at Turkey Creek and Cane Creek and Cloverdale, where we are headed now, and at every other prominent place somewhere near here, or near the line of Mexico. Our present Department commander doesn't understand these things, and he doesn't undertand anything about Indians. Now, you boys can plainly see what I am explaining to you. We are perfectly harmless to the Indians, and they know it as well as we do.

"There is always one thing a man can do under circumstances of this kind, and that is, just go on and keep in touch with both the soldiers and Broncos. We are merely scouts, and can only show the soldiers how and where to go. After we get them up to the Indians we can do no more, for it is the commissioned officer who commands the troops and not the scouts. You boys do as I tell you, and while the soldiers may be censured by the President and the people, if we do our part everyone will know it, and we will never be blamed."

Sieber felt better after he had had a good growl; said he was a fool to expect anything else, and that was an end to his growl.

Daylight found us on a hill overlooking Cloverdale, and the whole place seemed alive with Indians. Sieber said they had been joined by another big band, or had run into them there at Cloverdale.

The Mexico line was about a mile south of Cloverdale. Sieber said we would stay and watch the Indians all day, and that in the evening the hostiles would cross over into Mexico. "And in a day or two after they are gone," he added, "there will be troops enough here to whip them, but they will be in Mexico and perfectly safe, as no army officer would think of crossing the line, as he would lose his commission if he did."

We stayed close to the Indians to see all that there was to be seen, for that was all we could do. Sieber estimated that there were five hundred of them. We could see dozens of women and children who had joined our bunch during the night, or had been at Cloverdale when our band got there.

Along about three o'clock in the evening we saw they were getting ready to go, and as some of the advance guard started off in an easterly direction, we got ready and struck out that way, knowing the main band of Indians would cross still further east. We figured that there was

57

still a big band that had not arrived yet; they were evidently waiting for the entire bunch before crossing into Mexico. This advance guard showed us that they were all going towards a place on the line, or close to the line, called Agua Blanco. We pulled out in the same direction, leaving the main bunch of Indians to come later, as we knew they would.

They could all have crossed the line right where they were camped, at Cloverdale, but a short distance south in Mexico the country grew very rough, and was hard for a big bunch of Indians to get through and all of them keep together, and if they went over by Agua Blanco, they could cross over into Mexico and have good open country to travel in. Also, from Cloverdale, the San Luis Pass opened through the San Luis Mountains into a large open country or plain in Mexico called *Llano de Janos,* or Janos Plains. Any Indians that had kept farther up the Gila would naturally come in from the east and turn down this plain by the Agua Blanco.

Well, what they did do was this: The main bunch went through the San Luis Pass, and the picket or advance guard went over by Agua Blanco, striking the trail of Indians who had come from farther east and gone into Mexico ahead of them. The pickets may have struck some of the Indians belonging to the eastern band, for at night everything in sight was in Mexico and all headed, so we calculated, towards the Sierra Media, in Mexico. From a spur of the San Luis Mountains we could distinctly see four bands crossing into Mexico at sundown.

Sieber swore softly, and seemed, in a gratified, knowing way, not to care much. When it was dark we turned back and went toward Cloverdale again.

At Cloverdale we struck some new soldiers, and they

58

had a pack train and some grub and grain with them. Major Tupper was in command, and as scouts he had Sage and some twenty Apaches. His troop consisted of more than forty men, and Major Tupper was glad to see us. His Apache scouts had informed him that we were in the country, but that we were most likely on the flank of the Broncos.

These scouts had seen our trail and followed it a short distance, and they could see by the route we took that we were on the lookout; that we were watching to the south towards where the hostiles would naturally be. All the elevations that we rode onto commanded a view south, and had our trail been made by the Bronco pickets, the elevations that we rode over would have been places that commanded a view to the north, whence troops were likely to come. On one high point, where these scouts of Tupper's turned back, they found a quid of chewing tobacco; they were then satisfied it was Sieber, and they knew Micky and I would be with him.

Major Tupper was an old Civil War veteran and he wanted to "get a lick at the Indians." He had rations for twenty-five days more, and was not trying to get back to the post by the easiest route. While the men got us up a really good meal, he made a good many inquiries about the country to the south, Mexico. Sieber thought at first the old man was just talking, but after we got through eating Tupper kept on talking. Sage said to Micky in Apache, that the old Captain, meaning Tupper, was not afraid to cross the Mexico line in pursuit of the Broncos.

Sieber understood what Sage said and he turned to Major Tupper and inquired, "Is that so, Major?"

Tupper asked him what was so. Then Sieber, seeing that Tupper could not have understood Sage and the Indians, asked him if he cared to cross the line after the Indians.

59

Tupper did not want to talk before the soldiers and scouts, so he and Sieber went off out of camp and had a talk. In about half an hour they came back; Tupper gave command to "get-a-going," and in about an hour we pulled out for Mexico. It was about three o'clock in the morning.

Sieber and Major Tupper seemed to have settled the thing between themselves. I finally ventured a word at Sieber, and asked him if that old man thought he could whip three hundred Chiricahua braves with forty soldiers and twenty-five scouts.

"Why, the old man is crazy to get a chance," said Sieber, "We must be very careful and not let him get too many of his men killed."

Before sunup we went into camp in the rough hills, but Sieber, and not Tupper, was running things then. Every horse was kept in the low places and not allowed to go on top of any ridge or hill. Soldiers were all made to keep under cover. Sieber put some of the Apache scouts to watch the soldiers and keep them out of sight, for if we were to strike the Broncos it must be a surprise to them, for as Sieber said: "If we try to surprise them and they surprise us, we are gone fawn skins."

Sieber took Micky and me about nine o'clock in the morning and we went on to try to locate the Indians. We felt sure they were camped at the Sierra Media.

This Sierra Media means "Middle Mountain," and is a very rough, small mountain in the middle of the Janos plains.

On the west side of this mountain was a fine, big spring. At that time of year there was bound to be lots of water there and it took lots of water for that bunch of Indians when they were all together. There we felt sure the Indians would camp to rest up, for they were tired, and their stock was all tired, and the place was inside of the Mexican line, about twenty miles. The Indians knew we dared not cross the line, so they would feel perfectly safe, but it was necessary to use a great deal of caution in attacking them, for if we made a mistake they would kill all of us.

When we got within six or seven miles of the place where we thought they would be, we went up on a big hill and, Sieber took out a telescope he had borrowed from Tupper, and as it was a long concern, two or three feet long, we built up a pile of rocks and threw some limbs on them to disguise the rocks. Then we strung out that old telescope and focused it on the point of the Sierra Media where the water was. We had to build this rest for the telescope so we could steady it to see well. Sieber lay down and looked a long time; then told me to take a look. I did so, and there were the Indians and horses as natural as could be.

"Now," said Sieber, "all we've got to do is to 'ketch 'em'."

CHAPTER NINE

A Daylight Surprise — "And the Fight Was On" — Horn Saves
Sergeant Murray under a Hot Fire — Casualties and Booty —
Colonel Forsythe and Reinforcements — Indians Clash with Fifth
Mexican Regiment, Chihuahua Cavalry — 167 Killed, 52 Captured
— Forsythe Versus Garcia — Horn Interprets — Armed Force of
Americans on Mexican Territory — Under Arrest; the Surprising
Behavior of the Arrested — Sieber's "General Big Kick" to
Department Commander

THIS WAS ABOUT NOON, and Sieber told me to go back to
the command and move them up to the place where we
were; that we would likely get there by sundown or before, and to wait there till he came, as he said he and Micky
would go into the camp before he came back. He gave me
more details, and cautions, not to shoot or make a fire, but
to camp as soon as I got the soldiers up to this point.

I went back and reported to Tupper, gave him Sieber's
instructions, and we pulled out for the place where we were
to meet Sieber. Major Tupper was "tickled" to get a chance
to get at them, as he said, he wanted anyhow to have a
scrap of some kind and to capture a pony for his little girl.

We got to the appointed place quite a while before sundown, and camped, fed the stock, and prepared to make
battle. The only question was, would the hostiles move
camp again that night? Sieber felt sure they would not, as
they were tired and, as they thought, free from pursuit.

It was close to midnight when Sieber got back to where
we were. He said he left the hostile camp about ten o'clock
and that they were singing and dancing, and Micky told
me he heard the wedding drums beating and could plainly

62

hear the chants they sing at weddings. Sieber said Micky wanted to get a few ponies and bring back to Tupper, as he seemed to want ponies worse than anything else. While Sieber and Micky got something to eat, I got their change of horses. We left six soldiers with the pack train, which remained there, and we started out for the hostile camp.

We went up a swale that ran close to the camp and had to wait a good while for daylight to come. We were within less than a thousand yards of the camp, but they had so many horses running around that they had not heard us.

Sieber, Micky, Sage, and I all knew every foot of the land, and we were each put to pilot some soldiers for a charge when we should be discovered at daylight. There were nine soldiers in the bunch I had to guide. Micky Free was assigned to go with Major Tupper. Tupper was spoiling for a fight, and anyone that went where Micky would go in a scrimmage was bound to see the biggest part of it.

Just at daylight five Broncos came close up to where Sage and his squad were waiting. They saw the soldiers as soon as the soldiers saw them—and the fight was on.

The soldiers with Sage made a run at those five Indians, and got every one of them, and they were the only Indians killed, that is, that we were sure of.

The sergeant with Sage told me Sage killed three out of five with his six-shooter, as they ran. Sage rode his big, white war horse, and he could run right over the Indians. These five Indians were on horseback and were just starting out, evidently, to round in their loose horses.

As for my part of the fight, I did not get to see much of it. Murray, a sergeant, was in charge of the bunch of soldiers I was guiding, and as we charged toward the camp we saw about a dozen Indians in a little bunch of rocks and we took a run at them. When we got up close to the rocks, we

63

were not forty yards from them when we saw them. Old Murray got a shot in the side, gave a big grunt and fell off his horse. I looked around and saw him get partly up so I stopped (for we were going at a run), went back, and got off. I could see that he looked awfully white. He said he was shot in the side. His horse had gone on with the rest of the men in our squad, and I tried to get him on my horse, and I finally succeeded, but when I tried to start, I saw the horse had a hind leg broke.

The Indians were firing terribly fast at us, so I pulled old Murray off the horse, took him on my back and carried him about forty yards, then I gave out and had to put him down. Both of us had dropped our rifles, and he told me to go back and get them. My horse was still standing there, both rifles lying on the ground; but the Indians that were in that little bunch of rocks had undoubtedly gone, as they did not shoot at me any more.

I went back to Murray. He was sitting up swearing, and he said he felt better. "But listen," said he, "to that damned racket."

Well, there were "things doin' " all right just then. Indians were yelling and squaws were yelling. There must have been a thousand dogs barking, and horses were running every which way. There were probably three thousand horses there, and it was not very light yet. The soldiers had been ordered previously to get all the horses they could, but the horses would not leave the Indian camp, and the soldiers could not drive them away. At sunup we heard the bugler with Tupper sounding "Assembly," and as Murray could walk pretty well by this time, I headed off towards where I heard the bugle.

There we found all the command except one soldier who had been killed. Micky and several of the soldiers had a big bunch of horses and mules. Tupper sent several soldiers to get the dead man, and we pulled still farther away from where the hostiles had taken shelter in the rocks. After a little we stopped on a slight rise and waited for the men to come up with the dead soldier. When they came we laid him in a gulch, put a government blanket over him, and piled rocks on the blanket. We put Murray on behind another soldier, Micky roped a horse for me out of the bunch they were holding, and we started back to our camp. The hostiles afterwards told me they thought there was a big bunch of soldiers concealed somewhere close, and that we were just trying to draw them out. It was lucky for us that they did think so, for they could have come out and cleaned us up in a minute.

We had a big lot of horses, and I think there were eight different ones had saddles on them. We caught a big pinto mule with a saddle on, and I took that saddle and the horse Micky had roped for me as my share of the booty. Tupper took all the ponies himself; I think we counted 260 at that time. When we got back to the pack train and had something to eat, Major Tupper was the happiest man I ever saw.

About an hour before sundown Murray and I saw a dust up towards the line and we thought it might be more Indians coming, but we soon saw they were following the trail of our cavalry, and we decided they must be soldiers, which they proved to be. It was a colonel named Forsythe, and his scouts had assured him that there were troops ahead of him, so he came on and went into camp where we were located. There were five troops in this command, and there were now men enough to make a good fight. It was the first time since the outbreak, ten days before, that we had seen soldiers enough at one time to make a good fight. Of course, our outfit was pretty well worn out, having been up all the previous night. Forsythe was not in very good shape himself, but the sight of the captured ponies made him want some ponies of his own.

Forsythe sent for Sieber, and asked him if we could get him up to where he could get a lick at the Indians and get a few ponies. Sieber said he could, if we would go promptly. Then Sieber told him we would have to pull out at once. Sieber thereupon told Micky, two of the Apache scouts, and myself to go back to the hostile camp, and if they had gone, or were getting ready to go, to send back the two Apache scouts to a place named by him, and that he would meet them with the soldiers. Micky and I were to keep on after the hostiles and join him and the command at a place called Panuela. Sieber said if he got there first he would wait for us, and if we got there first to wait for him.

When Micky and I got back to the Sierra Media, where we had left the hostiles by the hundred in the morning, we found it as still as a graveyard. We looked around and found a trail, and it headed direct for the Panuela, and we sent the two Apaches back to Sieber. It was ten o'clock at night, but there were so many of the Indians they made a trail that even at night could be followed as easy as can Capitol Avenue in Cheyenne.

At the Panuela were two or three horses dropped by the hostiles. Micky and I had just reached this water and got a drink when we heard the troops coming, and in a few minutes they arrived. We told Sieber we were on the trail. Forsythe was keen to keep on, and as it was about one o'clock at night, we had to travel pretty lively to get across the plains before sunup.

We traveled on till just about daylight, and then left the Indian trail and turned into the hills at a place called Sousita. The soldiers and their mounts were all completely worn out, and Forsythe ordered camp.

While the soldiers were going into camp, we scouts went up to the top of a peak near there, so we could look ahead. At sunup we could plainly see the dust of the hostiles, not more than eight or ten miles ahead of us, and instead of going towards the Ojitas, as we had supposed they would, they were pulling into the Carretas Cañon.

While we were watching this dust, the sound of rifles was heard by all of us, and by the troops going into camp, also, and a great cloud of dust came up where the Indians were. We could not for a while understand what it meant. Finally we concluded the Indians had run into the Mexican troops and were fighting. We could not see anything but dust and smoke.

After we had eaten breakfast, Forsythe was so anxious to know what the row was where we could hear the firing, we again pulled out for Carretas to learn the exact cause of the trouble. About two hours' march brought us to the place, and, sure enough, it was the Fifth Regiment of Chihuahua Cavalry, under Colonel Garcia. They were just returning from Sonora, where they had been fighting all winter with the Yaquis, and had been camped on Carretas Creek that night, and on this morning the guards reported a big dust coming across the plains headed for the point where the regiment was camped.

Colonel Garcia was an old Indian fighter, and knew in a minute that it was Indians. They were still a couple of miles away, and coming up parallel with where the Carretas Creek runs out and sinks into the plain, Garcia threw his men out down this creek, and concealed in the brush on the creek and under the creek banks. He let all the bucks, who were mostly in the lead, pass on, then he struck the rear of the Indian column. The rear of the Indians consisted principally of squaws and children, and any loose horses there might have been. Garcia slew them all—women and children. One hundred and sixty-seven were killed and all dragged close together by the time we got there. They were killed all around over the country for a distance of about a mile square, but Garcia had dragged all of them together. There were also fifty-two women and children captives.

Garcia's command saw us coming when we were within half a mile of them. They did not know what to make of us at first, and then they recognized us as American troops. Colonel Garcia and about a dozen of his officers came to meet us, and his orderly was blowing his bugle for all he was worth.

Forsythe halted his command, and several of his officers and all the scouts went forward to meet the Mexicans. When we got within one hundred yards of them, they halted; we rode up to them and civilties were exchanged. Colonel Garcia did not have any one who could speak English and I was put in to do the interpreting.

Colonel Garcia immediately told Colonel Forsythe that we were an armed force of Americans on Mexican territory and that we must consider ourselves under arrest. He said he was Justo Garcia,, colonel of the Fifth Chihuahua Cavalry, and asked Colonel Forsythe who he was. Forsythe told him who we were and that we were following the Indians whom he, Garcia, had just engaged. We saw the pile of dead Indians and Garcia told us of the prisoners.

Colonel Forsythe was then informed that his command would be allowed to retain their arms for the present, and he and several of his officers were invited to go further up the creek where there was good water, and have breakfast with Colonel Garcia. Forsythe accepted the invitation. We all went further up the creek and made camp. Garcia and his command had not had breakfast, as the Indians came onto them too early in the morning to allow them time to get breakfast. That regiment of Garcia's, which he said was one of the best in the Mexican Army, had twelve burros for their transportation. They had no grub and no clothes, and many of them did not have a cartridge after their fight with the Indians.

Colonel Forsythe had five troops of cavalry and there were about thirty of us scouts, Indian and white together, and he had about fifty pack mules loaded with grub and ammunition. Forsythe soon saw that breakfast with Garcia was nothing at all, so he asked Garcia to have breakfast with him, which he did. After breakfast, which was about ten o'clock in the morning, Garcia told Colonel Forsythe that he would have to go to El Vallee, the head of the district and would have to remain a prisoner till such an invasion could be settled by their respective governments.

Garcia asked Forsythe to be his guest during the time he would be detained and said he hoped there would be no hard feeling between them. Garcia said he would have to dismount Forsythe's troops and confiscate the rations, and was going on at that rate when Forsythe interrupted him and said:

"I know I am violating an international agreement and I knew what I was doing when I came in here, and I know what I am going to do now. I am going to mount my command and go back as I came down here, and that was without order or command. I will not submit to go anywhere with you and your command. I will now bid you good day."

Forsythe ordered the troops to get ready for a row if it was necessary to have a row; he ordered the packers to

69

pack up, which they did in a very few minutes, and we mounted and pulled back toward the United States line.

Garcia did not attempt to stop us or to interfere at all. He had given the Indians a very severe blow. While he had killed only women and children, he had captured more than four hundred horses, and the Indians would not learn for a long time that it was an accident or a scratch that we ran them into the arms of the Mexicans.

This was the thirteenth day since the outbreak at San Carlos. Sieber, Micky, and I returned to San Carlos and the remainder of the troops went to their respective posts.

Sieber, as chief of scouts, had to make a written report of the whole trip to the Department commander, and in that report he said that from the time the Indians broke out at San Carlos and killed Chief of Police Stirling, till we quit them on Carretas Creek, in the state of Chihuahua, Mexico, that the scouts had been constantly on the flank of the hostiles, assisting and ready to give correct information to any one of the different troop commanders we came in contact with. He then gave the details very much as I have described them. He made a "general big kick" against the idea of sending detachments of from 20 men to 40 men to chastise a bunch of from 260 to 320 Chiricahua braves. He also got in a roar about the transportation and poor condition of the field organization and the lack of available troops for a pursuit such as we had just been on. He said, also, he had again employed me on his own responsibility and wanted me kept on regular; also predicted a big, general row all over the Reservation and on the Mexico line. He said that on our recent raid we had engaged the Indians three different times and all the Indians killed were five killed by a bunch of nine soldiers and one scout. Spoke also of the number of captured horses.

The Department commander sent this report on to the Secretary of War. He notified Sieber in a personal letter what he had done, and said he could do no more, as there was not sufficient money appropriated with which to do anything.

WE STAYED AT SAN CARLOS a while till I could get my affairs straightened out with the beef contractors, then we all went up into the White Mountain country. By "all," I mean Sieber, Micky Free, and myself.

Old Pedro, my friend, was very glad to see all of us, and the first night I got to his camp he kept me up all night long, telling him of the Chiricahua outbreak and raid. He made me go over the story again about how the Chiricahuas ran into the Mexican troops. He asked all the details of the raid and the exact route taken by each band of Indians after they parted and broke up into smaller bands. Of course, he knew all the hostiles well, and as I would describe certain parts of the raid, the old Chief would say: "Yes, that was Natchez," or "That was Chihuahua," or "That was old Loco, himself."

After I had told him the whole story, it was daylight and Sieber had got up and come to the fire where we were sitting, and then the old Chief showed his wisdom.

"Sibi," said Chief Pedro, "this 'Talking Boy' and I have been up here all night talking of this raid of the Chiricahuas. This boy has told me the whole and I am sadly disappointed in one thing. I can't see the work of that chief of all devils, called Geronimo. He was not in the raid. Where was he? Things are bad now, but they would have been far worse had he been there."

Afterwards we learned sure enough that during this raid Geronimo had been laid up with a shot through the shoulder. Chief Pedro could tell them all by their actions as described by me. He said he was very tired, as he was not used to being up all night, and for us to make ourselves at home and not to leave, as he wanted to talk to Sieber and me, both, on the following night. We did not calculate to go away anyhow, so we did as he said.

That night Pedro sent for Sieber and me about ten o'clock, and we again talked nearly all night about troubles we were going to have on Cibicu territory, or with the Cibicu Indians. Pedro told us they were all bad and that they were making lots of trouble for Indians who were actually trying to be good and peaceful. Sieber asked the old warrior what could be done.

"I will give you 150 warriors, all good, picked men," said Pedro, "and you can go over there and kill a good many of them, and then come back and rest up a while, then go back and kill some more, and keep that up the rest of the summer. By winter time there will still be trouble, but there will not be so many mean Indians to help out with it."

Sieber explained to the old man that we could not do that. Sieber asked me in English, so Pedro could not understand, if I thought it would do to tell Pedro how things stood in the Department, and how poorly equipped we were for a big Indian war, such as we thought there was going to be.

"I know what you think, and maybe it was what you were were saying," said Pedro, "and that is, that your soldiers are not prepared for so much war as you both know there is going to be. Both of you are well acquainted with both sol-

diers and renegade Indians, and you know that while your
white soldiers are without fear, they can never meet the
Apache in battle where the white soldier will have a chance.
Brave though your soldiers may be, you must remember
that while the Indians are renegades and outlaws, they also
are brave as any, and perfectly well acquainted with all the
country, and can live like the wolf and evade the white
soldier, who has never had such training as the Indians.
A mad man, though his will be ever so good, cannot overtake, in the mountains, a bad man who is trying to get away.
I am an old man, now; I am very old, and am a chief. I
have fought the white soldiers many a time, and I know just
how they act in battle and on the trail, and I am better
able to give you truth than any other man you can find,
be he white or red. I cannot read in books, I cannot write
on paper, but I can look at the forest, and the mountains,
and on the ground, and I can read every sign there. I can
look at the action of a bad Indian, and can tell you how he
feels and what he will do. Sibi, you are a great hunter. You
know what kind of a place to go to for deer and turkey.
When you see a band of deer or turkey you know what they
will do and how they will act. I am an old, broken-down
warrior, and many years of my life have been spent at war
with Americans and Mexicans, and I know them as you
know them, and as you know the deer and turkey; and now
I am going to tell you what you know well, and you may
think I am a fool to tell you, but there is going to be a great
lot of war, of which this last outbreak is the starter, and it
will continue for many years. Apache soldiers you will have
to use, for, as brave as your white soldiers are, they cannot
endure the hardships necessary to overcome the bad
Apaches.

"Those Cibicu Indians will break out soon and they will

have to go north to the Mogollons, as they are not Mexico Indians. So it will be war on the south from the Chiricahuas, and war in the north from the Cibicus, and many and many a white settler and traveler will be killed. Take my advice and my warriors and go at it at once. Now, good night, and think this over, and remember it is I, Pedro, a wise chief, who tells you this; remember, also, that I never talk two ways."

After Pedro had gone to bed Sieber said to me:

"Tom, that is exactly what you and I have said all the time, and it would be a great thing for the settlers of this territory if we could take the old man's advice and his warriors and go at these bad Indians; but the government would never tolerate such a thing, and all we can do is to do as we are told."

In a few days we went on to Camp Apache, and Sieber reported to the commanding officer there, as was his custom when he went into a government post. The commanding officer told him to come to the adjutant's office the next morning, as he wanted to have a talk with him.

The next morning Sieber and I went to the adjutant's office at nine o'clock, and I was ordered out, as the adjutant said he had no business with me. Seiber told him I was the interpreter, and it would be necessary for me to know of anything that was going to be done.

"My business," said the adjutant, "is not with an interpreter; it is with you, who are the chief of scouts."

I was turned out, and went and sat down and waited for Sieber to get through. When Sieber came out he looked so grave and solemn that I did not speak to him till he spoke to me. At last, when we got to our camp and sat down, he sent an Indian woman to find Micky, so we could talk. Then Sieber, Micky, and I held a war council. Sieber had to talk in Spanish so that Micky could understand, and then he told us what we had to do.

"I am ordered," said Sieber, "to take you two boys and go with a detachment of soldiers to Cañon Creek, and from there to Cibicu, and see these Indians and arrest five of them who are making all of this trouble, as the adjutant says, and we are to take a lot of those same Indians with us to show us who these Indians are. We are to arrest them and confine them here in the guardhouse."

Sieber then named several Apache scouts who were attached to the fort, and said we would go with them.

"Dead Shot and Dandy Jim are both sergeants of the scouts," he continued, "and they will show us the men we are to arrest. There will be a detachment of about twenty men to go with us. Now, those are my instructions."

We were all paralyzed by such an order, for this reason: Dead Shot and Dandy Jim were two of the worst of all the bad men, and they were capable of doing anything bad and nothing good. They were both Cibicu Indians, and entirely in sympathy with anything the bad Indians on Cibicu wanted to do. Sieber, as chief of scouts, had made a strong protest against enlisting these two at the time they were enlisted, as he knew them well and knew their reputation with the other Indians. They both, also, had considerable influence with all bad and turbulent Indians, and were sworn enemies of Sieber and Micky; but as for myself, I knew them by reputation only.

"There will be men leave this post in the morning who will either be brought back dead, or else will be left dead in the mountains," said Micky, for this is a trap that we are going into, and they will try hardest to kill us three, for they think we have no business to come up here and interfere with them. A rabbit trap will catch a wolf, but it won't hold

76

him," added Micky; "so we will just act as though we suspected nothing. We won't be able to find the Indians that we are going after, but we must make the bluff."

Micky suggested that after we got started he would look after Dead Shot, and for me to look after Dandy Jim; "and," said Micky, "we will civilize them." Sieber said that was his idea exactly, as he himself would have to be with the soldiers all the time.

Such was the trip we started on the next morning. Luckily for the soldiers, there were about thirty men of them, but Dead Shot had told the adjutant a dozen would be enough. "Those Indians are not bad, and are not renegades," said Dead Shot; "they will all help the soldiers to arrest these bad men, and it is a good thing to send the white scouts, for they tell lies on all of us; and when they see how things are out there, they will have nothing to say."

At Cañon Creek we camped and found there a lot of Indians. Among them was a captive (Mexican). His name was Suneriano. Suneriano had been captured by these Indians when a small boy, and had never left them. At this time he was married; had a couple of women and half a dozen children.

'Way long in the middle of the night one of his kids, a girl about nine or ten years old, came and woke me. She crawled down beside me, or rather was crouching there when she awoke me. Se told me she was sent by her father, who was Suneriano, to tell me that we would all be killed on Cibicu Creek; that there was a trap laid for us, and that Dead Shot was going to lead us into it. She said all the women and children were then up in the mountains, and we would find only warriors. "There are about sixty of the men," she said. She then went crawling away on her stomach and disappeared. I did not sleep any more that

77

night, and so quietly did this little girl come and go that Micky, who slept within six feet of me, did not hear her.

At daylight I told Sieber what this child had told me, and he in turn told Captain Hentig, the officer in command of the escort. Sieber did note tell Hentig how he got the information, but just told him the condition of things out there. Hentig told Sieber that if he was afraid he could take his two men, meaning Micky and me, and go back to Camp Apache. Sieber replied no, that we would go along to pilot the scattered soldiers back to Camp Apache.

About noon we got to Cibicu Creek, and Sieber spoke to me and told me to watch my man, and to tell Micky to watch his. We could not see any Indians where there should have been lots of them camped, and Dead Shot said they had probably moved down the creek; and there it was that he came to understand that we understood what he was trying to do, for Micky said to him: "Dead Shot, we are onto your game, and I am going to stay close to you all the time, and if any thing goes wrong you will be stealing moccasins in the camp of the Great Spirit just as soon as the fight comes off."

(Dead Shot was accused by the squaws of having once stolen a pair of moccasins from a woman of Pedro's band. This is the lowest crime an Apache brave can commit.)

Dead Shot saw that Dandy Jim was in about the same fix that he himself was. He appealed to Captain Hentig, but had to do so through Sieber, as he and Hentig could not understand each other. Hentig ordered us to leave them, and we told him we were not doing as Dead Shot accused us of doing. Hentig then ordered Micky and me to get behind, which we did.

Dead Shot wanted to go down the cañon, but Sieber swung up the side of the cañon, and then it was that the In-

dians in ambush opened up on us, for they saw that Sieber
would not go into their trap. They were not prepared for
such a move as we made, and consequently did not do a
great deal of damage. Dead Shot and Dandy Jim being in
front of the soldiers while Micky and I were behind, they
both made a run and got away as soon as the firing started.
About ten minutes after the fight started, Captain Hentig
was killed. There were eleven men wounded in the fight,
but none badly. Our Indian scouts all left us. There were
five of them.

We saw the renegades running to get on a high point
directly over us, and Sieber yelled to Micky and me to get
up there first, which we did. We beat the renegades to the
top by about forty yards and this saved the whole party.
Had the renegades reached this point we never could have
gotten out of Cibicu Cañon. This point was the commanding place, and five soldiers came up and helped Micky and
me to hold it. Sieber got Hentig's body on a pack mule, and
when we were all ready they came up out of the cañon.

We turned off the trail and buried Hentig in the hills, and
then started to make our way back to Camp Apache. We
had to leave all trails and stick to the mountains, but were
not bothered any more, for it got dark about the time we
started, and we traveled all night, daylight finding us at
Camp Apache minus Captain Hentig and our Indian scouts.

CHAPTER ELEVEN

The Fort Fired Upon, "This Means War." — Horn Sent to White
Mountains and Returns with Sixty of Pedro's Picked Braves — "Tom
Horn and His War Dogs" on the Renegade's Trail — Indian Atroc-
ities — Chaffee, Sieber, and Kehoe Join the Chase, "Tired, But
Full of Fight." — At Bay in Chevlon's Cañon — Blocking the Only
Exit — A Deadly Trap — Heavy Storm Stops Fight — "Major
Chaffee Too Wet and Cold to Swear." — A Bear Story

SIEBER WANTED TO REPORT TO the commanding officer,
but before he could find him and report, the Indians commenced to fire on the fort. They commenced about sunup,
and kept up their firing for about an hour. There were not
more than one hundred of them, and the nearest of them
were three hundred yards away. They did not hit anything
except a pony belonging to one of the children in the fort.
The pony was in a small shed, and the bullet passed through
the shed. In about an hour the soldiers were ordered to go
up on the hills and drive the Indians away, which they did.

This meant war. Until this time the Indians were allowed
to do as they pleased. Now telegrams were sent to Camp
Thomas, Camp Grant, Camp McDowell, and Camp Verde,
in response to which troops began to come in after a couple
of days.

Two hours after the renegades had been driven off the
hills I was sent to Pedro's camp, about twenty miles away,
and by ten o'clock that night I was back at Camp Apache
with sixty volunteers from Pedro, and they did sure look
"fighty." All of them had rifles of their own, but that night
I made all of them put their own guns in the government
storehouse, and gave each of them a Springfield carbine

and belt and all the ammunition they wanted. My object in this was to have them all armed with guns that used government ammunition. Their own guns were good, but shot all kinds of ammunition.

The second day, Colonel Eugene A. Carr came in from Camp Thomas with two troops of cavalry. He was the first to arrive, and he, as ranking officer, took command. Lots of the Indians from both Cibicu and Cañon Creek were coming in. They camped close to the post and said they did not want to be classed with the ones who had killed Hentig and fired on the post. Many of them said that while they lived on Cibicu, they were under the influence of the renegades, who lived there, and that they had to do as the bad ones said.

Well, we started out to find the bad Indians, and we knew from the information we got from the other Indians who had come in that there was a band of about sixty of the turbulent ones. We could not learn anything from the rest of the Indians except where these sixty Indians were.

"Horn, you take your war dogs and find them," said Colonel Carr to me.

I had previously told him I could find them within a few days sure, for my volunteers knew the country so well that the renegades could not get away.

"Find them," said Carr, "and go at them; then send me word and I will come, and come a-runnin', too."

I started out and went right straight to the renegades. When I struck their trail, I knew they were headed in the direction of Green Valley. I sent word back to Camp Apache to Carr, and kept on after them. In Green Valley I found they had taken a lot of horses from old man Tweeksbury and a lot from Al Rose. About ten miles farther on I found they had killed Louis Huron and Charley Sigsbee. All of the settlers thereabout had joined me. I left them to bury the dead men and look after one of the Sigsbee boys who had been wounded, and who had killed one of the renegades after he was shot.

I was all alone with my "war dogs" as Colonel Carr called them, and they were very anxious to strike the renegades, who were not more than six hours ahead of us. It was night, though, and we had to camp and get ready for a big ride on the next day. Our horses were a little tired and my main man of these Indian volunteers, whose name was Tul-pi, said we could start as late as daybreak and yet strike the renegades before night. We camped and Sigsbee let us turn our horses loose in his pasture where the feed was fine. Sigsbee gave us a sack of flour and we killed a yearling heifer belonging to Stimpson, and proceeded to "fill up." Tul-pi had put out guards around on the hills, and pretty soon they yelled there was American cavalry coming. It was perfectly dark, but they could tell from the sound of the horses' feet. I got on one of the guard's ponies and went to meet the cavalry, for my men were all Indians and I was afraid we might be taken for hostiles.

It proved to be Major Chaffee, Al Sieber, and Pat Kehoe. Chaffee had started from McDowell and had come through the Green Valley at a guess, and he had struck it right. Sieber and Pat Kehoe had been close to Camp Apache, and had met the courier I was sending back to let Colonel Carr know I was on the trail, so on they came after me. They had run into Major Chaffee in Green Valley.

Well, we all camped, and as they had been traveling all day and it was now past nine o'clock at night, they were a tired lot, but they were all full of fight.

After everybody got filled up we had a war talk, and I told Major Chaffee what my war chief had to say, and that was that we could strike the Indians the next day. Sieber and Kehoe thought the same thing, but all of us knew we would have to make a long, hard drive to make it.

At daylight, Major Chaffee cut loose from his pack trains, and went away. About ten miles from where we camped, the Indians had camped and then we knew we would get them that day. How we did go. All my men were mounted on their very best war ponies, and all had had a good night's feed and rest, so everything was in shape for a big day's ride. The cavalry troop were in like condition and all extra traps had been left with the pack train.

About ten o'clock we came to the Meadows ranch, on the east fork of the Verde, and found old man Meadows killed, Hank shot all to pieces, and John also badly shot up. We left the doctor, a couple of soldiers and a couple of citizens who were following us to help them, and learned from the ranchers that the renegades had most likely seen us coming when they left the Meadows ranch. Mrs. Meadows swore the Indians were not half a mile ahead of us.

As soon as we left the Meadows ranch we could see that there was a change in things, for the renegades began to go faster and to drop horses. About noon we struck them as we went up out of the basin on to the rim. We struck only a few, and that formed the rear guard they had thrown out. My men killed one and shot another so we caught him in about a mile. He soon died. He proved to be one of the men who had mutinied when Hentig was killed. We overtook him at a place called Crook's Springs. I was trying to hold some of my men out so as to keep us from running into a trap, but Major Chaffee said the renegades were traveling so fast they could not lay an ambush for us. Anyhow, we were traveling so fast I could not keep my men out. Tul-pi said we would get the renegades when they were crossing Chevlon's Fork, a very deep cañon a short distance ahead. Sieber and Pat thought the same thing. Chevlon's Cañon was a deep cañon that could be crossed in but a few places on account of its depth and the precipitous nature of its walls. We all knew this crossing we were coming to, and Sieber told Chaffee to send five men with Pat Kehoe to go below, and the Indians could never get up on the other side.

As we came to the banks of the cañon, the renegades were just starting up on the opposite side. We opened fire on them, of course. About halfway up the side of the cañon, on the opposite side, the trail would have to run around on a wide bench for a ways to find an opening in the bench to allow them to pass through. Then there would be a place in the trail leading straight away from us. The distance was just about six hundred yards, and when they came to a place that led straight away from us it made fine shooting. Going up over the last rim was a place about sixty feet long, and no one could get out of the cañon without going through this place. Sieber and the first sergeant of I Troop (Chaffee's), whose name was Woodall and who was a famous shot, took up a position with me to command this last slide, to stop as many Indians and horses as possible.

It was a deadly place for the renegades. We had been at them an hour, at least, before they got up to this place, and they were pretty badly demoralized. Pat Kehoe had gotten his five men down in the cañon below them, and they could not go that way. Up the cañon it was impossible for them to go, so up the slide they had to go. Not a horse ever did get up that place. There were three started up at first, and the one in the lead was a gray. I suppose we all thought the same thing, and that was if we could hit the lead horse he would fall back on the others and knock them down like tenpins. We all fired at the gray horse and down he came, struggling, and back he knocked the two behind him. We all felt good, for if Sieber and Woodall felt as I did, each of them thought his shot had done the work.

"Good work, men!" cried Major Chaffee; "keep that hole stopped and we have got 'em." He did not use just these words, for Chaffee, in a fight, can beat any man swearing I ever heard. He swears by ear, and by note in a common way, and by everything else in a general way. He would swear when his men would miss a good shot, and he would swear when they made a good shot. He swore at himself for not bringing more ammunition, and he would swear at his men for wasting their ammunition or shooting too often. Then an Indian would expose himself and he would swear and yell: "Shoot, you damned idiots! What do you suppose I give you ammunition for—to eat?"

The gray horse got stuck in the trail and no other horse could get up till he was gotten out of the way. Several renegades tried to get him out of the way, but it was an awful place to work to much advantage, for we were all good shots, and while the distance was close to six hundred yards, we had the range down so fine, and we were perhaps fifty feet above them, so that for that distance the spot was for us ideal. After they saw they could not get the gray horse away from the place where he had fallen, another tried to lead his horse over the gray one, and down that horse went; not on top of the gray, but nearly so, and that blocked the trail completely. No more horses tried to go through, but several Indians ran up on foot.

About four o'clock there came up the heaviest hail and rain storm that I ever saw in my life. There was heavy pine timber all over the country. The storm came up suddenly, and it got so very dark that we could not see across the cañon. Then the hail and rain commenced. Wah! I feel cold and wet from it yet! That hail and rain punished us pretty well, I tell you. It was over in twenty minutes, and the fight was over, also. All of us were so cold and wet we could neither see nor shoot, and there was a regular torrent running in the bottom of the cañon.

After the storm was over we went back a short distance and waited and wished for Chaffee's pack train. About six o'clock we were all surprised to see the pack train come in, but in the meanwhile we had some fires started and were feeling better. We soon got something to eat, for there were many willing cooks that night. The pack train had seen no hail nor rain and was perfectly dry. Our horses were all doing well, for the grass was as fine and fresh as I ever saw anywhere.

After dark Colonel Carr and a couple of troops of cavalry came in. He had made a very long march, having come from Cañon Creek that day. He also went into camp, and considering how wet and cold we all had been at four o'clock, we thought now we were in luck.

A lieutenant in Chaffee's troop, who was afterwards killed on San Juan Hill (his name was West), in telling some of the officers of Carr's command how wet and cold we got, explained everything about it to his own satisfaction by saying: "Why, Major Chaffee got so cold and wet he had to stop swearing." (Carr and his command had not seen any rain or hail, either.)

On the following morning we were all thrown out to cross the cañon and see what damage we had done the day before. We found a sad-looking outfit up on the side of the cañon. Out of more than a hundred horses, the renegades had only about twenty that were not killed or wounded. We found twenty-one dead Indians and one wounded squaw. Some of the soldiers afterwards said that there were a couple of wounded bucks, but that Micky had stuck his knife into them. Micky had come up with Carr the night before. I don't know if Micky did this deed or not; but I am afraid he did.

A squaw had been shot on the shin bone by a Springfield rifle ball, and the bone was of course shattered in a thousand pieces. The soldiers, some of them, ran onto her, and were getting ready to carry her back to camp, under the direction of the army surgeon; when they were all ready to start with her, she began to scream and motion, and kept pointing to a pile of rocks and brush, and one of the soldiers looked to see what there was there that she was making so much fuss about, as they could not understand what she was saying. The soldier found a little old papoose, about ten months or a year old, concealed under that rubbish. One of the men carried it along over to camp. There the surgeons cut her leg off, and she was sent into Camp Verde along with a few wounded soldiers we had.

All the rest of the troops, except Major Chaffee's, returned to their respective posts, while Chaffee and his troop, my volunteers and I, started out to see if we could find which way the escaped Indians had gone.

The wounded squaw told Tul-pi that there had been about forty-five warriors in the party, and she thought most of them were killed. She said they all knew that a lot of Pedro's warriors were with the soldiers, and they were all very mad because Pedro would send his men out after them. The woman said the Cibicus learned the morning of the day of the fight that these men of Pedro's were after them.

We could not learn anything of the ones who had escaped, for most of them had gotten away before the hail of the day before. Nearly every evening a hail storm or a rain storm would come up, and as all the men we were after were on foot, the signs of them were soon obliterated.

We stayed around there on top of the mountains for about ten days. We even went as far down as Chane's Pass, where there was a sheep camp. We camped within about a mile of the Pass, and several of us went down to see if they had seen any sign of the scattered renegades, but found they had not.

The foreman of the shearing pens (they were shearing) told us a big, long-winded story of a bear that was packing a sheep off every night, and how they had lain out by the shearing pens all night watching for him to come back so they could kill him.

We went back to camp, and about one o'clock that night a sheepherder came to our camp to see if he could get our doctor to come down to the shearing pens. He told us that the bear they had been laying for for several nights had made his appearance. The bear, from what we could learn from the herder, had come along about midnight and the two men who were lying there fired at him. The bear grabbed one of the men and nearly ate him up before all of the men belonging to the camp could get the bear to let up on his victim. The companion of the wounded man had gone for help as soon as the bear grabbed his partner, and in a couple of minutes nearly all the men in camp were there. The bear had been very busy in the meanwhile, and when all the camp got around him he had dropped his man and skipped out. Our doctor, or rather surgeon, went down with the herder, and I followed a few minutes later with Sieber. The man the bear had been doing business with was still alive, but he was the worst used up man I ever saw. He was crushed and bitten and broken in every bone and muscle, so our doctor said. He died before morning. Some of the men in the sheep camp said the bear had been eating sheep meat till he was tired of it, and when he met a hog he thought he would have a mess of it.

Finally we got word to leave the top of the mountain and go back home. Chaffee went back by way of Camp Verde and I went back to Camp Apache and disbanded my volunteers. The scattered renegades had all returned to Cibicu and Cañon Creek and were hiding among the other Indians.

CHAPTER TWELVE

Horn "Gets" the Four Bad Indians Wanted at Camp Apache —
Horn Is "Threatened" with a Government Medal for Bravery —
"I Did Nothing Very Great." — The Medal Still Waiting — Sieber
and Horn Before Investigating Committee — Border Justice to
Horse-Thieves Dealt under Horn's Directions — Unexpected In-
terruption by Department Commander and Department Inspector
— A Row and Reconciliation — A Clever Indian Trick

I HAD BEEN WORKING since early in the spring and had not
received any pay and Sieber had had a good deal of correspondence about it. When we got back to Camp Apache I
was informed by the Quartermaster that my pay was all
straightened out and was at San Carlos, for me to go there
without delay and get it.

The commanding officer at Camp Apache wanted to get
the rest of the Indians who had mutinied when Hentig was
killed, and asked me to go and see if I could do anything
toward catching them. I sent a man to Jon Dazen, a bad
man and a big chief on Cañon Creek, to say that if he did
not bring in these four Indians right away, I would go to
Pedro and get a lot of his warriors and go down there and
look for them.

Jon Dazen did not want me down there with Pedro's
braves, so in four days after I sent him this word, he came
into Camp Apache with the four men the commanding officer wanted. They were Dead Shot, Dandy Jim, Loco, and
another man whose name I do not remember. (These bad
Indians were later, in 1882, hanged at Camp Grant.)

I was not in Camp Apache when these Indians were

90

brought in, as I had gone to Pedro's camp to see and council with him as to how to get these Indians.

"Go back to Camp Apache," said the old warrior, "and in a few days they will be brought in. Those bad men down there have had enough of you and of my men, and to keep you from coming down there with my men they will surrender the men you want."

And, sure enough, when I got back to Camp Apache, the men were all in the guardhouse, heavily ironed.

I then proceeded to San Carlos to get my pay, now so long overdue.

Everything was quiet there. The only excitement they had had right at the Agency during the summer was the killing of Charley Culvig who had been made chief of the Agency Police after Stirling was killed. Colvig, or "Cibicu Charley," as he was called, had gone up the San Carlos River one day on some business or other, and at the place called Ten Mile Pole, he was shot and killed.

His killing had not created much trouble, as the Indian police with him had killed the man who shot him, and that was all there was to it.

Sieber went to San Carlos and located for the winter, and I was left to look after things all over the Reservation. Sieber, after he located at San Carlos, sent and got Sage and made him chief of police.

I received a long complimentary letter from the Department Commander, General Wilcox, along in the fall or early winter, telling me that I was an excellent man, and that he had taken proper steps to have a medal presented to me for bringing old Sergeant Murray out of the fight after he was wounded on what was called in the letter Tupper's Battle Ground at the Sierra Media in Mexico, and also for

91

saving the balance of the command after Captain Hentig had been killed on Cibicu; describing how I, under heavy fire, took one man and gained a high commanding point over the troops and kept them from getting demoralized and annihilated, by yelling to the soldiers to keep cool and to send up another man or two; that with the assistance of two more men I could whip all the Cibicus in the hills; also, for my excellent service with my volunteer force from Pedro's camp.

That was the first time I learned I had done anything very great.

On the famous Tupper's Battle Ground, (I had always considered that was no fight), I thought at that time, and I think so now, that we were bent not so much on fighting as we were on getting a lot of ponies. I know there was no thought of whipping the Indians, for we knew we could not do that, and the only thing we could do was capture a lot of horses for Major Tupper to "show off." Of course I brought old Sergeant Murray out of the fight, but I had taken him in also, and I could not very well leave the old man alone; for he was an old Civil War veteran, had been soldiering for about twenty-five years, and after he was knocked off his horse he could not walk, and if I got him away from under the Indians fire I had to pack him. So, actually, that is all there was to that; but the way it was described on paper, it did look great.

There at Cibicu I was afraid Sieber would get killed, for I could have run away myself easily enough, but Sieber kept with the soldiers and he and some of the men were carrying Hentig, who was dead. I could not run away and leave Sieber. He would not leave the soldiers, and when I saw that, I knew I would have to fight the Indians away till they got out. I know I was not thinking at all of keeping the soldiers from getting killed nor demoralized, as this great letter said, but I knew Hentig was dead, and I was wondering all the time what they wanted to monkey with a dead man for. The reason I yelled to Sieber to send me a couple more men was because when Sieber started in to get them out I knew it would not be worth while to tell him to cut loose from the soldiers and run up to where I was, for I knew when he started to do anything, he would do it. So I had to hold off the hostiles to let Sieber get out. I never thought of saving the rest of the command.

As for my now famous volunteers, Pedro's warriors, had I not taken them with me Pedro would have thought I had no confidence in him nor his braves. So the whole letter, while highly complimentary, was simply based on some account of these affairs as reported to him by some army officer, and in reality there was nothing extraordinary about any of it.

By the way, that was the last I ever heard of that medal.

Along before Christmas there came to San Carlos a delegation of army officers to see Sieber and me about our raid into Mexican territory. "In violation of the international agreement between the United States of America and the Republic of Mexico," I think this summons read. There were eight officers in this investigating committee, and two of them were Mexicans, though they spoke English fluently.

Sieber was sworn in and told his tale, and then I was sworn in and told mine. I don't remember now the names of these officers. I did not know their names at the time, except of one of the Mexican officers, which was E. Milo Kosterlitzki. He was a Polander by birth, a very gallant and courteous officer, whom I afterwards got to know intimately.

All we had to do was to tell them what we knew, and

I was asked who I got my orders from, and I told them I got them from Sieber, the chief of scouts. I was asked if Major Tupper gave me any commands, and I told them no; I was asked if Colonel Forsythe gave me any orders, and I told them no. I never heard of anything being done about the affair afterwards. Everything was done very quietly, and Sieber told me to keep my own council in this matter.

Along early in 1881, while I was camped about twelve miles above San Carlos, Indians kept complaining to me about Mexicans stealing their horses, and several of them wanted me to do something about it. I rode down to the Agency and saw Sieber, and asked him what I could do.

"Organize your 'Injuns,' and the next time any horses are stolen, go after them," said Sieber.

I went back up to camp and called up all the sub-chiefs, and from them learned that Mexicans had come in on the Reservation on two different occasions, stolen horses (always taking the best war ponies), and headed, on both occasions, towards the source of Turkey Creek, keeping on to the Mexican settlements on the Little Colorado River.

I then made arrangements for six different Indians to keep up a good horse apiece each night, so they could be gotten early in the morning, and for them to keep that up until more horses were stolen, and to let me know as soon as possible after the horses were stolen.

Along in February word came in, about dawn one morning, that the Mexicans had stolen a bunch of horses and gone. In ten minutes after the word came in, I was started with two men, the way the Mexicans had been seen going, about an hour before daylight, by some squaws that were camped up in the hills gathering mescal. By sunup there were six of us on the trail of the horses. We soon saw they were not more than a couple or three miles ahead of us, and then we concluded they would come up out of the cañon close to Turkey Springs. One of my men said there was a trail we could get over that we could make a cut-off and either overtake them or get ahead of them. These Turkey Springs were on top of the mountains, and the Mexicans would have a down-hill swing from there, if they could make it. The government road also ran by the springs.

We took the cut-off on the Mexicans and got in ahead of them all right, just at the Turkey Springs. The first the Mexicans knew, we were ahead of them. I yelled to one of them to surrender. He started to run, ran right up to one of my men and was killed. The other two Mexicans were killed also, but one of them ran about half a mile before the Indians got him. Finally, my men came back and said they had killed the last one over in the head of the gulch, and had his horse, saddle, and gun. The horse, by the way, was a war horse belonging to one of the Indians.

About this time, Indians who had started later than we did began to come in, and some of them had been close enough to hear the shooting. Half an hour after we got to Turkey Springs we had all the horses, and the three Mexicans were dead. Everybody felt good, and as two of the dead Mexicans were close to the springs, and one of them was off some distance, one of the bucks said he did not get there in time to help kill them, but that he and his partner would go and drag the one up that was over in the head of the next gulch. So away they went.

I wanted to bury the Mexicans, but the Indians said, "No, let them lie by the side of the road here at the springs, and any other Mexicans coming along will see them, and, as all Mexicans are horse-thieves, when they see these dead Mexicans they will decide that it is not good to steal Apache horses!"

95

Just then we heard the tramp of cavalry horses, and as they were on the government road, I got on my horse and went to meet them, for by this time there was a large bunch of Indians at the springs.

It proved to be the ambulance of General Wilcox and his escort. He was making a round of the government posts with the Department inspector. They were right on us, and came on up to the springs, as they were going to stop there for feed and lunch. Of course, the first things they saw were the two dead Mexicans, and, as I had never met General Wilcox personally, so that he knew me, I told him who I was, and he said, "Yes, yes."

Then he saw the dead Mexicans and asked me what it meant, and asked me where the troops were, and I told or was telling him how it all came up, but I could see that he was mad. To make bad matters worse, just then up came the two Indians who had gone after the Mexican in the next gulch, and now they came, dragging him, with each of them a rope tied to the dead Mexican's feet. General Wilcox did not know at first what they were dragging, but as Indians and soldiers gathered around the newly arrived, the General saw what it was. I was trying to explain it all to him, but he did not want any explanation, and oh, what a raking he did give me!

I can't remember all the things he said of me, but none of them were very complimentary, and perhaps that is the reason I can't remember them.

Among other things, he said it was no wonder there was so much turbulence on the Reservation, when a white man of my position and influence with the Indians tolerated such things as this. "And not only do you tolerate it," he said, "but I believe you encourage it. I have a notion to have

96

you arrested by my escort and take you to Camp Thomas and put you in irons."

I wanted to explain it all to him, but he would not let me talk, and would keep telling me not to talk back to him, but he would not quit upbraiding me. I was getting pretty tired of it, so I thought as Sieber always swore and raised Cain when he got in trouble that I would try the same game on Wilcox. I tore loose at him, and I did my best to equal Sieber or Major Chaffee, but I was a novice in the art compared with such accomplished veterans. Still, I could see I was making an impression, so I kept on and "gave him the other barrel," and really I guess I did pretty well. My Indians all came around, and, while they did not understand one word that was being spoken, they knew I was mad, or they thought I was, and they knew it must be the horse-thieves that had caused the trouble; at any rate, they were with me heart and soul.

General Wilcox was a fine-looking soldier. An old man he was at this time; his hair was perfectly white. He was dressed in civilian clothes, and the Indians knew he must be a man of importance, but it did not make any difference to them who he was, for they were with me, body and soul.

I guess I swore and tore along at a pretty fair rate, for the old man seemed paralyzed for a while. Then he ordered the officer of the escort to drive me and the Indians out of camp. We started in a minute after we got the order, and then General Wilcox called me back and said: "What are you going to do with those Mexicans?" I told him I guessed we would leave them, as we had no use for them at camp. He ordered his escort to bury them, and then told me to skip, and said he would take my case up with Sieber, my chief of scouts.

Every time I would start off, he would call me back and have some more words with me, but he kept getting in a better humor all the time, and finally wound up by asking me to stay to lunch with them! This I could not do, as I had all my braves, who would have had to go hungry; and, though it was now noon, I explained to the General that we had all had to start before breakfast, and were as hungry as wolves; that, though it was forty miles to camp, we did not think much of the return ride.

General Wilcox then called the officer in charge of the escort and made some inquiries about the rations, and we were given a sack of flour and some bacon. This I told the Indians to cook and eat, and in a short time we were all eating.

General Wilcox had his youngest son with him, and the boy was looking at a fancy buckskin bag one of the Indians had; was admiring it and wanted to buy it. I spoke to the Indian, telling him to give the bag to the boy, but to take nothing for it. The Indian then gave the boy the bag. Young Wilcox insisted on giving the donor a dollar, but the Indian spoke to the other Indians to get in a bunch. This they did, for they well understood the game proposed. The Indian who had given the bag then crowded into the bunch of Indians. The Indians immediately scattered out again, and young Wilcox did not know which of the Indians had given him the trinket. This caused a big laugh among the soldiers and Indians, and, as the whole outfit was now ready for the road again, after bidding us good-bye, and after being told by General Wilcox that *may be* I understood the Indian question better than he did, and cautioned me "not to do so any more," they pulled out, cheered to the echo by my outfit.

Charley Wilcox, the boy who was with his father, General Wilcox, on that trip, is now the business manager for William Cook Daniels, of the old firm of Daniels & Fisher, Denver, Colorado. He was for several years reporter on a Denver newspaper.

We all got on our horses and struck out for camp as soon as the soldiers left, and it was late when we got back, as we rode slowly, having ridden very hard in the morning. Our ponies had gotten a couple of hours' rest while we were at Turkey Springs, but we were forty miles from camp.

The next day I went down to the Agency and told Sieber the whole thing just as it happened—of the row and reconciliation with General Wilcox. Sieber said I was doing well for a boy! to get such a complimentary letter from the Department commander one month, and to fall out with him the next was a good way to keep the government in mind that there was, in their employ such a man as Tom Horn!

Nothing more was ever done or said about any of that affair so far as I ever heard, but we lost no more ponies by Mexican horse-thieves.

CHAPTER THIRTEEN

Orders to Report at Camp Apache, Camp Verde, and Fort Whipple — Sieber and "Sieber's Boy" Enjoy a Fine Trip — General George A. Crook Supercedes General Wilcox as Department Commander — More Depredations — Sieber and Horn, "An Armed Force," Invade Mexico — Red-taped, Long-drawn Elaborate Investigation — Governmental "Censure" — General Crook Arrives — Big Indian Council — United States–Mexican Treaty — Sieber and Horn Revisit Tombstone — A Too Warm Welcome

THERE WAS NO MORE DOING until April, when Sieber was ordered to bring me, come around by Camp Apache, report to the commanding officer; to go from there to Camp Verde; report there, and then to come on to Fort Whipple and report to the commanding officer there. We were instructed to take all the time we wanted, and to look well over the Reservation, so as to be able to report the condition of affairs to the commanding officer at Fort Whipple on our arrival there.

We took three horses apiece and struck out. It was a delightful trip, and we enjoyed it to the limit.

When we got out of the White Mountains and out among the settlers in Pleasant Valley and Green Valley and Strawberry Valley, and on the Verde River, we were treated by the settlers to everything they had to give us, and we lived fat and enjoyed the trip as I never enjoyed a visit before nor since. Sieber was a great favorite with all the settlers, and I was called "Sieber's boy," so, for ourselves, on that trip all was lovely.

At Camp Apache, when we reported there, we were just told to go on, but at Camp Verde we were told by the adjutant to wait there for further orders. We stayed at Camp Verde about six weeks, and were then ordered back to San Carlos, and to go in a leisurely manner and to keep a good lookout among the settlers of the Tonto Basin to see if any of them had been molested by the Indians during the spring and summer.

Before we left Camp Verde we had heard that General George Crook was coming to take command of the Department of Arizona. Sieber was glad of it, as he said Crook was a good Indian man.

We had been waiting for a long time to hear some news of the Chiricahuas, in Mexico, but, beyond a few reports that they had been raiding in Mexico, we did not know anything of them. We got back to San Carlos in July, and, for the first time since the Chiricahuas broke out, we heard of them. A bunch of raiders had come back up from Mexico, killed a man close to Stein Peak, crossed over within ten miles of Fort Bowie, killed a man and his son, and stolen a lot of horses at Theo White's Ranch, then had gone down through Rucker Mountains and into Mexico again. It was said there were about twenty or twenty-five bucks in the party.

From San Carlos we were ordered to Fort Bowie as fast as possible. We got there two days afterward, and went over to Pinery Cañon, struck the trail, and followed it back to the Mexico line. The Indians crossed the line at the Guadaloupe Cañon; Sieber and I were alone, but, as the Indian trail was three days old, we had no cause for alarm.

The Sixth Cavalry were going to New Mexico, and the Third Cavalry were coming to Arizona, so rumor said; sure enough, that fall saw a great change in the Department. General Crook did not show up in person till the summer following, but he was running things, so it was said.

101

Sieber and I were now kept at Fort Bowie, and were given to understand that Bowie would be our headquarters from that time on. We got all our ponies together. We had about twenty-five between us, and we hired an old Mexican to herd and look after them for us when we would be away.

There was no more raiding during the fall and winter of 1881, but we frequently saw where little bunches of Indians would come up into Arizona from Mexico, camp a few days, and, as there were no settlers down there, in these cases we were not bothered.

Early in the spring of 1882 there was a bunch of renegades from Mexico crossed the line at Dog Springs, and raided up within two miles of Deming, New Mexico; from there up on the Membres River and over within six miles of Silver City, then down toward the Gila settlements. The first man they killed was at the old Yorke ranch, across from the Stein Mountains, and there they were run into by a bunch of cowboys and white men who were after them.

These boys struck the Indians just at sundown. The Indians were led, some of them, by a white man named Jones, and the cowboys were led by a cowboy named Buck Tyson. They were trying to run up behind the Indians, as they could not get ahead of them. They did finally overtake some of the rear Indians, and had a little running scrap. One of the squaws had to drop her kid, which was eight or ten months old, and the white man, leader of one of the outfits, picked it up—"captured it," the cowboys said. All of the other Indians escaped in the fast-gathering darkness; and as the pursuers' horses were completely worn out with the long chase, they all turned back home.

Sieber and I struck the trail of the renegades as they went back across the line. We ran upon them at the Hot Springs, just across the line. Sieber killed a buck, and I ran up and captured his squaw. We were alone, in Mexico, and as we decided we must hold our prisoner, we turned back, traveled all night and reached Camp Rucker, where we found a bunch of soldiers, and turned our catch over to them to take her to the guard house at Fort Bowie.

Sieber and I both told the officers that we captured the squaw on the head of the Guadalupe Cañon, in Arizona; but some of the Mexican guards found the body of the dead buck at Hot Springs, and found our trail leading back into the United States. Thereupon the Mexican government again sent a protest to the American government about "armed bodies of men" from the United States entering Mexico. We swore up and down when we were "jacked up" about it that it was in the United States where we got the squaw and killed the buck.

By the time this thing came to a head, the squaw had been sent to San Carlos from Fort Bowie, and the agent there asked her where she was captured, and she said: "Right at the Hot Spring." Now, there is only one Hot Spring in that part of the country, and that is in Mexico.

Sieber and I were certainly "in the soup!"

Captain Smith was in command at Fort Bowie, and we were summoned from the southern part of the territory to report to Fort Bowie immediately. The detachment of men who brought us the summons had been looking for us eight days and had started back to Bowie when we ran upon them, and they gave Sieber the dispatches from the commanding officer at Bowie. We questioned the officers who had the dispatch as to what was wanted with us, and he said his orders were to scour the Mexican line till he found us and delivered those letters, and that was all he knew. We knew it was some more of that Hot Springs business, so we went on in with the soldiers.

When we got in and reported to the commanding officer, he told us to go over and report to the adjutant. We went to the adjutant's office and sent an orderly to tell the adjutant to come to the office, which he did immediately. We were called into his office, and he dismissed the clerk who was there. He then informed us that he had a very disagreeable duty to perform. I could tell Sieber was mad, for he knew it was some more of the Mexico business, and we were both tired of it.

The adjutant got out a great elaborate report of a military investigation that had been made by certain commissioned officers of the United States of America, or something about like that; that this investigation was instigated because of certain reports made by certain officers of the Mexican government; that the Mexican government claimed that an armed body of men from the United States of America had crossed the international line between the United States of America and Mexico without authority; that this was done in violation of some treaty or other, and the Mexican government asked that such steps be taken by the proper authorities of the United States to prevent such things in the future.

"Now," said the adjutant, "the officers who are making this investigation have found that you, Al Sieber, chief of scouts, and you, Tom Horn, scout and interpreter for the Department of War of these United States, did, as an armed body of men, cross this so-called international line between the United States of America and the Republic of Mexico, and that you did this without the order or sanction of the military commander of this district, of which Fort Bowie is headquarters. The order of the commission that made this investigation is, that you be censured for the violation. Gentlemen," continued the adjutant, "that is all.

Now, let's go down to the sutler's and get a drink, and you will please do me the honor to dine with me this evening at seven o'clock."

We gladly accepted the invitation to dinner; went down to the sutler store and fixed up about the drink; then went and hunted up our greaser herder and turned our tired horses out. So ended the second invasion of Mexican territory by "armed bodies of men from the United States."

"What a h——l of a row those greasers keep kicking up!" was Sieber's comment. "We are in big luck, though, to get out of it so easily, because I told General Crook that we did not go into Mexico at all, and I guess he thought it was funny if I did not know where the line was, for I was at the head of the party that made the preliminary government survey through there."

From Bowie, after our "reprimand," as we called it, we were ordered to report at San Carlos as soon as convenient. So, in a few days we went up there. General Crook was coming to San Carlos, and was going to reorganize everything in the entire Department.

We stayed at San Carlos a couple of weeks before General Crook came down. He came by way of Camp Apache, and there were about a couple of thousand Indians following him. We are going to have a big Indian talk. And we did have a big Indian talk, and it lasted for a week.

Old Coaly and Suneriano did the interpreting. Sieber and General Crook would talk together all night, or a big part of it, and then General Crook would talk to the Indians all day. General Crook wanted to enlist Indian scouts to go after the Chiricahuas, and he wanted the support of the Indian chief to do so. The Indians, on their part, wanted to be started in the cattle business and they knew that if they could get General Crook interested he would do it for

105

them, or take the proper steps to have it done. A whole week it lasted, and then General Crook went back to Whipple, and Sieber and I went back to Bowie.

General Crook was at this time working to get a treaty fixed up between Mexico and the United States, so that we might cross the Mexican line in pursuit of the Indians. It seemed as though the matter had been referred by the Mexican government to officers of the Mexican Army in the states of Sonora and Chihuahua, in Mexico, and that Colonel Garcia had made a strong protest to the Mexican government against the treaty, saying that, as military commander of the district of Gallajano, in the state of Chihuahua, which was the only part of the state infested with renegade Indians, was entirely under his control, and cited as a fact that he had killed two hundred, as he said, and captured one hundred in one fight; that he had understood the American troops had made some slighting remarks about his engagements with the Indians on that occasion, to the effect that he had let the men all get away, killing only women and children. He said, so Sieber understood from General Crook, that fully one-half, or more than one-half, of the Indians killed by him were grown men with arms of warfare in their hands, and, therefore, he did not consider there was any need for the Americans to come into Mexico. That report of Colonel Garcia had to be gotten over some way, and that way was being worked as fast as the red tape at Washington, D. C., would permit.

Before we left San Carlos, we took the squaw we had captured at the Hot Springs, in Mexico, out of the calaboose and gave her a pony, and took her to Fort Bowie, and told her to go and find the Indians in Mexico, and tell them to send up someone to talk to General Crook.

We lay around on the border for several months waiting

106

for a messenger from the hostiles in Mexico, or from our treaty with Mexico. There was nothing doing, and those were dull days, indeed.

Sieber and I went over to Tombstone and stayed a week to break the monotony, and we did sure break it to a finish! We knew a great many men in camp, and everybody knew of us as members of the pioneer party that located the camp. Well, that trip to Tombstone was worse than any campaign we had been on yet. Every one of the pioneer party that we met had done well. Some of them who were in the party did not do well, but we did not see any of them. Every one of them insisted on buying us a new suit of clothes and hats and six-shooters and champagne. Wow! but it was, as old Ed Clark told us, "a brave struggle we made," but the combination was too strong and too swift for us. We left one morning about three o'clock, so as to avoid the rush. We got the city marshal to bring our horses out behind a place they called the "Bird Cage"; he came in the cage and called us out "for a minute," and we got on our horses and "hit the pike."

Well, I think I am safe in saying that we were drunk, and as we were not allowed to drink anything but champagne, for my part, I did not get steady for ten days.

107

Indian Troubles Begin in Earnest — "Peaches" and Horn as "Talk-Carriers" — Geronimo Would Have a "Peace Talk" — General Crook Goes to Meet Geronimo — Smugglers Versus Custom Guards — "Not Honest, but Honorable" — Geronimo's Hostages and Camp — Horn Must Interpret — An Indian's Tribute to Horn's Tutor (Sieber), "The Old Mad White Man, a Man of War and a Man of Truth"

THE EARLY PART OF 1883 began to start trouble. Peechee, a Chiricahua warrior, came in from the hostiles in Mexico, went to an Indian camp up on the San Carlos River, and told the Indians in camp that he wanted to be taken by them to the Agency, as he had a big talk to make.

These Indians took him to the Agency as he requested, and there he said he wanted to see General Crook, to have a big long medicine talk with him. The agent put the Indian in the guardhouse and put a close watch over him, and wired General Crook that this man said he was from Geronimo's camp in the Sierra Madre in Mexico and had come to see and have a talk with him (General Crook).

The General wired from Fort Whipple, where he was, that he would start for San Carlos as soon as he could make arrangements to do so. He also wired to Fort Bowie for Sieber to meet him in San Carlos. Of course, Sieber and I had heard of this man's coming in, and we knew that the squaw had gotten to the hostiles' camp in Mexico. I mean the squaw Sieber and I captured at the Hot Springs and over whom we got our, by this time, famous reprimand. The officers at Fort Bowie were forever joking us about our "invasion of Mexico with an armed body of men" and our consequent reprimand by the investigating committee.

We knew that this man—who, in all government dispatches, was called "Peaches"—was a messenger of more "peace." Geronimo was one of the greatest and most eloquent talkers in the entire Indian tribe, and when he sent in word that he wanted to talk, he always said he wanted to talk "peace." When there was war to be made, he never had anything to say, but just went to war; but he could stay on the warpath only so long, and then he would get all filled up with talk, and he would send to the government to get someone to talk to. This is what the rest of the Indians always said of him.

We went to San Carlos, and in about a week General Crook reached there also. We got this Indian, Peaches, and took him to General Crook's camp, and the preliminary part of the big tallk was on!

Peaches said that his talk was all from Geronimo and no one else; meaning that such chiefs as Ju, Loco, Chihuahua, and Natchez were not in the talk. He said Geronimo wanted to talk and wanted to surrender, and come back again to the Reservation and not go on the war path any more. He wanted General Crook to come to Mexico with a good big body of troops and escort all the hostile Indians who wanted to come up to the San Carlos Reservation, in case terms could be agreed upon between Geronimo and General Crook. Geronimo said he knew that American soldiers could now come into Mexico, for he told of the fight at Sierra Media and on Carretas Creek, where they ran upon Garcia, and he knew we followed that far, at that time. He also knew how Sieber and I alone struck the little bunch of Indians at the Hot Spring and knew that the Hot Spring was in Mexico.

109

So he said we would not have as an excuse that we could not cross the line any more, as we had crossed it whenever we liked. He said that in the talk Sieber and I had with him in the Terras Mountains, three years before, that Sieber had told him it was only a question of time when arrangements would be made between the American and Mexican governments so that we could cross, and he knew those arrangements had been made or we would never have crossed the line. Geronimo said he was tired of the war path, and, in fact, made the same old talk as in former times.

We then turned the Indian loose, made arrangements for him to get his meals with the escort of General Crook, and told him to be on hand again in the morning.

Sieber and General Crook then held a long talk by themselves, and they did not know what to do under the circumstances. Negotiations were on foot to bring about the treaty to allow us to enter Mexico, but General Crook had not heard anything concerning them and did not know what progress had been made in the matter. The General said he would wire Washington and see what he could learn. This he did, and the next day got a reply and an order to come to Washington immediately.

We concluded to turn the Indian loose for good, give him a horse and some grub, and we made arrangements for me to meet him in two moons at a place in the San Luis Mountains, Mexico. General Crook said he would give Geronimo his answer at that time.

The Indian was given a horse, and Sieber and I took him to the Mexico line and turned him loose; at least, there we left him, as he had been loose all the time. General Crook went to Washington, and when he returned Sieber and I were again summoned to meet him, but this time he came to Fort Bowie.

110

"A Man of War and a Man of Truth"

The General had sent me to meet the Indian at the appointed time, and when I found him with a squaw at the place where he said he would meet me, I told him General Crook wanted him to come with me to Fort Bowie to get his message from the General in person.

Peaches then took his woman off to one side, and I guess he told her what to say to Geronimo. Anyhow, he soon came back to me; the squaw got on her pony and pulled out south. Peaches and I got on our horses and struck out for Fort Bowie.

General Crook was waiting for us anxiously, and was greatly relieved when we came riding into the fort. We had a talk with him that same night. General Crook told him that he must go and tell Geronimo that he, the General, would get together an outfit big enough to furnish an escort for all the Indians who wanted to come to the Reservation, and for Peaches to go and tell Geronimo this, and that our command would go directly to a place in the Sierra Madre called Rio Viejo, and for a guide to meet us on the Rio Viejo to take us to Geronimo, wherever he happened to be. Also sent word he wanted to take all the Chiricahuas.

The Indian was again turned over to me to take back to the Mexican line, which I did. When this Indian, Peaches, and I were together, he would tell me anything I asked him and we got to be great friends. We understood that as far as we were personally concerned, that we did not amount to much, and at the same time we knew that we did amount to something as "Talk carriers," as he called it.

I left the Indian at the head of the Guadalupe Cañon and returned to Fort Bowie. There I found great preparations being made for our expedition into Mexico, but no one know where we were going to. Many soldiers and officers

111

had seen the Indian and me going and coming, but they did not know who nor what he was. I think the general supposition was that the Indian and I were spying on the Chiricahuas, and that we were going to Mexico to surprise the Chiricahuas. I told all of them that I did not know where we were going and I did not know if I would go along or not, and gave them answers of all kinds except the truth.

Some report had come out in the newspapers that there had been some kind of an agreement entered into between certain ministers of the United States and Mexico. The article said that negotiations were instituted to get a regular treaty, but that the treaty could not be brought about and that in place of a treaty this was simply an agreement. Putting together what they knew and what they could guess at, they knew we were going to Mexico, but that is all they did know, and they were not sure we were going there. All cavalry, of which I think there were three troops, were ordered to take rations for sixty days. All the mules in the Quartermaster's Department were turned into pack mules, and a couple of pack trains also came in from New Mexico.

All the scouts were brought from New Mexico and a good many Apache scouts were enlisted. After all the transportation had been put in shape, the packers were laughing to think that they would not have scarcely any load.

The evening before we were to pull out, the Quartermaster sent down extra flour and sugar enough to load all the pack mules down to the guards. The extra flour and sugar were for the hostiles we were going to meet.

At last we got under way, and we headed direct for Mexico. It was amusing to hear the different surmises as to what we were going to do and as to where we were going. The troops we had were of the Third Cavalry. Lieutenant Gatewood of the Sixth Cavalry, was with us, and in command of the Apache scouts. Captain Emmet Crawford, of the Third Cavalry, was in command of the cavalry escort. We had five pack trains and about fifty Apache scouts.

We went down past what we now called Tupper's Battle Ground, at the Sierra Media and on to where Colonel Garcia had his famous fight, and then we crossed the Sierra Madre to get on the Yaqui River slope and over through Bavispe, a good big town, kept up by the guards of the Custom Department. (This town, I will say now, was shaken down to its very foundations by earthquakes in 1887.)

On we went, past the town of Baserac, only two leagues from Bavispe, and the earthquare that razed Bavispe to the ground only cracked one adobe wall in Baserac. All residents of this part of Mexico at that time who were not smugglers belonged to the custom house guards in some capacity or other, and there was the hardest of feeling between the two classes. There was always more or less war between the guards and the civilians, (or smugglers, to use the correct term). Smuggling was a great business in those times. All the smuggling to amount to anything was in the shape of overalls, women's shoes, buttons, needles, thread, and little trinkets. The difference in the price of things in the United States and Mexico was about as follows: Overalls costing 47 cents to 50 cents a pair in Deming, or Silver City, New Mexico, sold in Old Mexico for $2.50. Ladies' shoes costing $1.50 a pair, sold for $5.00. Buttons costing 20 cents a gross sold for 25 cents per dozen.

From this it will be seen that there was big money in the business.

All smugglers were, of necessity, brave, daring fellows who had to bring their cargoes of smuggled goods right in under the very nose of the custom guard, and there was many a fierce fight between them, for a smuggler would as soon die as lose his cargo, and would sooner die than loose a mule. (All smuggling was done on pack mules).

Thus, the residents of Bavispe were all guards or else belonged to the custom service in some other capacity, and all of the residents of Beserac all said, when the earthquake shook down Bavispe, that it was the wrath of God being inflicted upon the guards. And as only one house in Baserac was cracked, and that man was a brother-in-law to one of the guards and supposed to be in sympathy with the guards, it made them all the surer that smuggling was far more legitimate than belonging to the guard service.

These fellows were a good lot of citizens, so far as honorable conduct went. In fact, a common saying among them was, "We are not supposed to be honest, but we are honorable."

From there we kept on down to Bacadebichi and over by Nacori (where we buried Captain Crawford three years later, as I will relate later on). There we left the Mexican settlements and turned into the Sierra Madre proper and crossed over to the Rio Viejo. There the command was camped for a couple of days till I could go up to the head of the river and see if I could find our man to guide us to the hostile camp.

I looked for two days for my man before I could run on him, and then I met him coming down the Rio Viejo. We returned to our camp and I found General Crook very uneasy for fear I had been taken in by the Indians.

Next morning we started for the hostile camp, guided by Peaches, who said it would take us five days more to get there. We kept out a very careful line of guards for the pack trains and soldiers. General Crook said he had no fear of treachery, but it was well to be careful.

It was a lovely country we were passing through. Limes

grew wild most everywhere. On the second day from the camp on Rio Viejo we camped on a stream that our guide said was called "the stream with the old houses on it," and for miles up and down the creek were peach trees by the thousands, all of them loaded down with fruit. Some of the peaches were as ripe as could be without rotting, but more of them were very green. The guide said there were ripe peaches there five months in the year. General Crook said we would name this place "The Peach Orchard." There were many more streams in that part of the country with peaches on them, but none where there were so many as here. There were lots of signs of Indians, and our guide said the whole outfit of hostiles had just left that part of the country.

The night before we got to the camp of Geronimo we were joined by about twenty Indians, young men and young women. One of them, who was in command of them, apparently, said that they were sent by Geronimo as a hostage, and that they should remain with us till after our big talk. They requested to be put under guard, but they were told by General Crook just to stay where Captain Crawford ordered them to stay.

We found Geronimo camped in one of the most lovely places one could imagine. He sent several men to show us where to camp, but we picked a camp to suit ourselves.

Geronimo, Ju, and old Loco came during the evening and paid their respects to General Crook and arranged for a big talk on the following morning.

A big talk it was, sure enough. General Crook had for his interpreters two Mexicans named Antonio Dias and Montoyo. Geronimo started the war tallk by saying that these interpreters were of Mexican blood and that no Mexican was a man of word, meaning they could not speak true.

115

He said that he wanted only peace and harmony in the big talk that was coming off, and that there would be many days of it, and that some of it would be of such a nature that only Geronimo and General Crook should know, and it would necessarily have to go through the mouth of an interpreter, and he must preferred that I should be the one to do the interpreting. He then went on and told of all the preliminary work that led up to this meeting, the part I had taken in all of it, and of the confidence the government must have in me to have me attempt such an undertaking; that the "old mad white man" (meaning Sieber) had raised and trained me; that he knew Sieber to be a man of war and a man of truth, a man who could always be found in a peace council or leading a war party, and that I, as a pupil of such a man, must be a good man and a truthful one, and that I had come to his camp with Sieber on a former occasion to see and talk to him; and he said Antonio Dias was of the Apaches who were not truthful, and he finally wound up his harangue by saying that I was the only one who could do the interpreting.

This was not what we had figured on, for General Crook had instructed me this way: When the talk got started, I was to circulate around among the women and warriors who were not in the council and use my influence to get all of them to go to the Reservation. We knew that old Geronimo would talk to General Crook all day and to his own people all night, and we knew also that Geronimo was popular as a chief, because, while he would make a big bluff of a talk, that he would wind up by doing as the majority of the most influential Indians should decide.

In other words, some of the Indians did as they pleased, regardless of Geronimo or anyone else, and on our side there were certain things that General Crook wanted the

Indians to know, and he did not want to talk it to them or to promise it to them in council, and my duty was to let the Indians know these things. We talked these things over and our councillor, Sieber, said that old Geronimo was onto our job, and that he did not want me going around among the younger men and women to do any talking so as to influence them to go back with us; but as Geronimo had requested that I do the interpreting, the only thing that General Crook could do was to say that Antonio was an old man in council and had been engaged in interpreting for twenty-five years; that I was a young man and not as experienced in such things as was Antonio, and for that reason he had brought Antonio to do the interpreting. General Crook also told Geronimo that I was being raised by Sieber as a warrior and that a warrior was not supposed to be an interpreter.

Geronimo replied that Sieber was the one white man he knew who always represented the government. He said: "Sibi is always with a government council or government war party. White soldiers come and go, and I have seen many of them for many years come and go, but Sibi, the mad white man, is always here." He added that "Sibi" was not a good man to be with, as he was a man of iron and nothing would turn him, and that he did not care to talk, but that his words were all from his heart; that there was no room in his heart for anything that he did not think was right, that his words were as wise as those of any chief, white or red; that he was respected by the Indians, though as iron he was, and that being raised by him was of itself a guarantee of faithfulness in war or in council.

I was all puffed up by the time Geronimo and General Crook got throuugh discussing me. Antonio was then set aside and I took the interpreter's place.

CHAPTER FIFTEEN

Synopsis of General Crook's Speech in Geronimo's Council — "It Must be War or Peace!" — Deep Impression Made by General Crook — What Will Geronimo Do? — Sieber and Horn Summoned as Advisers to the Tribe Council, the Only White Men Admitted — "Take Your Knife, Tom; Stand While You Interpret; Forget That You May Not Live One Minute, and Think Only of the Talk" — The War Chief Speaks — Etiquette of an Indian Council — The Eloquent Silence of the Red Man — Sieber's Advice, "Words of Wisdom and Truth"

GENERAL CROOK was the first man to do any talking, as he had taken the first steps to bring about this talk.

He told Geronimo that eleven years before, when he was in command of the Department, he had left all the Indians on the Reservation at peace, drawing their rations and seemingly content; that when he left, he had no idea that any of the Indians would ever go on the war path again. Then he had been called away by his government to go to another part of the country, and that from time to time he had heard of the Apache outbreaks as they occurred. He said he did not know what made men with as much sense and judgment as Geronimo do such things, and leave a place where everything was given them that was given to the white soldiers. He knew that they had a grievance of some kind, and that he wanted to hear what it was, and he wanted to adjust the grievance in any way that he could that would not hurt Geronimo or the people with him, and that before he left the Sierra Madres he wanted to get Geronimo and every Indian in the mountains to go back with him, and he wanted the influence of Geronimo to help him do this; that the time for war was past, and it was now time to leave the war path and its hardships and go and settle down on the Reservation. He told Geronimo that the Chiricahuas had committed many depredations which laid them liable to arrest and prosecution by the government, but that if they all went back that he would see that none of them were taken away and tried by the civil courts, and that if they would go back to the Reservation and be counted regularly and draw their rations, he would locate them on any part of the Reservation (that was not occupied by any other Indians) that Geronimo might choose.

"There is always more or less trouble in a big Indian camp," continued General Crook, "and I will make soldiers of your men to keep peace in the camp. I will keep a company of twenty-five men all the time, that may be selected by the long-nosed, ugly soldier." (Lieutenant Gatewood was so called. Gatewood was, perhaps, the homeliest man in the service.) "This officer will have no other duty than to look after you and your interests, and to adjust your troubles. He will see that you get your rations and clothing, and everything that you are entitled to by the government. Now, you know what it is that the government has done, and will do, and all that it can do I promise to do for you.

"I have just came back from the place called Washington, which, you know, is the head of our government, and there I met officers high in rank belonging to the Mexican government, and I made arrangements with them to permit of my crossing the line in pursuit of Indians committing depredations in the United States. I have come to you as a brother and as a personal friend, to tell you all this and

119

to conduct any and all who want to go back in safety. When I leave here, I must be informed by you if you want war or if you want peace.

"Formerly conditions were such that we could only pursue renegade Indians as far as the Mexico line. Now I can follow them to the end of the earth. If you do not go back now, and if I cannot persuade you to go back, then I must say 'War!' I am an old man, and would be at peace with all the world, but my people living in New Mexico and Arizona must have protection, and I am there to protect them. I could not do so while our laws would not allow me to cross the Mexico line with my soldiers. Your young men could live here in the Sierra Madres and raid up into our country, and it was seldom we could run onto them while up there.

"The Chiricahuas are very clever, and can easily dodge the cavalry when they have only to dodge them long enough to get back across the line of Mexico; but from now on, Mexico will not protect you. I am telling you all this so that you will know how we are fixed, and so you will know what a refusal to go with me means. It means war, and if you do not go with me now peacefully, I will return as I came to this country, but I will go with a heavy heart. I will then organize a war party and send it to this country and will make several divisions of it, so as to be able to operate all over the mountains at once. Then will the Chiricahuas be doomed, and I, an old man, will go with a heavy heart to my grave, for the war will be long and bitter, and my days will be passed in restlessness, and my nights without sleep. I cannot go out myself, for the hardships will be too great for me, so I will have to remain at home; but, as I said, without rest or sleep. Geronimo, you will go from this council to a council of your own people, and you may think that I have spoken too severely to you. I can talk to you only as I have, for about this talk there must be no misunderstanding. This is a council of great importance to me, as I could not begin a war on you without giving you a chance for peace. I will listen to what you have to say tomorrow."

That ended the big talk for this day. Of course, there was a great deal more talk than I have written down here, but this was all there was said of much importance.

There must have been two hundred warriors in the council, and every one of them got up and went back to their camp as silent as shadows. General Crook's talk had made a deep impression on them. General Crook himself was very grave, and went to his tent and stayed out of sight of everyone. All the officers that heard the talk went back to their camps and began to make preparations for a fight. They thought that Geronimo would resent such talk as the General made to them. Sieber also went off to one side of a hill and sat by himself. Anyone who knew Sieber knew that he wanted to be alone.

We had started the talk very early in the morning, and it was now close to noon. The whole camp looked more like a funeral party than it did like a war party or peace commission.

Micky Free came up to me and said, "Tom, what do you think Geronimo will do?" Of course, I could only guess, and I guessed that he would take a big lot of renegades to the Reservation, but I knew there were warriors with Geronimo that Geronimo himself could not control, and I did not think they would return with us to live in peace on the Reservation, for they were not men of peace. I asked Micky how some of the bad ones, whom each of us knew personally, could go and live in peace. "There," said I, "is Mas-say. How can you expect a man like him to give a serious thought to peace? Mas-say loves the war path, and many of the more restless ones will follow him. They are, every one of them who follows such a devil as Mas-say, men who want the excitement of the war path, and for peace they care not."

Micky asked me if I had known beforehand that General Crook was going to make such a talk to the renegades as he had just made. I told him I certainly did not know what General Crook intended to say until he said it. "Then why did you go and put on your big white-handled six-shooter before you went into the council?" asked Micky. I told him I did so because Sieber had told me to.

"I saw Sieber had his pistol, too," continued Micky, "I could see it where it pushed up his hunting shirt. And when it came around to the part of the talk where General Crook said, 'War or peace, I will have,' I saw Sieber slip his hand up under his shirt and put it on his pistol. It would have been a sad day for Geronimo if he had made any kick at that point, for it would have meant a general row right there. I could see Sieber was watching Geronimo like a hawk. Look up there. Do you see him now?" asked Micky, "When Sieber goes off by himself like that he knows that there may be serious trouble, and Sieber can tell when trouble is liable to come. He can smell it as easy as I can smell smoke. Well, we will just watch him, and do as he does. He is never wrong and he won't be wrong this time."

Micky could not keep still, and I did not feel very easy myself.

All the soldiers were close to camp and close to their guns. All the renegades were as silent as mutes. Not a dog nor a child in the entire camp was making any noise. We could not visit any one for every one seemed to want to tend to his own business.

Presently Sieber called to us to come up to where he was, and we got our rifles and went up there. Sieber began to laugh at us, and said we were standing around like a couple of lost squaws. He said we need not look so solemn as the talk the General made was all right, and he felt sure that the worst of the campaign was over; that when the renegades did nothing in the first twenty minutes after the council was over there would be no danger from them afterward.

We could see many Indians gathering around Geronimo and he stood talking to them. We could see his gestures, and could hear the hum of his voice, but could not distinguish a word he said. None of our party were allowed in Geronimo's council. We watched them for a long time and finally saw him turn and point at us. Sieber said to me that he and I would be sent for by Geronimo before night. "And if you are not with me when he sends, you must come and leave your pistol and take only your knife," said Sieber.

Along in the middle of the afternoon, after I had had something to eat, a small girl came to me and said Sieber would talk with me. I went up to his camp, and he said: "Well, Tom, the summons has come. We are to go to Geronimo. Now you watch me all the time, and that will keep your nerves steady. You tell Geronimo for me, exactly as I tell you to tell him, when I am asked to talk. Stand while you are talking, forget that you may not live one more minute and think only of the talk. No one but Geronimo knows what he will say to us for this is a very critical period, and anything of the least importance may start the war or may prevent it. So don't you say anything at all except as I tell you to say it."

123

We then went over to Geronimo's council. I had felt a little nervous ever since General Crook's council broke up, but now that we were stepping right into the lion's jaws, I did not feel near so shaky. As we were getting up close to the council Sieber looked at me and smiled, asked me how I felt. I told him I was not *much* scared.

The first time Sieber and I had gone into Geronimo's camp, entirely alone in the Terras Mountains, I was not scared or shaky at all, and the Indians all seemed not to pay much attention to us, but it was the actions of the Indians here that made one feel the gravity of the situation. Not a smile on the face of anyone, and, in place of not being noticed as in the Terras Mountains, here every Indian of the two hundred was looking at us and watching our eyes and faces as though they would read our very thoughts.

A place was made for Sieber on a blanket and he was motioned to sit down. Then everybody sat but me. I was left standing as was my place to be, for there is etiquette in a hostile Indian camp just as there is in a ball room of the "Four Hundred" in New York.

Who was it that said the silence of an Indian chief is eloquent? It might have been on this occasion, but if it was I did not appreciate the eloquence of it. I am sure as I stood there amid that silent eloquence I was the most uncomfortable man in Mexico. Oh, how I did want someone to say something. At last, Sieber said to Geronimo:

"You would talk with me?"

"Yes," said Geronimo, "I would talk with you and I have asked you into my council to give me advice and to talk with you, not as a warrior of one nation talks to a warrior of another nation, but as two warriors talk as friends and brothers when a question of gravest importance confronts them in their respective positions. You heard the

124

words of General Crook. You may have known what he would say before he came here. They were words that make a man feel sad to hear, and I know that it made General Crook feel bad to say them. I had no idea he would speak so straight, and I can not now realize that such words have been spoken. General Crook said that I must say if it is to be peace or if it is to be war.

"When a man like General Crook says that to a man like me, it does not leave anything for me to do but say 'war' or 'peace.'

General Crook knows what war is, and he is a man of peace. I, Geronimo, the war chief of the Chiricahua Apaches, for the first time in my life feel that I am getting cornered. True, only the men belonging to my tribe know these mountains well, but with a man like you, a man of iron, as war chief of the white scouts, you will soon know these mountains as does the wolf. Yours is an Indian's knowledge, with the brains of the white man. You are without fear, and, although an old man you have never felt yourself tired. Sieber, man of war, man of peace, man of council, tell me what you think of my position."

Sieber rose and said:

"Geronimo, I cannot answer the questions you have asked me in one minute. I will go to my camp and think well over them and will come again tonight and you and I will talk this over. It will not be well for these men to be present when I talk to you and when I do talk, it will not be General Crook nor the government that talks, it will be myself and my advice will be from no mouth but my own. Send someone for me tonight when you get ready and I will come."

Sieber did not wait for an answer, but went back to his camp alone.

125

After Sieber had gone, Geronimo said to me, "What do you say, boy? Do you like peace or do you like war?"

"I can say only," replied I, "that I can merely act as interpreter for men who have grown old in war. I am a young man yet and have not had experience enough to act as councilor."

"Ah," said Geronimo, "you are cautious. You are being well fitted. Your teacher, the iron man, is raising you to suit himself. He has an apt pupil, and you a chief for a teacher. You are in good hands, but you were nervous when you came with Sieber a while ago. Were you afraid of Geronimo?"

Yes, I told him, I had felt nervous. That I was embarrassed also to have to translate the words of such great men as himself and General Crook and Sieber in a case of this kind.

"Well, talk and visit with my men here. You will always be safe in my camp," said he, "though if we meet in battle, then everyone must look out for himself."

I did not feel much like visiting and soon returned to camp. I was going to Sieber's tent, but he told me not to stop, but to go on to my own tent. "Geronimo's people are watching us, and we will not talk together until after we talk to him tonight."

An Indian council, I will say here, is not a regular discussion of any question, but only by one side at a time. If General Crook talked, no one else was permitted to talk at that meeting. So it was when Geronimo sent for Sieber; only Geronimo could talk then; and according to the custom of the Indians, one must deliberate before speaking. Consequently, Sieber, instead of answering Geronimo at the time he was in the camp to listen to what he had to say, could not [*sic*] make an answer only by appointing a meeting with Geronimo so he could answer him.

It was close to ten o'clock at night when an Indian kid came and told me to get Sieber and to go to Geronimo, which I did.

Geronimo was alone, with the exception of one woman, who was there to build the council fire and keep it going. (Such work as building up a council fire was beneath the dignity of such men as Geronimo and Sieber.)

All three of us sat down in a circle on some skins and Sieber said to Geronimo: "Now we will not be in council, but will just talk to each other as brothers and warriors, as you said in council this evening."

Sieber then began: "Geronimo, you asked me for my advice. You must have known what it was when you asked me to give it. I am for peace all the time when peace can be made to answer. I am in favor of war only when I know there can be no peace. You, Geronimo, do not like peace, else you would never have left the Reservation years ago when you were there. The last time I talked to you in the Terras Mountains I told you that the time was not far off when the Americans could come into Mexico in pursuit of you and your men. You see that I knew how things were bound to come out, for we are here. Now I say to you in all faith and honor that the Chiricahuas can not resist the white man successfully since we can come to this country. If you continue to war with the white man now and under these circumstances, you and all your people will be exterminated. It takes you ten years to make a warrior out of a ten-year-old boy. General Crook can make many hundreds of soldiers in a single day. The white man cannot be exterminated. You and I have seen this country when

127

it was an Indian country. We have seen it when there was no business here except getting in rations for the soldier and his horse. We have seen it from that day to this when there are towns everywhere, and ranches and settlements where once there were only Indians. Now we see the railroad and the telegraph, and with this command is a corps of men who can signal words with a sun glass as the Indian can send a signal. Here I see you Geronimo, the proud and able war chief of the Chiricahuas, surrounded by the last of your tribe and they number about six hundred souls. You are driven to these mountains as the last place of refuge. Here now are two hundred men or more in the very heart of the country you have come to as a place of refuge and these two hundred men are Americans and can find their way here again. I ask of you now what can you do?

"You must go to the Reservation now or else make up your mind to die on the war path and see the last remnant of your tribe die with you. Your men are brave and fearless, and your influence with them is as you want to make it. Not one of them is afraid to die, but all men who are used to facing death every day of their lives like to get the best of any fight that they are compelled to make. I have fought and know what the feeling is when I know that I cannot win the fight. My heart gets heavy when I know that I have to lie close in the rocks all day and creep away when the darkness comes and can only take my rifle with me and cannot tell when I may get something to eat and at times something to bind up my wounds. I cannot tell you how I feel then, but this I can say: that it is not well for any man to be so, be he white or red.

"I never walk into a trap that I can see and still I have walked into more than one trap. Among all the warriors in the Chiricahua tribe not one knows more of the mountains

128

or of war than I. While you have been growing weaker in men day by day and week by week, my position has become stronger and stronger, until now, I know that the white man will rule. Can I make you believe that? Yes, I will answer that question. I can make you believe it, for you know I speak only the truth. I am an old man. You know when I was a young man. Twenty-five years of my life have been spent with the government, and during all of that time my one business has been to hunt down the Indians who were marauders and enemies to my people. Some men never get killed, and I must be one of them. You know if my words have ever been words of wisdom and truth. I always do my best. Sometimes I have made mistakes, but never have I told an Indian a deliberate lie. Geronimo, I say to you, take my advice and tell General Crook tomorrow that you and your people will go with him to San Carlos. Now you know that you cannot hold out, and from here there is no further place for you to go. How can I say more?"

Geronimo sat for a long time and did not say a word. At last, after a long sigh, he said:

"Sibi, your words have touched me. They have struck deep into my heart. I will consider well what you have said, for I know it is the truth; but I am and always have been a proud man, and such words from you make my heart heavier than even the words of General Crook. I talk to the General in the morning; you, of course, will be there. I will not forget what advice you have given me."

I was past midnight and we all started to our camps. The woman who was to keep up our fire had gone to sleep; our fire had nearly gone out. Geronimo gave her a slight kick and told her to go to her tent. So ended our first day in the Chiricahua camp.

CHAPTER SIXTEEN

Geronimo Answers General Crook — The Red Commander Outwits the White Commander, and the Government Is Made Accessory to Theft — Horn Becomes Chief of Scouts to Succeed Sieber — Tribute to Sieber — Twenty-five Apache Scouts Enlisted, Micky Free as First Sergeant — Their "Military" Appearance — An Apache's "Outfit" — Christmas Dinner at Camp Apache — Gatewood's Troubles With Geronimo's People — Horn Orders Chiricahuas Counted at Sunrise and Sunset — Joins His Scouts at Camp Thomas

THE FOLLOWING MORNING, bright and early, we went to the council of General Crook. Only a few of the Chiricahuas were present. By that, we, who were acquainted with their ways, knew that Geronimo was going to promise to go back with General Crook to the Reservation.

Geronimo commenced his talk to General Crook, and if ever an old horse-thief did try to make a squaring talk for himself and his people, that man was Geronimo. What a great confidence man he would have made!

"I listened to your talk yesterday," said Geronimo, "and it made me feel that I had done some great wrong. Perhaps I have done wrong, as a white man looks at my actions. I know that a white man does not see as an Apache sees, and I know what is life to a white man is death to an Apache. My influence with my people is great, as you have said, but there are warriors here whom no one can control. Within the last year some men of my tribe have raided into the American's country. This I am not going to deny. It would be idle for me to attempt to deny it, for this young man who does your translating and this old man who always leads your war parties [meaning Sieber and myself] have met my people raiding up in your country. This old man here, Sieber, killed one of my young men, and this interpreter ran up to one of my women and caught her by the hair and dragged her from her horse and took her captive, and took her to San Carlos, and she was the means of bringing about this talk.

"You complain of my people raiding and killing up in the American's country. Do you not think I should complain of your war chief killing my warriors? Well, I make no complaint of that kind, for so, and in that fashion, do many of my young men want to die. I know, and my men know, that sooner or later all will get killed who keep up such a life; and now I am going to tell you that a life of this kind no longer pleases me. I have grown old on the war path, and what have I accomplished? Only this: today I stand before you as a supplicant. Today I am going to ask of you what I, the proud war chief of the Chiricahua tribe, never thought to ask of any white man. I ask you to take me to the Reservation, and there to do with me as you see fit, and as your judgment says is right for you to do. I will go with you tomorrow, or when you say.

"There are a good many of my people who are not here now. They are all scattered through these mountains, and I will summons them as soon as my runners can get the news to them, that they must come. It will take several days to reach them, for I know not where they are. I now only wait for you to say: 'Geronimo, summons your people and come with me.' I am under your orders from now on. I will have my family move my camp up here to your camp, and here I will remain till we are all ready to start to the United States. Give me the order to bring my camp here, and to send and gather my people to go with you. No one could say or do more than this."

131

"I will do as you say," said General Crook.

Lieutenant Gatewood was then called and told to arrange to issue rations to all the renegades each day, and to arrange to count them each day, and to take entire charge of them.

He told Geronimo that Gatewood would attend to all of that. He told Geronimo to bring his camp up to the soldiers' camp, and that his family would also draw their rations, and then he told Geronimo he would talk to him again in the evening. "For," said General Crook, "Lieutenant Gatewood will be busy with you most of the day."

Geronimo and Gatewood then went about the ration business, for that is the joy of every renegade's heart when he wants to make peace. Flour and sugar cut a big figure in all they do when once they conclude to accept it.

General Crook asked Sieber to go with him to his tent, as he wanted to talk to him. Siber said he might want me, and for me to come with them.

When we got to General Crook's tent, Crook asked Sieber what to do next.

Sieber said: "That talk was all right, and Geronimo will do as he said he would; but the old wolf has something up his sleeve, and I think this is what he intends to do. I think his men have gone now—that they left last night to raid and rob out in the Mexican settlements, so as to get stock—such as mules and horses—to take up with them, and to save my life I can't think of anything to do to stop them. We could call Geronimo up and tell him not to do this, and he would say that he would not think of doing such a thing; but he was cute enough to send these men away before he made his talk to you. Now, when they come in with their stolen stock, he will say they were not here when we first came here. If he gets cornered still more closely he will say that he or no other can control some of his men. I think we will have to take hundreds of head of stolen horses and mules to the Reservation with us. There is some consolation in knowing that they think of staying, or they would not take that trouble."

Sieber then told General Crook how he and I had taken them, or a good many of them, up out of the Terras Mountains three years before, when General Wilcox was Department commander, and that while many of them did not go at that time, the ones who went did this very same thing; that the Mexicans raised a big row, and were upheld by the newspapers; that Sieber and I were accused by *El Fronterizo* (a Mexican newspaper published in Tucson, Arizona) of standing in with the Indians and encouraging them to do this thing, and then protecting them after they got to San Carlos with their stolen stock.

"Now, that same thing is going to occur again," said Sieber, "and you will be blamed in place of Tom and me. Now, I can not think of any way to stop this—can you? We can send and tell Gatewood to make a good count on the bucks and find how many there are here. When they came to council yesterday, I counted 193 warriors. In my opinion there won't be ninety-three for Lieutenant Gatewood to count today."

General Crook called his orderly and sent word to Gatewood to count the bucks and report to him the number after he had given them rations.

Late that evening Lieutenant Gatewood reported 41 bucks and 362 squaws and children. General Crook sent for Sieber, after Gatewood made his report, and told him of the count. "We cannot do a thing to help ourselves," was what we all concluded.

At least 150 warriors had gone in the night to steal horses

from the Mexicans, and the American troops, with General Crook personally in command, were to protect them in it, and give safe transportation to the Indians and their booty to the United States.

"We must stop it at any sacrifice!" cried General Crook. "Call Geronimo immediately," said he to me. "I cannot and will not tolerate such a thing as this. I should be court-martialed for it."

I went and brought Geronimo to the General alone. Geronimo no longer looked down hearted and broken in spirit, as at our previous talks. He was smiling and looked as happy as a king. When he had taken a seat, General Crook said to him:

"Where are all your warriors who were here at the talk yesterday morning?"

"They are gone into the mountains to find and bring back the scattered Apaches," replied Geronimo. "I want to take all of them to the Reservation, and some of them don't know that I am going. I have just sent them word by the men who have gone from this camp. Last night I spoke with them and told them to go, and most of them, or maybe all of them, left last night."

General Crook said to him: "You have sent them off to rob and steal stock to take to the Reservation. Why did you do this? I cannot allow you to get stock in such a manner to take up there."

"I don't think they will rob or steal," said Geronimo, "they have only gone for the rest of my people and will soon return. Maybe we had better all go up to the line and let my young men come and join us there. Many of my people are between here and the line, and we can pick them up on our way. No one can tell where they are and no one can

134

call back the men who have gone after them. We will have to wait here till they come back, or better still, we can go slowly north and wait for them in the San Luis Mountains."

"But I won't allow them to take stolen horses to the Reservation," said the General.

"Oh," said Geronimo, "you need not pay any attention to a lot of howling Mexicans. They are only good to raise horses for the Chiricahuas. My men won't steal. They have a good many horses cached in the mountains and they will likely pick them up, but they won't raid and steal now."

"I may send for you again shortly," said the General, and Geronimo went off smiling.

"He has got all the best of us and he knows it," said Sieber. "We had as well pull out for the line, for so long as we camp here, so long will we see no more Apaches."

Nothing else could be done, so next morning we set out for the line. General Crook said he felt like a horse-thief himself, and Sieber went along swearing softly to himself.

"I knew that old wolf was cute, but I was going to do something to prevent this very thing," said Sieber, "and now he has got the best of us on the one point we were going to guard against. No wonder to me now that he came up and offered to go with us without any more talk. Do you know that Geronimo knew we would try every way in the world to prevent this very thing, and that was the way he took to get the best of our talk. He knew we thought he would want to talk several days and that he would then consent to go. But instead of three or four days' talk, he says, 'All right, I am ready.' There will not be a Mexican in Mexico, or a newspaper in the United States that won't swear we allowed them to do this, and that we just shut the other eye while they did it. Of course we may be mistaken and the bucks that have gone may not raid the Mexicans, but one who knows the Apaches can only think that is what they are going to do."

The next day, as I said, we pulled out toward the United States and the renegades with us, but there seemed to be no one but women and children. Slowly we kept on and not an Indian joined us.

Gatewood counted them morning and night, but they were always the same number. We were twelve days getting back up on the San Bernardino. We did not come back the route we took going down, for old Geronimo had said we might find more of the renegades in the Terras Mountains. We did not find an Indian. From the San Bernardino we pulled over onto the Cajon Bonito to catch any that might come in that way.

We had been on the Bonito about three days and calculated to start toward Fort Bowie the following morning. After night, twelve Indians came in and reported to Gatewood for rations. Gatewood gave them rations and reported to General Crook. He sent for Geronimo and asked about the men who had just come in. Geronimo told him there were twelve. Crook then asked if they had brought in any extra horses, and Geronimo said they brought in fifty head. General Crook told Geronimo that he would make them turn all of those fifty loose in the morning. Geronimo told him that would make all the Indians go back on the war path again.

General Crook then said he would pull out of Mexico, so on the following morning we did so. The General told Geronimo that he would leave soldiers on the line to escort any Indians that came in, back to Fort Bowie, and there he would wait for them. Rations were getting scarce. We no sooner got to Fort Bowie than the renegades began to come in in a stream. Every bunch of them had a great drove of horses, and soon after the Indians commenced to come in, Mexicans also began to come. All wanted their stock, and the Indians refused to give it up.

I guess there were more than a thousand head of the stolen horses and there were several Mexican lawyers on the ground, and things began to look interesting.

Arrangements were finally made to pay the Mexicans for their stock as they could prove it. And on that basis that part of the trouble was finally settled, though even until now I do not know where the money came from to pay them.

About this time Sieber was taken down with the rheumatism, and some of his old wounds broke out, so he was sent to the hospital. General Crook went to Fort Whipple, and Captain Crawford, Gatewood, and I were left with the Indian problem on our hands.

We were ordered to take the Indians to San Carlos, which we did. Geronimo then wanted to move up on Turkey Creek, close to Camp Apache, and in the fall we moved them all up there.

Sieber got no better, and he sent for me to come to Fort Bowie in November. There he told me he had made all arrangements for me to be chief of scouts, for he said he would never go on another trip. He said he was old and worn out. That was the last time he ever did go on a trip. He was still kept at Whipple and San Carlos by turns and drew $100.00 a month, but the only thing he ever did after that trip was to sit around and give advice regarding the Indians.

No white man ever knew Indians as Sieber knew the Apaches. The Apaches, in turn, had the greatest respect for him. His courage was only matched by his regular bull-dog hang-on-and-stay-a-long-time qualities. All quartermaster's men told of how he, one time, lifted a pack mule up and set it on a ledge from which it had fallen. This was an example of his strength.

For myself, personally, I always thought he was the greatest and best man I ever knew. Some said Sieber was no fit company for man or beast. That was because he would go for days at a time and never speak to anyone. No one knew where he came from originally. A few people in Arizona had known him in California, but before that he was a blank. I don't think anyone ever did ask him where he was born or raised, for he was not the kind of man that one cared to ask such a question. His face always looked stern, and perhaps savage, to one who did not know him, but to me he was always good and kind and never, unless in the heat of battle, did he speak loud or cross. He was spoken of by the Indians as the "man of iron," and of iron he must have been. He was shot in Indian battles twenty-eight times with bullets and arrows, and the twenty-ninth time he was crippled for life. That was when the Apache Kid broke out, as I will describe when I get to it.

Captain Crawford was now stationed at San Carlos with his troop of cavalry. I also put in a big portion of my time there. All the Cibicus were as good and quiet as mean Indians could be. The hanging of Dead Shot, Dandy Jim and Loco had a good effect on them.

About Christmas time, Gatewood sent word for me to come up and see him, as he was having some trouble. He did not say what it was. I mentioned to Captain Crawford that I was going up to the Chiricahua camp and asked him if he wanted to send any word up to Gatewood.

Captain Crawford said he would go with me and we would stay and have Christmas dinner with Gatewood.

I had enlisted twenty-five Apache scouts and Micky

Free was my first sergeant, so I told him to detail a scout to take some messages from Captain Crawford and myself to Lieutenant Gatewood, also for him to get ready five of his men as an escort for the Captain and myself to go up to Gatewood's camp.

We started a couple of days before Christmas and got there on Christmas Eve. Gatewood complimented us very highly on our military appearance.

Crawford said we looked a good deal more like a band of border outlaws than we did like the military commander of San Carlos and the Chief of Scouts. The only thing military in the whole outfit was our rifles. We all had Springfield rifles, but our clothes and horses and equipments were of every kind of buckskin to calico shirts, and from corduroy pants to no pants at all. There was not a soldier's uniform in the whole outfit. Crawford and I both had Mexican saddles, as did Micky, but the rest of our escort had no saddles at all.

Usually the Apache just puts a raw-hide or hair rope in a horse's mouth and that is a complete outfit for him. The Apaches said that the Americans were always leaving something in camp; but an Apache never. With an Indian rig (a horse-hair rope), you had all that was needed. When you went into camp, the rope was used to stake out the horse, and when you wanted to move, all you had to do was to tie it around his under jaw and you had a bridle and no traps or parts of your equipment were left in camp.

We had a big Christmas dinner with Gatewood. The Chiricahuas were also given ten head of steers for a Christmas treat. Gatewood waited till after dinner and then he told Crawford and me his trouble. He said he could not keep his count of the Indians anyways near the same. One count day there would be six hundred, and the next count day there would be from five to fifteen short, and he could not get any satisfaction out of Geronimo about where these people were. Geronimo said he did not know. Noche was in charge of the Chiricahua police, and he said he did not know where these people were when they were missing. Gatewood had counted them the day we got to camp and they were twenty-two short.

I concluded that it was now up to me, for as chief of the scouts, it was my business to see to such things. I called Micky, who was having a good time in the Chiricahua camp, and told him that we would count the Chiricahuas at sunup next morning and for him to tell Geronimo that I would expect to find every Indian there, as none had permits to be absent.

Micky said: "Well, I have learned that there are about fifteen bucks gone back to Mexico to steal horses, and if my information is right, you won't find them here."

A correct count next morning revealed the fact that there were twenty Indians missing. As chief of scouts, I asked Geronimo, chief of the camp, where they were. He said he did not know. I told him then, that his people would have to be counted at sunup and sundown every day. Geronimo did make a strong kick at this, but he had to come to it. He said his people did not want to be herded like goats and that they were not molesting anyone and counting them so often was an imposition.

While we were listening to Geronimo trying to square himself and his people, the soldier who carried the mail up to Turkey Creek from Camp Apache came in. Captain Crawford was looking over the latest San Francisco *Examiner* and found an article copied from a Mexico paper saying that the Apaches were still raiding in Mexico. Told of the place and the number of Indians supposed to be in the

140

band. Geronimo was still talking when Captain Crawford called to Gatewood that he had found his missing Indians. He brought the paper over and read the article and I translated it to Geronimo. He swore that the paper lied, but as some of his people were missing, he could not make a very good showing in a talk.

I sent Micky to San Carlos for the balance of the company of scouts and made arrangements for them to go to Camp Thomas, where I would meet them. I made arrangements to have the Indians in Geronimo's camp counted twice a day, and then I went to Camp Thomas to meet my scouts.

CHAPTER SEVENTEEN

After the Raiders — Apache Smoke Signals — Apache Humor — Horn Gathers His Scattered Scouts and Is Joined by Twenty Troopers (Lieutenant Wilder) and a Dozen Cowboys — In Ambush for the Raiders — "You Must Obey Me; I Will Cut the Throat of the Man Who Does Not Do as I Say!" — The Five Minutes' Fight, Not a Foe to Tell the Story!

I MET MY MEN and they were all in good shape. Each had two war horses, and an extra one to carry a little grub and to herd on. I struck out for Fort Bowie and there made arrangements with the quartermaster to bring me grub and grain to old Camp Rucker. I then went on towards the Mexican line to try to intercept the renegades as they came in. I scattered out my scouts and gave each sergeant in charge of his four men a district to work in, so I could cover well all the country that these renegades would have to pass through coming back to Arizona.

My scouts were enlisted men and could not again go into Mexico, but I was a civilian and could go alone anywhere. I went into the Terras Mountains in Mexico. I felt sure the renegades would come through that way.

I was making camp on the very top of the Terras Mountains and, as it was quite a bit after night, I was thinking of building a fire, and I knew, also, that it was not the proper thing to do, because if the renegades did come through there, they could see or smell my fire. I was on the side of the mountain, where I could plainly see a place on the Bavispe River called Los Pillares. I was hobbling one of my horses that I called "Pilgrim." When I got him hobbled, I saw he was looking intently at something in the distance, so I glanced down towards the Pillares and on one of the Pillares(*Pillares* in Mexican is pillars, or buttes), I saw an Indian signal fire. Of course I knew what the Indian was trying to do. He was trying to signal some Indians, and he did not know where they were. I knew the signal was not there when I started to hobble my horse, and was sure I would learn something before morning. Presently the signals were repeated, and they plainly said to me: "Answer!" After an hour they were repeated, "Answer!" Of course I did not build any fire, but wrapped myself up in my blankets, for it was cold (it was the first half of January), and set me down to wait and see if the signal was answered.

About ten o'clock the man doing the signal act had received an answer, but I could not see the point his answer came from. He signaled, one long flash and four or five small or short ones, then two flashes and two again. The signals meant to me that they "were all right and would wait there two days." I knew that the rest of the Indians had asked them from some distance to wait for them two days.

I knew now that it was time for me to be moving to get my scouts together and try to intercept the renegades in Arizona. I was not going to bring my men into Mexico, for I had had enough of that. I traveled all night, and after sun-up next morning rode into Slaughter's ranch, on the line at the head of the San Bernardino Creek. I saw John Slaughter and told him I wanted the best horse he could let me have. I then told him where I had been and what I had been doing. He gave me a good breakfast and told one of his Mexicans to saddle up one of the best horses on the ranch while I ate. I told Slaughter I wanted to leave my two horses there that day and night, for I had ridden very hard, and wanted a

143

Mexican to bring them on to Camp Rucker the next day.

This he promised to do (and did do), and then I got on my fresh horse and was ready to pull out. Slaughter came out and said: "Tom, that is the best horse on this ranch, but I have got three thousand more, so you can keep that one. I know you never spare your own horses, and I am going to give you that one, so you will have no excuse to spare him."

I pulled out for Rucker, about forty miles away, but I was on a good fresh horse, and I let him go. I was within about fifteen miles of Rucker when I saw someone coming down out of the hills to intercept me, and I saw, also, that it was an Indian, in a very great hurry.

It proved to be one of my scouts on the lookout for anything he could see. He saw me at a distance and recognized me, but he could not make out my mount, as I was riding a strange horse to him.

I learned that the squad he was with was only a short distance away, so we went to where it was. I wanted all of the scouts, and I wanted them that night. They were on the head of the Guadalupe and up at Skeleton Cañon, and on the southern point of the Chiricahua Mountains. I started a scout for each of the squads of scouts, and told them I wanted every man of them by daylight next morning. I then went to a place called Tex Spring and waited for them, for that was the place we were to meet. I kept one of the scouts with me, and when he and I got to the spring I told him to keep an eye open and look after my horse, as I was going to sleep. It was about two o'clock when I lay down and pulled my blanket over me, and, as I had not slept a wink the night before, I was soon dead to the world.

It was after dark when someone touched me, and I woke and found Micky standing there. "May we build a fire?"

he asked. I told him yes, all the fire he wanted. He said all the scouts were there but six, and these would be in soon, sure. He said: "We are hungry, and some of our horses are tired." I told him to send all the horses to herd and make ready to stay there all night, and as soon as they could get something to eat, I would talk to them. And I told him to tell the rest of the men that I saw the signal fire of the Chiricahuas the night before on one of the Pillares. Micky said: "Now, where were you when you saw them?" I told him on the top of the Terras Mountains, and that I left the top of the mountains about midnight. He went and gave orders to send out the herd, and we soon had something to eat. We had just got through eating when up came the rest of my scouts.

A strong sense of humor runs all through the Apache race. When these last Indian scouts reached camp, the sergeant with them came up to me and saluted me, as he had seen the American soldiers do, in a very business-like way. Micky said to him: "Why do you salute your chief? He is no soldier. He is a citizen. I am the ranking soldier of this outfit, and if you want to salute, I am the one to be saluted." "I can't salute you," retorted the scout; "here is too much mixture in you for me to attempt it. You are part Mexican and part something else, and I don't know what that part is. I know I never saw anyone else like you. I know only Americans, Mexicans, and Apaches. You are none of these and you are all of them, and as I am only Apache, I will have to balk." This is the kind of talk and josh that you could always find in the Apache scouts' camp.

Micky made them eat, turn out their horses, and then we had a talk to see how we could get a lick at the renegades. I told them all I had seen, and Micky said the same as did all the rest—that the signals I saw sent from the Pillares

145

were to the effect that the ones at the Pillares would be joined by the others in two days. I told them that it was just about the same time the night before that I saw the last of the signals. It was seventy-five miles to that place, so going there was out of the question for two reasons. We would not have time, and we could not go into Mexico. Now, the question was, what would we do and how would we be able to get a lick at them?

Just then one of the scouts on herd came in and said there were soldiers coming. I got on the scout's pony and went to meet them. This was always customary, as wild Indians and tame scouts all look alike in the dark.

The soldiers proved to be Lieutenant Wilder and twenty troopers of the Third, and he was glad to find me. General Crook had learned that I had gone towards the line with my scouts, and he was afraid I would invade Mexico again. Wilder had dispatches to that effect for me from General Crook. Wilder, of course, went into camp there with me. General Crook's dispatches to me said that Lieutenant Wilder would remain with me in command of the outfit, as it was necessary to have a commissioned officer in command of enlisted men, and that my scouts were all enlisted men.

Wilder came over to my fire after he got his camp straightened out, and I told him what my dispatches contained. That I had an order from the adjutant general for him to take command. I then reported to him what I knew and what I had seen from the top of the Terras Mountains, and that I was sure the renegades would come up in two days, or three at most, and I wanted to try to get a lick at them.

Wilder was a trump. He called me Chief, and said he would do anything in the world I told him to. "Now, you want those Indians," said he, "and nothing was said to me

146

about Indians; but we will give them a little chase just for luck."

We all concluded to go to bed and wait till morning. Wilder was all right, for he had two blankets, and he offered me one of them, as he said he had a piece of canvas besides his blankets. I would not take his blanket, and the next morning I saw his good piece of canvas—it was about four feet square!

Next morning we started to go to the southern end of the Chiricahua Mountains to pick out a place to take up a good position, that we might cover all the ground to the Mexican line. We were joined by six San Simon cowboys. Micky had met one of them the night before and told him that I was at Tex Spring; that I had just come up from Mexico, and was sure to have some knowledge of the renegades, as I had twenty-five scouts there on the line, and had just sent word for all of them to join me at Tex Spring, to get there before daylight, sure.

The cowboys were always ready for anything, and so they came to help us out if they could. They were all well armed and well mounted. Our force was all right now, if we could just make the correct guess and intercept the Indians. The boss of the cowboys said for me only to tell him what to do and he would do it.

One of my scouts reported a band of men of some kind coming across the flat. They proved to be John Slaughter's men, and I sent one of the cowboys to head them off and bring them directly to us. When they came up, I found they had my two saddle horses that I had left at Slaughter's ranch. The Slaughter men were five in number, and all were Mexicans except the boss. who was a Texan. They wanted some of the row if we could get them into it. They were armed, as Wilder said, like pirates and well mounted. I

147

knew there were only twenty or twenty-one Indians in the bunch, and at least three and maybe five of these were women. So we all knew that if we could strike them, they were ours.

The San Simon cattle boss wanted to get at them so bad that he could hardly be controlled. He said he wanted to get in a place where he could get right up on the edge of them. I just wanted a man or two like him, so I put him with Micky. We could not figure that the renegades could or would come any other way than by the mouth of the big open cañon called Dry Creek. They would come from the Pillares, where they would all get together, and Micky and I figured that they would come up in the Wild Bull Hills, as the Indians called them. We calculated they would then try to make the southern point of the Chiricahuas Mountains from there in one night. It would be forty miles, but it was open country, and they would be bound to cross the Mexican line from where they were in the night. Then I knew they would have a good big lot of horses, and by crossing in the night, and in the neighborhood of the San Bernardino Ranch, the horses they had would not make so conspicuous a trail to be seen and followed by anyone, as there were hundreds of head of horses on the San Bernardino Ranch. I knew, also, that the renegades would figure on this same thing. It would also make the best route to the Reservation.

Well, we camped there, and I put in the day figuring out the exact way the Indians would come. If we could make the right guess on the exact place they would come through, then we could get them easily. I took only Micky with me, as he and I were the only ones among the scouts that knew every foot of the country. We finally decided that the place the Indians would come would necessarily

148

be the mouth of Dry Creek. We kept a good watch during the day, thinking we might see something, but nothing showed up.

That evening I placed all the men just where I wanted them and we waited and watched the best we could during the night, but not a sign did we see of the regenades. We put in the day eating and sleeping, and of course kept a good lookout. In the evening I took more precautions than on the previous evening, as I figured we would strike them about daylight next morning.

Next morning, when it got light, there were no Indians on hand, but we saw a big dust off to the south, and we knew it was the renegades with their stolen horses. They were fully ten miles away. At first we could only see the dust, and it was quite a while after sunup before we could distinguish the Indians. The herd of horses kicked up a great cloud of dust, and the Indians were enveloped in the cloud of dust, so we could only make out one once in a while.

Instead of coming up into the mouth of the Dry Gulch, where we thought they would, they kept on around the foot of the mountains in the open. As soon as I could determine for sure which way they were going, I arranged my men, and a fine opportunity we had.

The renegades had no idea we were near, and as they got close to us, I could plainly hear them singing.

I arranged for Lieutenant Wilder and his troops to strike them in the lead, and the cowboys, led by Micky, were to take them in the rear. I would keep my Indian scouts with me, as I had misgivings about the wild soldiers and about the cowboys, wilder still; and as it was to be a fight on horseback, I knew everybody would be more or less excited. The San Simon cowboys were led by a wild kind of fellow, and

149

he asked me if the man I was putting with him was anyways timid. "If he is," said he, "you keep him and let us cowboys go it alone." I told him that if Micky acted timid, to come back and tell me, and I would shoot him. I told him to follow Micky and he would be in the fight. I had told Micky how to do, and not to start the fight, but to wait and let me start it. I told him that I would expect him to control the cowboys till he heard my yell and shots from my party.

Now we were ready and the Indians were still half a mile away. We were waiting for them to get behind a hill, then my men would get in position. Micky ranged up his cowboys and addressed them in Mexican, which they all understood. (Micky could not talk English.) He said to them:

"Friends, I will take you into this fight, and then each of you do as you please after the fight gets started. You want to do as I tell you until the chief says to start, and then we will go. Till that time, you must obey me and I will cut the throat of the man who does not do as I say. That is all. Come on."

A more recklessly brave man than Micky never did live at any time, and as the cowboys wanted to fight so bad, I knew that if they followed Micky they would be in it.

I got down as close to where the Indians would come, as I could get. They were coming slowly and we had plenty of time. The herd would come within two hundred yards of where my party were concealed. Just when they got to where I wanted to strike them, one of the renegades gave a yell. "Un-Dah!" he yelled. (That meant "White men." I was going to start the fight by firing, and this renegade that gave the yell was looking towards where I knew Wilder was. I was on the ground and was going to shoot at this Indian.

150

He checked up his horse an instant and I blazed away at him. That was the signal, and few men ever saw such a sight as I saw there. Soldiers rode at them from the front, Wilder at their head. Cowboys charged them from the rear, and as I saw them come over the hill I looked to see where Micky was. He was all right and leading the cowboy charge.

I wanted to turn the renegades out into the flat country, so I took a run at them myself, enough to make them think that I had the main body of men with me. Sure enough, they turned for a minute towards the flat. In a good deal less than a minute after I fired the first shot, soldiers and cowboys and renegades were all mixed up, and most of my scouts went away and left me. I had got soldier blouses from Wilder's men and put them on my scouts, so that if they did all get mixed up, my scouts would be easy to distinguish from the renegades.

If any hostiles got away from that fight, I never saw nor heard of them, and I do think that not one escaped. A squaw turned towards where I was and there was no one after her and she was coming directly toward me. I stopped her, and I think she was the only one of the entire party that was not killed. After the fight was over, she told me there had been fourteen in the party. Eleven men and three women. We found and counted ten dead men and two dead women, and I had one woman alive, which accounted for all the women, but there was one man shy, and we could not and did not find him. He never returned to the Reservation, and I do not know what ever became of that one Indian. My opinion always was that he escaped in some way, and was wounded so that he must have died in the mountains.

I don't think the fight lasted five minutes. We, on our side, had one dead cowboy, a Mexican from San Bernardino

Ranch, and two wounded cowboys. Micky Free had a big slash in his left arm and one soldier was shot in the neck and one in the stomach. We were in big luck to get off so easy. The cowboys and Micky did most of the killing, as they had the best show and all of them were riding picked horses, and as the San Simon boss said, they did go right up to the edge of them!

There were 118 head of stolen horses and I did not know what to do with them. I would not touch them, and Lieutenant Wilder would not have anything to do with them. The San Simon boss would not have anything to do with them, so I got the Slaughter boss from San Bernardino to take them back and turn them loose at the Slaughter ranch.

We buried the San Bernardino Mexican. He had tried to rope an Indian and did rope him and pulled him off his horse; then the Indian got up and killed him.

Some of the cowboys wanted to scalp the dead Indians, but the San Simon boss would not let them. We stayed around there till close to noon and then we all went our different ways.

Wilder and I both wrote out our reports of the fight, and Wilder sent a couple of soldiers on in to Bowie with them. I tried to get Wilder to take charge of my prisoner, but he respectfully declined. Wilder was going back by the Tex Spring and I was going up over the Chiricahua Mountains, and I made arrangements to meet Wilder at old Camp Rucker in two days, and we would go from there to Bowie together.

CHAPTER EIGHTEEN

Horn Wins the Approval of Both Burke and Sieber — A Breathing
Spell — Visiting the Big Ranches — Back to Camp Apache — The
Chiricahuas Becoming Restless — The Verge of Another Outbreak
— Intercepting More Apache Raiders — A Surprise and a Scatter-
ment — A "Big, Healthy, Greasy Squaw Treed." — Brandy as a
Persuader to Telling Tales — Geronimo and the Entire Tribe Break
Out Again — The Mexican Rendezvous — Planning
to Thwart the Renegades

FIVE DAYS AFTER THE FIGHT we got into Bowie. All this
happened in the month of January, 1884, and it was the
last day of January when we got into Bowie. Major John G.
Burke met us there, or at least he came in the first day of
February.

Major Burke and Captain Roberts, both of whom were
on General Crook's staff, had a long talk with my prisoner.
I was not present at the talk. Major Burke spoke Mexican,
or Spanish as he called it, and he used Micky as interpreter.
Burke came, after he got through his talk, and asked me
what I was going to do with the squaw. I told him it was
up to him. He said I might send her up to Turkey Creek
with the rest of the Chiricahuas, so she could tell them that
the renegades that were missing would not come back. I
sent Micky and a half-dozen scouts with him to take the
woman up to Turkey Creek, and to come back by San
Carlos and get all their traps and horses that they wanted
and come back to Bowie, as Burke said I must make Bowie
my headquarters.

Major Burke was very much pleased with the way things
were going, so he told me.

153

When Micky and the rest of the scouts came back, I had a long letter from Sieber and he told me I was doing fine, to keep it up and do just as I saw fit all the time and never to wait for orders from headquarters, but when anything was to be done, to put out and do it and let the orders follow me up, as they had on this occasion. He said Major Burke and Captain Roberts were both old Indian fighters, and whenever it became necessary for me to do as I had just done (that was to go on my own hook, without orders), that Burke and Roberts would always send out a good young man to find me and take charge of my command, but that the young man would always do as I advised, just as Wilder had done, and any officer who would not do so would never be sent for me. Sieber said Burke and Roberts did not want to tell me this, but they wanted me to do so without being told.

After Micky got back from San Carlos, we lay around Bowie till we tired of it, and I took Micky and a couple more men and went out to look around the country a little and visit. The San Simon cow boss had pressed me to make him a visit, so we took in the San Simon Ranch for a starter.

We reached there the next day after we left Bowie, and at the ranch we stayed for six days, "hunting Indians." Well, it was certainly amusing to hear those cowboys tell of the fight we had out at the south end of the Chiricahuas. There were ladies there, also, and one of them asked me if I did not think it a very dangerous life to lead, being chief of scouts. She asked me how I knew the Indians would come the way they did come, and a great many more questions with about the same amount of sense in them. She asked me if I was not afraid my own scouts would revolt and kill me. She said they could do so any time out in the mountains. She said: "All the cowboys say that your man Micky is one of the greatest scouts alive and one of the bravest men, but I am sure he looks like a villain."

I told her that Micky was a gentleman and a scholar, and that I also considered him a judge of beauty, as he had told me that the white lady with blue eyes and blonde hair was the prettiest woman he had ever seen. Next day I noticed she had Micky in her house feeding him sweet cakes and giving him lemonade to drink!

We knocked around the big ranch and visited for about three weeks, and then went back to the post.

Along in the summer we went up to Camp Apache and to the Chiricahua camp on Turkey Creek. I was going to discharge my scouts in a short time, as they had enlisted for only six months at a time, and I wanted to see Gatewood, so as to know if it would be necessary to enlist any more.

Gatewood told me he was having an awful time. The Chiricahuas were unusually mean, were trading off all their horses for ammunition and whiskey, and that they were raising Cain with all the other Indians; in fact, that he could do nothing with them.

"They will not stay much longer," said he, adding that he was going to leave the camp and go and live in Camp Apache, twelve miles away.

I went over to Geronimo's camp and asked him why he could not behave himself. He asked me what he had done, and I told him that his people were not doing right. He said he could not do anything with them. I asked him if he was tired of life on the Reservation, and he said all his people were dissatisfied. I wanted to know why. He replied: "It will do no good to lie to you; they want to go back to Mexico." I told him if he ever left again, that General Crook would keep his word and go down to Mexico with a war

155

party and that many Indians would have to die. He said that they all wanted to go, and that only his counsel held them. I learned from his talk that Gatewood had good cause to feel uneasy, for when Geronimo said that only his voice for peace was heard in the entire Chiricahua camp, the matter of peace hung by a very slim thread, for Geronimo never had favored peace. He would talk peace, and talk it day and night, but he was in reality the war chief of the Chiricahuas, and was still looked upon as such by all the tribe, and the balance of peace, when left to him, was surely a slim hold on peace.

I went down to San Carlos, saw Sieber, and told him of my talk with Geronimo. I told him that the other chiefs would not talk with me at all. Sieber said: "That means war, and bitter war it will be now. I have just learned what Geronimo came up here for. He calculated to live here on the Reservation and keep sending raiding parties into Mexico to steal horses and bring them up here and sell them and start up a regular business, thinking we would be compelled to help him out with it. You and Wilder and the cowboys knocked it out of the first gang that he sent down, and now that he sees that he cannot do that kind of business in a successful way, he wants to go back on the war path, so he can keep up the devilment he loves so well. We will go to Bowie and see Burke, and we may be able to do something. At least we can not let this go without putting it to him plainly."

Sieber could not ride on horseback, as an old wound in his hip was giving him a lot of trouble, so he got an ambulance from the Quartermaster and we struck out for Bowie, which was now the Department headquarters. Sieber had to go around by Thomas with the ambulance, so

I went straight across the country and got to Bowie one day ahead of him.

When he came in, we saw Major Burke and told him that we thought Geronimo was going to break out again, and soon at that. We then went over the whole business with him and told him our reasons for what we thought. Major Burke told us that General Crook was in Washington and that he would write him a full account of what we had reported, and see what General Crook had to say. Burke wanted to know what we had to suggest to stop the outbreak. We wanted to take up the cavalry regiment and put all the bucks in irons and the women and children under guard and send them away. Burke wanted to know where we could send them to. I suggested that they be sent to Missouri, and Sieber said: "Yes, send them to Missouri or to h——l or some such place. That is all we can do."

I asked Burke if I should enlist another company of scouts, and he said I could not, as no arrangements had been made for them. He told me that I could hire nine Apache scouts for $30.00 a month and them furnish their own horses, and one man for $50.00 and furnish his own horses and that the Quartermaster Department would give me forage for two horses for each man. Told me to go to San Carlos and get them and report back at Bowie as soon as convenient, as he thought General Crook would soon be there. I went back with Sieber in the ambulance and took my saddle, as I had some horses at San Carlos I wanted to bring down.

I got my scouts as soon as my old company was discharged. I made Micky my head man, of course, and we were soon back at Fort Bowie.

There Burke told me that General Crook would be de-

157

layed some time in Washington, and hinted that now, as
my men were all civilians, I could cross the Mexico line, and
that we would not be an armed body of American troops.
I then told him how Sieber and I once crossed the line and
that our own government rounded us up for it, and he
laughed and said, yes, he knew all about our having been
"reprimanded by the investigating committee," and said
that he guessed it did not do much good, as the following
January I had gone into Mexico alone, anyhow, as far as
the Terras Mountains, when I located the Indians that
we cleaned up so well down on the south end of the Chiricahua Mountains. I told him one man was not an armed
body of men. He gave me to understand that if I did violate
the orders of our War Department and invade Mexico with
civilian scouts, that our government would stand by us if
we were arrested down there. And that if we made an invasion and were not arrested in Mexico, that he did not
think the federal courts would handle us very roughly here
in the United States.

Of course we would not be arrested in Mexico, for there
was no one there to arrest us. Burke told me to take my
men and go make Camp Rucker my headquarters, and that
he would send down rations and forage for us. He told me
always to leave two or three men in camp so they could
go and find me if I were away from camp when any message
came from headquarters.

We pulled out. We had about twenty-five extra horses
and every one of them a picked horse. We were well fixed
to do lots of scouting, but there were no renegades out that
we knew of. I always left three men in camp to feed and
look after our extra horses. Now, when we would go out,
we never had to take an extra with us, for we would make

only such trips as took us from four to six days. I never got any further orders regarding anything. Every month the Quartermaster's chief clerk from Fort Bowie would come down in his ambulance and pay us off. There was a troop of cavalry stationed there also, and with the troop and in command of it was my friend, Lieutenant Wilder. He put in his leisure time in wishing I could find some more renegades, and in drinking smuggled mescal. I always left word at camp with the men there as to about where I would be if we were needed. I was looking for General Crook to come, but did not hear a word more of him.

Along about the middle of November the long expected happened. At the head of Skeleton Cañon we heard some shots fired and a big bunch of "Diamond A" cattle came running through the hills. There were three or four hundred head of them, and we were sure it must be Indians. It was either Indians or outlaws, sure, and so we guessed Indians. Whichever it was, if we met them it meant war. There were eight of us, and we were all right to look out for ourselves.

Micky and I got off our horses and ran up to the top of a little butte, and there we saw about twenty-five Indians gathered around the carcass of a cow they had shot. There were squaws and bucks and children, and they were all gathered or were gathering around the cow so we could not get a count on them. They were coming from the north, toward the Reservation, as we saw several of the hindmost ones still coming up. There was water close to them, but if they camped at the water we could not get at them, as there was too much open country. They were about six hundred yards from us, but we could get a great deal nearer by going on foot. The only thing to do was to try and get a lick at them as they were butchering.

159

We rode as close as we dared to go on horseback and then left one man with our horses and ran up on a little hill that had a kind of a rough stony top and also a few scrub trees on it. We were only a couple of hundred yards away, so we tore loose at them. Well, I am telling you the truth when I say there was no more butchering done there. The women and kids commenced to yell and their horses were some that had been stolen in Mexico, and they most all of them got scared at the racket and started to run and we kept on shooting for a minute, and then I sent four of the scouts to bring the horses. The man we left with them was coming, but he was slow.

In a couple of minutes the horses were brought up. Micky and I remained and were shooting as well as we could, but we were not doing any good. When our horses came up, we mounted and went at the Indians. We did not have very good success, as they were well scattered now, and running, most of them on foot, and they were hard to do anything with, so we went back up the hill the way the rest of the scouts had gone.

We found Micky with two squaws and five children; we also got six horses and two mules with their equipments. We went down to where we had done the first shooting, at the beef, and there we found two dead bucks. I was afoot, my horse having been killed, and we had a bunch of prisoners. We did not notice for a while that we were one man shy, and then we heard a big racket up on the top of the hill. Micky rode up there and one of the scouts had a big, healthy, greasy squaw treed. The scout did not want to shoot her, and she had out her knife and swore she would cut his heart out if he put his hand on her. I did not see it, but Micky said it was a great battle. The woman said she would not be a prisoner, so Micky said: "Well, we have got too many prisoners, anyway." He drew up his gun as though he were going to shoot her in the eye, and she said: "Well, I will go with you." That made three women and five kids that we had, and the worst of it was we did not have the women the kids belonged to.

We loaded them all on the horses we had captured, after I picked out the best animal (and a very good one he proved to be after he got rested up a month or so), and for Camp Rucker we headed. It was getting late, and we wanted to get out into the San Simon Valley before night. We were thirty miles from Rucker, and we wanted to get there that night. The San Simon Cattle Company were boring a well out in the flat and I wanted to go by there and tell the men the Indians were out, as one of our captives said all the Chiricahuas had broken out.

At the well I found one of my men from Rucker coming to look for me to tell me of the outbreak. He had also come by the well to let the boys there know that the country was full of Indians. This outfit of mine settled the whole thing for the men at the well. They wanted to get away from where they were, and they wanted to do it quick. They had a good team of horses and a wagon, and a double-barreled shot gun. They could not go to the San Simon Ranch, as they would be going towards the Indians. When I suggested that they hitch up and go with me, they were very willing. I put all my prisoners and the traps that were on the captured horses in the wagon, as the Indians' horses were very tired. I put Micky in the wagon also, and we again started to Camp Rucker, where we arrived about sunup.

Lieutenant Walker had a full report of the outbreak from

Bowie, and he was ordered to co-operate with me and see if we could intercept any of the renegades that were coming toward the line. I told him that we were too late to do any more good, but that I would get something to eat and then have a talk with the captives. The women had refused to talk much and were as sullen as mules in a mud hole.

I got a big drink of brandy from the surgeon and gave to one of the women, and then all of them said they would talk if I would give them a dram. This I did, and a big one, and they then told me all about the outbreak. How everyone was made to leave all extra horses and camp traps and to make for Mexico in small bunches of about twenty in a bunch, and not to stop from the time they started till they got to the San Luis and Terras Mountains. They were all warned to be very careful on the Mexican line, as Geronimo knew that Micky and I were on the line somewhere. There is a mountain in Sonora, Mexico, called El Durasnillo. The Indians call it Cu, and there all the Indians were to rendezvous.

This was pretty good to know, so I sent a scout in to Major Burke and told him what I had learned as to the place the Indians would all come together, and suggested to him that he immediately notify Colonel Torres, at Hermosillo, Mexico, to that effect, so as to give him a chance to go gunning for them.

After I started my messenger to Major Burke, I tried to get Wilder to take my prisoners on to Fort Bowie, but he would not do it, as he wanted to go on down towards the line and try and find some more Indians. So I had to go myself to Bowie. I did not like to leave the line. I knew, also, that all the renegades were in the mountains safe across the line, but I had only ten men and I could not divide them and do any good.

162

I dared not send Micky in charge of my prisoners, for he would have killed all of them; so I sent Micky and another with Wilder and I loaded my squaws and kids into a government wagon and pulled out for Bowie.

CHAPTER NINETEEN

No More Bluff, but Real Old Business — Civilizing Geronimo a
Hopeless Task — General Crook Arrives — Preparations for War —
A Side-Trip Scrimmage — Danger and Irish Wit, Guns and Tongues
— Sergeant Nolan and the Indian "Ladies" — Plan of Campaign —
Chiricahua Band, Bent on Vengeance, Raid up to White Mountain
Camp — Hal-zay "Loses His Head" — Horn and Ten Scouts "Hit
the Trail" — The Language of a Cold Trail: Tracks, Side Trails,
Smell of Roasting Mescal, Shadows of Campfires Ten Miles Ahead
— "We had Located the Main Camp at Last!" —Sending
for Captain Crawford and the Troops

WHEN I GOT THERE, I found Burke had wired Colonel
Torres, the Mexican commandante of Sonora, Mexico, and
I learned also, that to the best of Burke's knowledge all
the rest of the Indians had gotten to Mexico in safety. Now,
it was no more bluff and no more talk for there would have
to be a great deal of campaigning to get rid of the Indians.
Major Burke actually told me he did not think Geronimo
could be made to stay on the Reservation. Every advice
that the government had ever had was that Geronimo would
not stay on the Reservation, and nowhere else but on the
war path. Every department commander wanted to have the
the reputation of civilizing Geronimo. I had helped, and in
fact been mainly instrumental in bringing him to the Reservation twice, and he had been brought up and put there a
couple of times before, and now Major Burke said he did
not think it was worth while to try to keep him there.

Sieber knew that a dozen years before, and had always
maintained that the wily chief would have to be sent away
if the government wanted to stop his raiding, and now Major
Burke, chief of staff for General Crook, admitted as much.

164

I got ready to start toward the line again, but I knew it was too late to do any good, so Burke told me to wait for reports to come in from the pursuing parties, as he said there were several out, and all of them specially instructed not to cross the line. One of my captive kids died in a day or two. It did not belong to any of the women we had and the women would not look after it. It was only about three years old and did not take kindly to government rations and the guardhouse, so it went to the Happy Hunting Ground. The rest were put in the guardhouse.

Reports commenced to come in that the troops pursuing the renegades had followed to the Mexican line and there abandoned the trail as per instructions from the Department commander. That was the report of every one of the commands that were in the pursuit of the renegades.

General Crook wired that he was coming from Washington, and for Sieber and me to meet him there at Fort Bowie. It was two months before he did come, and that threw us out into 1885. But General Crook was fixed for war when he did come. He had had a regular treaty made with the Mexican government, so we could campaign in Mexico the same as in the United States.

He ordered Sieber and me to San Carlos to enlist Apache scouts to go to Mexico, for we had long before decided that only Apache scouts could ever be effective on a campaign in the Sierra Madres. We enlisted one hundred scouts of the San Carlos and White Mountain tribes for a six months' campaign in Mexico, and all to go on foot. Under the new treaty we were to have any and all stock that we captured from the renegades.

General Crook went to work to establish heliograph stations and started a school in Bowie to teach men the art of heliography. He ordered cavalry stationed at all the prin-

165

cipal watering places anywhere near the line, and started out just as though he intended to make good his word with Geronimo in the Sierra Madres. Three pack trains and a good many team mules were sent to Bowie from Camp Carlin, Wyoming. Ed Delaney was boss of one pack train, and John Patrick was in charge of another, and Ben Groves had the third. Harvey Carlyle was master of transportation.

Things did sure look like war, and in June we pulled into Mexico.

Sieber had to stay at home, as he was crippled up, and too old for such hard work as we had before us.

We calculated to have a field headquarters and supply depot at Nacori, and we went there. I was busy all summer getting stations located for the heliograph. We made several little side trips while getting everything in order.

On one of these we ran onto a bunch of Indians in camp. There was a detachment of troops with us, or rather I was with them. I was looking for a place to put in a connecting station for the heliograph we were locating. The men who were going to do the work at the station (there were about twenty of them) met a bunch of Chiricahuas in a cañon. There was no commissioned officer with them, but they made a run at the Indians and caught thirty women and children. There were only about seven or eight bucks with the gang, and the bucks all got away. One of the squaws was run over by a soldier and hurt so that she died before a doctor could get his medicine to work on her. Excepting this squaw (and a crippled pack mule), there were none killed.

I got my mountain located where I wanted to put a station, but could not find my men to put up the glass. I started out the way I had told the soldiers to come and meet me, and I was coming to the conclusion they had made a mistake and got lost, and was thinking to myself that they had overruled my scout and gone to suit themselves, when I began to see all kinds of tracks on the ground.

There were Indian tracks on foot—large and small—cavalry horse tracks, pack mule tracks, and lower down a dead pack mule. The tracks showed me plainly enough that there had been a fight, and soon I saw where the soldiers had turned back, and could see they were guarding prisoners. Then I knew I would find them at Nacori, so I pulled out for there.

It was past midnight when I got to Nacori, and Nolan had not come in yet. I told Major Davis, who was in command, what had become of his "shadow men," and that they had no doubt camped, and that I had missed them in the night, but that they would be along in the morning.

At daylight I was on my way back to meet them. I had a whole lot of soldiers and Apache scouts with me. About nine o'clock we saw them coming. There were a good many more prisoners than there were guards. Sergeant Nolan had seen my Apache scouts, and thinking we might be renegades, he was trying to get the prisoners in position so he could hold them and make a fight, also.

I had with him two Apache scouts, and they were trying to make Nolan understand that we were of his own party. Nolan thought the scouts were frightened, but, as he was not very proficient in the Apache tongue (for he said there were no Apaches in Ireland!) and as the scouts did not know any English, they could not get him to understand. Finally one of the prisoners said to Nolan: "You fool! He white man soldier!" Nolan then saw that we were all right, and he slacked up and put up his pistol.

One of the men in his detachment used to tell afterward what Nolan said to the prisoners when he was trying to get them behind a reef of rocks, so he could guard them and make a fight at the same time. Martin reported that Nolan said:

"Ladies, there are people approaching that are your friends and are enemies of mine and the United States government. Now, I, Sergeant Nolan, do order you to get behind that reef of rocks, and I want you to be d——d quick about it, and not stand there gaping like a lot of low-down shanty Irish! Here, you little black-haired imp of the devil, let that pack horse go and come along here! To h——l wid yer d——n talk, and do ye moind! You think that you will be rescued, do ye? Not while Nolan is at the wheel; you won't lose your course. I will order a court-martial and hang every mother's son of ye to the yardarm!"

By this time Martin said Nolan was getting so excited he did not know what to do. He yelled to Martin to shoot those two d——n'd Apache scouts. "They have led us into this ambush!" Martin then got Nolan to understand that we were from Nacori. When Nolan did finally see that we were all right, he said: "God be praised! I was afraid I would have to take a life, and I was using my best judgment to act and conduct myself as a gentleman before ladies."

This soldier, Martin, never did get through telling what Nolan did and said there in two minutes. Nolan was very much worried as to what he should do with the ladies when they camped for the night, and he finally went over and told them in the choicest Connemara Irish that he had never read anything in any article of war that would seem to fit this peculiar case, and they would have to excuse him, but he could not offer them any bedsteads to sleep upon. "In fact, we don't have any with us, because we did not expect the honor or pleasure of your company."

Nolan never did hear the last of what he did and said on that trip; but he "got the grapes," just the same.

Nolan was all right!

We were very busy all the summer of 1885, getting transportation into proper condition, getting camps of soldiers established at all the principal water holes, and getting the heliograph in working order.

When we got the heliograph to working properly, we could send a message to Fort Bowie from Nacori in about an hour. It had to pass through seven stations; had to be received and sent again from one to the other, but such was the excellence of the management that seldom was a mistake made.

I was hastily called to Fort Bowie after we had all the stations established and working, and there met General Crook, who was having a battalion of Apache scouts enlisted to go to Mexico under Captain Emmet Crawford. With Crawford was Lieutenant Marion P. Maus, now on General Miles's staff, and Second Lieutenant Shipp, who was killed at San Juan Hill, in Cuba, in 1898, July 2.

The scouts were on the road to Bowie from San Carlos when I got to Bowie. General Crook said he would send for me as soon as Crawford arrived.

When Crawford did get to Bowie, we were all summoned to meet and talk to General Crook. He invited us to dinner, and after dinner he told us of his idea, which was to have us go to Mexico and stay there six months, and when we got on an Indian trail never to leave it so long as we could find one track to follow; to strike the renegades as hard as we could on every occasion; to kill all bucks and take all women and children prisoners; but that we must keep after them all the time. He then told us all the details of arrangements in Arizona, and he gave Captain Crawford a map of all the country where troops were stationed and where there were heliograph stations.

It was about December 1 when we finally left Bowie. We had heard, by heliograph, that a band of renegades had crossed the line close to Agua Azul, and that they were coming up the country. We thought they would come through the Dragoon Mountains, as that would be their best route up from where they crossed the line. I was now the one who, as chief of scouts, had to decide about such things, and how I did miss Sieber, for he knew everything!

I put out men in the Dragoons and men as far west as the Whetstone Mountains, to try to get them as they came up, and in that way to keep them from raiding in the settlements. Always before, we had been compelled to wait until they had done their raiding, and then follow their trail back.

Our helio was doing its work well. All the settlers were requested to notify the helio stations as soon as any Indian sign was seen. This was the first bunch of Indians we had ever heard of as they came up from Mexico; and this information came, thanks to the helio.

Well, they were a war party bent on revenge, and not on robbing. They were not seen again until they got to the Reservation, and there they ran into old Nad-is-ki's band in the White Mountains. The men were nearly all away, so they struck a camp mostly of women and children and killed twenty-one of them. One of the raiders was also killed, and they cut his head off and took it into Camp Apache. It proved to be Hal-zay, the Indian Sieber and I met on the Bavispe River when I first went with Sieber to the Chiricahua camp. A party of men had gotten after them there the next day, and they had come back south and crossed the line way up by Alamo Hueco.

170

We headed then for the Car-Cai, in Mexico, knowing they would cross in there. Now, one thing we knew, and that was that they were going to try to do so much damage to the Indians on the Reservation that the Indian men on the Reservation would not go to Mexico to hunt them. They made remarkable rides while up in Arizona, and the troops were within sight of them several times; but as there were only eleven came up in the first place and one of them was killed, only ten of them got back. They did not steal any horses except what they had to have to make good time, nor kill anyone except one Mormon at Ash Cañon.

Well, I struck their trail in the Sierra Madres, and as it was ten days old when I struck it, I knew we would have to be very careful or we would not get up to them. I left the command and took ten men and pulled out on the trail on foot. I made arrangements for Crawford to wait two days where we were camped and then follow on down by Nacori; then on to the crossing of the Rio Arras.

I kept on the trail of the ten knowing they would go to the main band to tell of their raid on the Reservation. I soon saw that they did not know exactly where the main band was, and there had been rain enough in the mountains to wash out any very old trail.

After we got across the Arras, I struck more Indian signs, and saw where quite a bunch of Indians had come in from Saguaripo in that part of the country; then I sent a man back to tell Crawford that we were coming upon more Indians, and wrote him what I knew. I also told the man I sent back to bring the command to the mouth of a big cañon we could see in the mountains ahead of us.

In a few more days I found more tracks coming in, and knew then that the reason the Indians we were following did not know exactly where to find the main band was

171

because the main band, or anyhow, all the bucks, had been raiding in Sonora. All that were coming in had lots of horses.

Pretty well up the Arras we found where a bunch of cattle had been brought in on the trail and also found where a big lot of Indians had been camped but had moved on south into the mountains.

Here also all the trails leading away had been made at the same time, and then I knew that we had struck the main bunch. (There were many beef carcasses, showing they had killed all the cattle and jerked the meat.) There were about four hundred of the Indians, but many of them, as I knew, were women and children. Here I sent two men back to Crawford, and told him all I had learned and asked him to come with the outfit and camp till he heard from me again.

I left the trail and took up a course parallel with that of the renegades, for I well knew their custom of leaving a few men behind the main party to give warning if anyone was in the track of them. I traveled all day, and then at evening began to cut across to see if I could strike their trail. I sent a couple of men to two different mountain tops to see if they could see any sign or shadow of campfires. Two of the scouts who went up on one of the hills came back about midnight and said they had seen the shadow of campfires reflected on the clouds in the sky and that the Indians must be camped a long way up the river.

I sent two more men back now to bring the outfit on up to the point where we were and to wait there for further orders. We went on the next day, and about noon we could smell the smoke from pits where the renegades were roasting mescal. Then we knew that we were getting very close to the main Indian camp, as they have to take a week gen-

erally to roast mescal and they would not be doing it unless they felt very safe.

We lay off and slept the rest of the day after we began
to smell Indians, and we calculated to do the most of our
work from that on, after night. When night came we were
all on the highest point around there, and as it began to
get dark we began to see shadows of fires and they were
not ten miles from us. We had located the camp at last.

Now the main thing to do was to get at them in good
shape. I had only four scouts with me now, but I sent two
more back to bring the command up to where we first
smelled the mescal smoke.

I did not know anything about where the command was,
as I had been sending word back to Captain Crawford all
the time, but had had no word from him. I was afraid now
that he was several days' travel behind me.

I did not know Crawford, but he had a great reputation
as a "go-to-'em" kind of a fellow, and no man would look
at him and call him afraid or negligent. He looked good to
me; he had a regular wolf snap to his jaw. Really the only
thing I was afraid of was that the country would be too
rough. When I was leaving him fifteen days before, he said:
"Now, Chief, you show me the way, and I will be there on
Hank Monk time."

Well, I was showing him the way, but I had not had a
chance to hear from him, and now that I wanted him I
began to be afraid he would be slow.

I took my last two men and struck out to get close to the
Indians' camp and see what we could learn about it by the
time daylight came. We were all night getting to a place
that suited me, and so when we did get where we thought
we would be all right, we all sat down and went to sleep.

173

I woke as the day was breaking and was plenty cold, as we had no blankets and we had not had anything to eat except meat, for ten days. As it began to get light, we could see some fifty campfires, and some of them were not a mile away from us. We saw the Indians going around in their own way, driving in horses, and they did have lots of them. At first I thought they were going to move camp, but I soon saw that they were merely getting in their horses to accustom them to the camp, as many of the animals had just been stolen and were not yet used to an Indian camp.

About nine o'clock I had learned all I could learn about them and the lay of the land, so we started back to get our own command. If Crawford was keeping up with me, he would not be more than twelve miles away, and if he was not, it was not my fault. About noon, or a little after, we were called by one of my scouts, and he said the outfit was very close there, and so it was. My two men and I were very hungry; Crawford had a dozen pack mules with him, and we soon had something to eat. Everybody was pleased at the news we brought, for the command had had a hard time keeping up with my orders.

I told Crawford all I knew, and he told me to go on and finish the job. "You have made a fine hunt of it so far, and you must take command now, and do your best, is all I can say."

I had everybody get ready for a whole night's work, and then I lay down and went to sleep and was wakened at sundown; one of the packers gave me some grub, and we pulled out.

CHAPTER TWENTY

Forces Divided Into Four Groups under Crawford, Maus, Shipp, and Horn — Attack upon Geronimo's Camp — Complete Rout — A "Sieber Bluff" — Horn Captures Nana — The Old Chief's "Growl" — Geronimo Sends Messenger; He Would Talk — Chiricahua Squaws as Mourners — Much-needed Rest

WE GOT TO CAMP all right, and I broke the command up into four bunches. I took the east side, and sent Shipp to the west side. The east side was next to the mountains and the west side was about a mile from the Arras River. I placed Maus to go to the south side, and left Captain Crawford on the north side. We were approaching the camp from the north. I wanted Lieutenant Shipp to start the fight on his side, next to the river, and make the Indians come towards me, if he could make it work that way; but at the same time I knew that any one of our parties might run into the Indians, and then the row would be on. Naturally I knew that the way the Indians would break would be towards the rough country, and the rough country was on my side.

We were all in position before daylight, and all we had to do was to wait; the longer we could wait, the more light we would have and the better would be the shooting.

One thing that was against me was the eagerness of my scouts. I talked to them, and warned them to try to keep from starting the fight as long as possible to give us better light, but they were all mad because of the raid that the renegades had made on the Reservation and the killing of the woman and children. They all knew that we would

175

capture some women and children, and I had instructed them that they must not kill any women or children, but to go at the bucks and kill all the bucks they could.

There were dozens of horses scattered around everywhere, and just as it was getting light, we could begin to see the women and children working around among the horses, and others beginning to build fires. Minutes were worlds to me just then, as it was still too dark to do any good shooting.

It was just getting light enough so we could begin to see everything quite clearly when two big bucks came directly towards where I lay. There were four or five scouts with me, but I knew that every one of my twenty-five scouts had a bead on these two renegades. They got up within twenty yards of where I was, and had not yet seen one of my men. No one spoke, but everybody seemed to fire at once, and those two bucks never smiled again.

Well, there were big doins' in that camp for the next half hour! Geronimo jumped up on a rock and yelled: "Look out for the horses!" And a minute afterwards he yelled: "Let the horses go and break towards the river on foot! There are soldiers and Apache scouts on both sides and above us. Let the women and children break for the river and the men stay behind!"

Towards the river they all ran, and I was thinking that Lieutenant Shipp had not got into the place I had assigned him, but had got in the wrong place. I could hear old Geronimo giving his orders as plainly as though he had been by my side.

I knew that my scouts could hear and understand, also. Geronimo kept on yelling to his people: "Towards the river! Towards the river!" I began to think I had been a fool to put Shipp on the river side, and that I should have put

Captain Crawford there. The time was very short, but it seemed ages to me. I knew that a scared Indian could outrun a mad one; that my long, hard work was about at a close, and I was thinking it was too bad; I was just saying to myself: "If Sieber were here what a scientific lot of swearing there would be!" Then my thoughts came to a close, for I found Shipp, and he was the "rightest" man in the world.

Shipp had a boy with him who could speak English. I don't know how much he could speak, but I don't think it was much. I think it was the opposite of much that he could speak. Anyhow, this boy, Charley, could, of course, understand the renegades, and when the fight started, and Geronimo commenced to yell to his people to go towards the river, Charley made Shipp understand it some way or other, and Shipp and his men lay still till the renegades got up within ten feet of them before they opened fire. Then they did good work and lots of it.

Instructions to the scouts did not amount to anything. They shot everything in sight. Women and children and everything else! When I saw the renegades were all going directly away from me, I told my men to go rounding in the horses, and to yell to all the scouts to look out for the horses.

I ran down the way the renegades had gone. With me was the boy, Chi-kis-in, the son of old Pedro, and my first friend among the Apaches. He was a man now, and was a good warrior.

Shipp and his men coming up in front of the renegades, as they did, stopped them short, for the renegades did not know how many scouts there were in front of them. They checked up a few minutes, but Maus and Crawford were still giving them a good, heavy fire from both sides. Then Chi-kis-in and I ran right into them all, and that did settle it! They scattered like quails. "Scatter and go as you can!" yelled Geronimo.

I lost some good shooting by running over a little ridge to where I heard him, to try to get a shot at him. I could not tell one Indian from another they were so thick, and all running, and it was sure enough run, too! So I could not distinguish Geronimo. Captain Crawford had told me to try to kill him if I possibly could, and I knew him so well that I thought I could recognize him at any distance; but there I was, convinced that all naked Indians looked alike to a man at some distance, and before sunup at that.

When I saw that I could not pick out Geronimo, I followed along, shooting wherever I could see a buck to shoot at, but I was getting down to where the women and children were, and things were pretty badly mixed up. Shipp was right in front of a big lot of women and children, and could have gotten all of them, but they could not surrender, as the scouts kept killing them so fast, and when that was stopped they were beginning to stampede.

Then I tried old Sieber's way. I ran down to my scouts and yelled and cursed and swore, and said some awful things, so Shipp said: but I was not on exhibition. I don't know what I did say. Shipp said I would yell in Apache and then swear in English, then more Apache and then more swear! I guess I was the central figure for a while, for Shipp said he quit looking at the renegades and began to watch me.

Well, whatever I did do, it had the desired effect. I got the scouts to stop shooting the women and children, and I got a lot of the women and children to surrender. I think we got only sixteen to surrender; the rest of them wanted to but were stampeded by my scouts.

Just as we were getting them rounded up, I saw a renegade trying to cross a little open swale about one hundred
yards away, and he was going a little lame. He was in sight
for a distance of about ten feet only. I ran and gained on
him, but he was on one side of a little ridge and I was on
the other, yet the gulch he was in was open and ran right
into the gulch I was in a couple of hundred yards below.
I beat him to the forks, or met him there. We were both
running and not more than twenty-five yards apart. When
I came in sight of him, I threw up my gun; he stopped dead
still and turned towards me. He was old Nana, a formerly
noted chief in war and council, but at this time about ninety
years old. He said to me as calmly as though he were going
to draw his rations: "I surrender." Then he commenced to
talk Spanish, which he spoke with as much fluency as the
ordinary Mexican.

"I am old," he said, "and no more fit for war as it is waged
now. At this time of my life all is changed. Now the best
warriors are the ones who start to run first, and their ability
as warriors depends on the length of time they can run after
they do get started. You have no men; I know you, you are
Sibi's boy, son of the man of iron, and he has taught you
to fight anyhow, no matter which is the superior body of
men, the ones you are with or the ones you are fighting.
Once the Apaches were so, but now they sit around the
fires and tell what they will do and what they can do, and
they won't do, and can't do anything. We had men enough
to make you a good fight, and we could get away in the
dark after we did fight you, but no, these braves must run,
run, RUN!"

The old chief then commenced to laugh. I had been grin-
ning at him, for when I had headed him off, he was cer-

tainly making a gallant play at a run himself, but he just
could not keep it up, as he had been lame for twenty years
from a wound in the hip.

"Yes," he said, "now you think I was running, too, and
so I was, but I will run no more and I will fight no more."

I had not made him drop his gun, so he still had it in
his hands. He swung it over his head and struck it on a
rock and broke off the stock, then kept on and bent the
barrel, threw it down, and said: *"Para sirvir usted."* ("At
your service"). I told him to come on to camp, and as several of the scouts had come around, we started back toward
where the camp was when we jumped it.

Shipp and his prisoners were ready and we all went back.
Nana kept up his roast on his own people, telling the squaws
how brave were the warriors under Geronimo. "Look,"
said he, "here are about twenty or twenty-five scouts who
have taken you prisoners. Where are your braves?"

"They are all gone," said one of the women.

"Yes," said the old Chief, "they have gone, and they
now have not got the best of anything. They are only even
with the world. Not one of them has even a blanket. They
have neither camp nor comfort; yet, up at Turkey Creek
on the Reservation, when it was left to you women to go
on the war path or stay on the Reservation, you all said,
'Mexico, Mexico, Mexico.' I now say, 'San Carlos, San
Carlos, San Carlos!' and there I will stay and die, and not
be trying to keep up with your strong young braves in this
great Mexican and American foot race. Did you hear your
great chief, Geronimo? He said, 'To the river, to the river!
run to the river!' Why did he not say, 'Fight, make the scouts
go to the river!' "

Well, this was only a small part of the cranky, roasting
talk of the old chief. He said to me: "You think the Chiri-

cahuas always run, but I tell you there was once a Chiricahua chief who said, 'Fight!' and his name was Nana."

Nana asked who was the captain, and I told him. When
we got up to where Crawford and Maus and the scouts
had all the horses rounded up, I left Maus and Crawford
to talk to Nana. Maus could talk some Spanish, and I told
Crawford who the distinguished prisoner was; as I was leaving, I heard Nana say to Maus: "My people have just had
a big foot race here, and the fact of my being old and
crippled and unschooled in the art of winning a cause by
racing for it, the fortunes of war of this kind have made
me your prisoner. I am at your service, sir, and only ask
as a favor that you will allow me to growl as much as I
want to. I ask also, that you will not ask me anything regarding the people that I have passed nearly ninety years
of my life with, for, while I don't admire their peculiar
tactics in battle, they are still my people."

I loved to hear Nana growl, for he was quite an ingenious
kicker, but I had to look after my men and the captured
property, and try to get something to eat.

We had a great many captured horses, but I never
counted them, as my orders were to kill most of them so
that the renegades could not get them to live on. We, of
course, got all the camp equippage of the renegades and
there was a big lot of plunder of one kind and another. Of
course, there was a good deal of quarreling about the division of the spoils, and to get everything straightened out,
I had to make another Sieber's bluff; so I arose in my wrath
and made the scouts pile up all the stuff and then I set it
on fire. I rounded up the horses and put a herd guard to
look after them, and that about squared everything. I then
went to look for something to eat. I found the packers had
come in, and I got a good meal, and as it had begun to

rain by this time, I got under a piece of canvas stretched up by the packers, and went to sleep.

I told Crawford to take some men and count the dead Indians, but he said he did not want them counted, and as I did not care for it myself, they were never counted by our party.

It was a damp, cloudy, dismal day, and was drizzling along in a small way all day. The stuff we found in the Indians' camp was burning and sent up a terrible smoke, that went straight up, and I thought at the time that it could be seen for many miles. There were old blankets, quilts, clothes, and raw-hide sacks, such as the Apaches used for packing, and everything else that one could think of, stolen on different raids.

Along in the middle of the afternoon, Crawford woke me and told me there was a woman in camp from the renegades who had crossed the Arras River and were only a few miles away. She said the Chiricahuas wanted to talk to Captain Crawford and me. I told her we would start away from there on the next day very early, and if Chihuahua wanted to talk, he had better come in and do so. We were out of rations and would have to go to the camp at Nacori to get more, and it would be five or six days' travel the nearest way we could go to get to Nacori, but I did not want to tell them we were about out of rations.

I sent her back, and told her I would talk to any or all of them next day. Nana said to the woman to tell the rest of the renegades that he was a captive and was going to San Carlos. I told him, not to San Carlos, but to the guardhouse in Fort Bowie. Any place, he replied, where he would not have to run foot races.

We had, I think, sixteen prisoners, and some of them were cutting up a good deal on account of having seen their

182

people killed, and an old squaw can always make her share of noise when she is doing the weeping act. They don't cry, they just pitch out one long screeching yell after another, all the time lying flat on their stomachs. A dozen of them in camp is no treat.

We were all tired and worn out, more especially the scouts who had been with me, and I, myself, was worn completely out. I always tried to carry a hundred rounds of cartridges on a trip where we were working as we had to work there, for we always calculated that if we got cornered in the day time, we could make a standoff fight till night and then get away. I never did make any calculations on getting killed. Well, a hundred rounds of 45-70 cartridges weighs eleven pounds when you first put them on, and at the end of twenty days, they weigh about as much as a small-sized locomotive.

It kept raining all night, and was still raining at daylight.

CHAPTER TWENTY-ONE

Unwarranted Attack by Mexicans Under Corredor — "For God's Sake, Chief, Can't You Stop Them?" — The Death of Captain Emmet Crawford — Lieutenant Maus in Command — Thirty-seven Killed, Fifteen Wounded — Horn as Truce-Bearer — "If I am Harmed, My Apache Scouts Will Kill Every Mother's Son of You!" — A Mexican Trick — Coming to Terms — Chihuahua Would Talk — Dissatisfaction Among Geronimo's Followers — Burial of Crawford — Horn's Reputation Increased — Lieutenant Maus Lauds His Chief of Scouts

ALL OF US BEGAN TO STIR at daylight, and very shortly after we saw Mexican soldiers coming toward us. I saw they were getting ready to make a fight, and I could hear their orders as plainly as I could hear Captain Crawford's, who stood beside me. I told the scouts to get ready for a scrap, and to listen to me and do as I said, and not fire one shot if they could keep from it.

I heard the Mexican commander say to his men to throw out flankers on each side of us, and for some of them to get ready to charge. I got Shipp out on one side to stop their flankers, and Maus on the other side to do the same, and told each of them to start the game when they were compelled to for their own protection. I yelled to the Mexicans many times that we were American troops from the line, but that did not stop them. They must have heard me, for Captain Crawford and I could hear them plainly. They had formed for a fight about three hundred yards from us. We had ample time to get into position, and we were in a strong natural fortification. I knew a thousand Mexicans could not move us.

Finally, I heard the commander ask if the men were all in position for the flank move, and the answer came back that they were all waiting.

"Follow me, *valientes!*" cried the Mexican captain, and at us they came on a run across a little basin, directly toward us.

Crawford said, "My God, Chief, can't you stop them? These scouts will kill them all!"

I ran out towards them, and Crawford jumped up higher still, on a big prominent rock, and had a white handkerchief in his hands. He could not speak Spanish, but he could swear in a moderately clever way, not like Sieber or Chaffee, but still he was doing very well. I kept on talking to the Mexicans all the time, and was also talking to the scouts telling them not to fire.

When they reached the middle of the basin, the Mexicans began to shoot. Some would stop and shoot, and then come on towards us on a trot, and others would do the same, so that some were coming on a trot and some were firing all the time.

One of my scouts yelled to me to come back, that Crawford was killed. I was half-way down meeting the Mexicans, and was out in the opening. I was wondering why it was that they did not hit me, and then all at once I wondered no more, for I was struck in the arm. My scouts saw I was hit, and they yelled, "Come back!"

I did not start right away, although the Mexicans were within fifty feet of me, but I yelled to my scouts to give it to them! All my scouts seemed to shoot at once, and how it did paralyze those Greasers! They went down in groups and bunches! Their advance was stopped as though they had come to the end. Some of my scouts wanted to be down where I was; and, Chi-kis-in and about a dozen came down and kept on shooting at some of the wounded Mexicans who were trying to crawl away.

I believe the Mexicans afterwards said there were 36 killed and 13 badly wounded. There were 154 Mexicans, so they said later. After all the Mexicans had gotten out of sight, one of them yelled over to us:

"O, you white man that talks Mexican, I want to talk to you."

I said, "What do you want? I spoke to you many times and you would not answer."

They replied, "Now we want to talk."

I had gone over to where I left Captain Crawford standing on a rock. Some of the Indians had said that he had been killed, and I wanted to see if it were true.

The scouts told me he was lying out in front of a big pile of boulders. I ran around there, and sure enough, there he lay. Shot in the center of the forehead, a glancing shot, but it had torn out a whole lot of his brains—I should say as much as a handful.

When I stepped around to where he lay I guess I was in plain view of the Mexicans, as they commenced to shoot at me again, and I tried to get Crawford back, but I had only one arm that I could use, and I could not lift him. I could not get the scouts to help me, as they do not like to do anything with a wounded man. So I had to drag him with one hand. It was about fifty feet from there to the sheltering rocks, but I finally got him around there. He was unconscious. I poured a little water down his throat, but he did not revive any.

The fight was going on again quite briskly, and it was not worth my while to try to stop it! Chi-kis-in came to me and wanted to scatter out our men and go after the

186

Mexicans and kill all of them, but I talked to them and told them not to do so until I ordered them.

Old Nana came crippling up to me and said:

"Captain, though I am a prisoner and an old man, I would like to take the rifle and ammunition of the dead Captain and help to entertain the Mexicans."

I gave him the gun and belt and told him to do as I told him, or rather as I told the rest of the scouts. He said, "I will do so. If this is a fight to the death, here I will die, for I will never be shamed by running, as I did yesterday."

I went around among my scouts and told them not to waste their ammunition too freely, as we were in the Mexican's country and two weeks' travel from the line, and maybe the Mexicans had taken in all our command. I did not know, and could not guess, why we had been attacked. I thought Mexico and the United States were at war, and that we were in it. I was sure the Mexicans did not want to do anything but fight, and I knew, also, that my men were wanting to advance awfully bad, and I knew, also, that if I did let my scouts go, they would kill all of the Mexicans, or nearly all, as an Apache has no fear of Mexicans.

I went and saw Lieutenant Maus, and had a talk with him, and told him how things were.

We could not make out why we were attacked by the Mexicans, unless Mexico had declared war against our country, and, as we had left Bowie on December 1, 1885, and it was now January 11, 1886, we had not had any word for a long time from the line.

Maus was now in command, as Crawford was dying, and I asked him if I should turn the Indians loose and make a ramp on the Mexicans. Maus said to speak to them again, and if they did not answer, to do as I wanted to, which, I tell you, meant go to 'em!

187

Just then I caught sight of Lieutenant Shipp and his bunch of scouts, right around over where the Mexicans were, and in a splendid commanding position. I could see that the Mexicans were getting excited, also, and so I spoke to them and asked them how they liked the entertainment. One of the Mexicans asked me who we were, and I told him we were a bunch of sports down from the United States, looking for some game, and thanked him for the nice little time we were having, and invited him to get his *"valientes"* together again, and try another charge.

He asked me what those Apaches were doing, getting up over them, and I told him that if they did not charge or run soon, my men were going to try it, and see how charging went; but as we were now on three sides of them, and a steep ledge in front of them, that they had better act as though they had some sense.

"What do you want?" asked the Mexicans.

"Everything you have," replied I.

They talked awhile among themselves, and then they asked what the soldier they saw (meaning Crawford) and I were doing with the Apaches. I told them that our business originally had been to hunt down renegade Chiricahuas, but that we were attacked by their outfit and that we had to defend ourselves, which we were perfectly able and willing to do.

Just here a loud yell broke out on the side of the Mexicans that we did not have guarded, and old Geronimo bobbed up and began to call to me. He shouted to me to give the word, and we would all strike the Mexicans at once and kill them all and get their piñole. Mexicans, when they go upon a campaign or trip, take only piñole, a kind of parched meal, and the Indians all like it—would do anything to get it. Some of Geronimo's men began to talk to the Mexicans in Spanish. I could easily distinguish old Jose Maria among them,.

The Mexicans were getting pretty badly worked up by this time, and they asked me to come over there to their camp. I went and saw Maus and told him I was going over, and then I told the scouts that I was going and to be sure to kill all the Mexicans if they killed me. I told Geronimo, also, that I was going into the Mexican camp, and I heard Jose Maria tell the Mexicans that if they harmed me that the scouts and renegades would combine and kill every mother's son of them!

Then I walked over. I went in among them and asked where their commander was, and they said he lay dead on the field of battle. I told them we had not had a battle yet, only a skirmish; that if their commander had been killed, they had better go back home and get a new one; that we were the same as Mexican troops, as we were; and were allowed all the rights and privileges of Mexican troops within certain limits and that we were within those limits, and that on this occasion, by our treaty, our rights and privileges were equal to their own. I told them that they had come and attacked us, and that we had merely defended ourselves.

One of them then asked me who I was, and I told him. "Well," he said, "we don't know anything of this treaty you are talking about, but we think it is all right, and we will let it go, though we have had many men killed and among them is Don Maurice Corredor, the bravest man that ever lived. We will have to take you with us to the city of Chihuahua to settle this thing."

I told them that I would have to decline the order or invitation, whichever it was, and they said they would take me anyhow, and that I was their prisoner!

189

Geronimo was closer to me than my own men and I spoke to him and told him what these Mexicans were talking of doing, and he yelled to my scouts what I had told him, and in a minute every scout and renegade commenced to yell and get ready for an advance. The Mexicans asked me what the Indians were doing, and I told them that I was chief of the Indians, and they did not propose to see me taken away.

"What did you say to the Indians?" asked the Mexicans. I informed them that I had told the Indians I was a prisoner. The Mexicans could see that they were surrounded and that they would be exterminated in a few minutes more.

"We will kill you," said one of them, "if the Apaches fire upon us."

"I know you will," replied I, "and I know, also, that you will never smile again after you do kill me, for no one but myself can handle or control those Indians, and when they know I am killed you will all be killed. Not one of you will escape."

All of the Indians were closing in now, and one Mexican said to me, "Go quick and stop them, and then come back and see if we can not fix this thing up."

I called to Geronimo not to fire till I told them, or till they saw me fall. I was in plain sight of the Chiricahuas and most of the scouts, and I stepped up where I could be more plainly seen by all of them. I then asked the Mexicans if they did not think it unnecessary to take me to the city of Chihuahua, as my presence was very necessary there with my scouts.

"Have you not got a commissioned officer with your outfit?" asked one, and I told him that there were two of them with the scouts.

"You go over and take care of the scouts, and send one of the officers over and let us talk to him."

190

"Neither of them can talk Mexican," said I.

"Well, if you can control the Indians, go on back to them," said one of the Mexicans.

I went back and told Maus all about the whole business; also that the Mexicans, such as were there, were a very uncertain lot and would not do to trust. Maus asked me to go and get one of the prominent Mexicans to come over and talk to him. I went back to the Mexican camp and asked them to send over a man or two, or a dozen if they liked, to talk to our officer.

Two of them concluded to go. Jose Maria, of the Chiricahuas, asked me what we were going to do, and I told him. "May I come over, too, and hear what they have to say?" And I told him yes, to come on. Jose Maria came down, and the four of us went over to our camp. I introduced them to Maus and told them who Maus was. The Mexicans then told Maus that they had made a mistake and did not know we were from the United States, that they were sorry for what they had done, and that they had suffered a much more serious loss than we had, as Maurice Corredor was a great man and would be a great loss to Mexico. I did not tell them of Crawford being shot. They wanted to know if we had any men killed, and I called a scout that had gotten a shot in the wrist, and told him there were our wounded.

The Mexicans did not know what to do and I could not see that we were doing any good, so I told them to go on back to their camp. We had not had any breakfast and it was ten o'clock by this time, so we went to work to get something for all hands.

Along about noon a Mexican came over and asked if I could let our doctor go over and attend to their wounded. I told Dr. Davis he could do as he liked, and he went over and dressed a whole lot of wounds for them. Dr. Davis said

191

one of them was shot eight times. While Dr. Davis was over there, one of them came over and asked for Maus to go over, as they wanted to talk to him. I told Maus not to go, as he could not do any talking to amount to anything, but he said he would go, and go he did.

About the time Maus went over, Dr. Davis came back and said he did not like the looks of things. That the Mexicans did not treat him right. Presently Maus sent over a note, saying he was held prisoner; that the Mexicans wanted us to divide our rations with them; they wanted our mules to carry their wounded and they wanted everything we had.

They talked of taking him to Chihuahua. I told the Mexican who came over with the note to go over and get men to take the mules and grub back; told him to bring four or five men. This he did, and the man who came back to receive the mules and rations said he was the man now in charge of the Mexicans.

He had four men with him, making five altogether. I told them that I was surprised that they should hold Lieutenant Maus as they were doing, and he told me that they were bound to have their own way, and we had better not make any trouble. I told him if that was their game, they should see how it was going to work. I told them to get upon a rock that was close by.

"What are you going to do?" asked their spokesman.

"You are playing a Mexican trick of bluff on us," said I, "and I am going to show you what joy means."

I made them get up on the rock, and then I called old Nana and Jose Maria, and about a dozen of my scouts, and told them to get ready to do as I told them.

I told them that as soon as I gave the word, I wanted them all to shoot into the Mexicans. By this time the Mexicans could see that they were going to be executed. I told

192

them to call over to their comrades and tell them just the kind of fix they were in, and after they told them that Lieutenant Maus must be sent back in one minute, or I would allow the Apaches to shoot them.

The man then commenced to tell his companions how things were, and that they would surely be killed in a minute if Maus did not appear.

For many a day we laughed at the way that Mexican did talk; Nana and Jose Maria were also telling them that they were all the same as dead men already, and how much pleasure they were going to have. I did not wait long till I told them that it was no use; that their friends had quit them, and they would have to die. Their friends wanted to talk, but I told them, "No savvy," and it was getting time for my lieutenant to be coming.

The talk of this man sounded so sincere that the lieutenant came over and said that the Mexicans were doing a lot of bluffing on him, but they would not do any more. Maus said the Mexicans demanded everything when he got over there, and he could not talk much Spanish, and the Mexicans could not understand a word of American, and I guess there had been big doin's.

Well, that ended the row. I told the Mexicans to come over and get a lot of extra horses I had, and I took about forty head of the best and turned the rest of the captured horses(and there must have been three hundred of them) over to the Mexicans.

The Mexicans came from the Chihuahua side of the Sierra Madre, and the horses belonged to the Sonora side, but I was not going to take any more horses to the line or to Bowie, as I already had enough of that.

Late that evening the Mexicans pulled out, and I sent half a dozen scouts to follow and watch them. They were in very bad shape, as they had a good many wounded. I let old Jose Maria go back to the renegades, and told him to tell Chihuahua, and any others who wanted to talk to me, to come on the next day to where we would camp.

Crawford was unconscious, and remained so till he finally died, three days later. He had a great hole in his head, and it looked as though a handful of brains had been shot out; but with all that, he lived until the third day, and died while on the way out of the mountains. We were carrying him in a travois, carried by pack mules. We were rather a sorrowful lot ourselves, as we pulled towards home. We did not want to bury Crawford there in the mountains, so we were taking him out to the nearest settlement, which was Nacori.

I had sent five scouts on ahead with dispatches from Maus to our camp at Nacori, and two others we sent to General Crook. From Nacori we could send in helio dispatches, and by the time we arrived at Nacori with the body of Captain Crawford, all the world knew of his death, and how it came about.

We buried Crawford at Nacori. The packers and soldiers had the grave prepared when we arrived there with the body. His body was taken up the next summer and sent to either Lincoln or Beatrice, Nebraska, where his mother and sister lived, and I always understood that it was buried at Lincoln.

To go back to the Chiricahuas. As we went into camp, the first day after we left the battle ground, a woman came and told me Chihuahua was close there, and for me to come out, as he wanted to see me. I told Maus I was going out to see him, and he told me to do as I liked, and to come back and see him, and tell him what Chihuahua wanted.

I went with the squaw, and joined the chief, and he said

194

he would follow Geronimo no more, as Geronimo was "all on the run and drink mescal." He said Geronimo was the war chief, and it was the custom of all other chiefs to obey the order of the war chief. He said Geronimo was too much on the talk; and gave me to understand that he was going to follow him no more.

He wanted me to make arrangements for him to meet General Crook and talk to him, and said he would be a renegade no more. Chihuahua was one of the most determined, and of the best hereditary standing of any chief in the Chiricahua tribe, but he never aspired to rank high as chief. Natchez and Chihuahua were half-brothers, and both of them grandsons of old Cochise, the most noted of all old-time Chiricahua chiefs.

Natchez was the greatest warrior, and the best man, physically, in the bunch of renegades; he was also a man of great personal pride and courage. So, knowing his pride, I asked Chihuahua to try to see if he could not get Natchez to come with him. He said he would see, but that he thought Natchez would consider himself bound to stay with Geronimo. I did all I could in a talk, and made arrangements to bring General Crook to meet him in the full of the March moon, at the San Bernardino Peak. I told him I could not be sure General Crook could come, but that I would take his message to him.

That evening several more women and children came in and said they were going back with us. We had now about twenty-five prisoners to take back. I never put them under guard at all, as they were all willing to go, and they were perfectly contented when not within the sound of Geronimo's voice. Geronimo certainly had an influence over them that controlled them when he was with them, but once away from him, they would do as they pleased. Now, for the first time, I could begin to see dissatisfaction in the renegade camp, and that was what I wanted to see.

At that camp on the Arras, where we jumped Geronimo, he could easily have given us a licking, or else a stand-off had he made a fight, and all the Indians in the renegade camp thought that I had planned the fight to come off just as it did, and ran them down the draw among my best scouts.

It was true I did send some of my best men with Shipp, but I did it because Shipp was young and inexperienced, and I thought he would need good men to take care of him, as I was sure we would have a hard fight. Of course, I never let on but that everything came out as I wanted it to.

Maus and Shipp knew different, but as they could not talk to either the scouts or the renegades, they could not give me away, and I took advantage of the wisdom I was supposed to have displayed. Then, too, the renegades all began to think more of me because I had headed off the scouts and would not let them kill any more women and children; and, taking it altogether, I was getting to be a great man in my own estimation!

* * *

[*Personal Recollections of General Miles*: On page 471, Captain Maus, in his account, says: "I can not commend too highly Mr. Horn, my chief of scouts. His gallant services deserve a reward which he has never received."]

WELL, after getting to Nacori and burying Crawford, we hired a large room in the town, our camp being several miles from there. We put all the supplies in the big room, left a guard of soldiers there, and we all pulled out for the line. I guess General Crook ordered the storing of the rations in Nacori for future use. I did not know anything about that.

We were stopped at the Batipita Ranch as we were on our way up, to wait there with the command till Maus and I could go to Bowie and report in person to General Crook. Maus and I left the command and went on in and had a long talk with the General, and I told him of the dissatisfaction among the Chiricahuas, and he made arrangements to come down as soon as he was notified by helio that the renegades were on hand.

Maus and I then went back and established camp on the San Bernardino Creek, about twelve miles below the line, to wait for the March moon. We would have to wait about six or seven weeks. A long and tedious wait it was, with a message coming in from General Crook every day to see if we had heard anything. We had a helio station in camp.

At last the welcome signal came. It was on the San Bernardino Peak. And, though it came at nine o'clock at night, I started out right away to go and find the messenger.

I found him to be a young buck, who said he was a nephew of Chihuahua. He said that Chihuahua would be there whenever I said the word. I sent him word to be there in four days, and then went back to report to General Crook by helio.

General Crook sent word back he would be there at the appointed time, and I went on back, leaving the General to follow. General Crook was very anxious, for, as I learned later, the Department was hurrying him up as much as they could, and he was depending upon me. But I could not hurry the renegades; and so it stood.

When the appointed day came along, all parties were on hand, and Chihuahua said that he did not have any more talk to make, but that he was willing to go to the guardhouse and stay there till Geronimo came in, for he said Geronimo would not stay out long now, as many of the men with him were much dissatisfied. There were about twenty-five men and a good many more women and children with Chihuahua.

All at once there was some commotion up on the Peak and a big bunch of renegades came into sight coming to our talk. Geronimo was at their head. The desire to make a peace talk was too strong in him to miss the chance.

I asked Geronimo if he had come in to surrender, and he replied by telling me to take him to General Crook. This I did, and he wanted to make a great long talk about the way he was treated up on Turkey Creek, and General Crook asked him what he wanted to do, and Geronimo said he wanted to have an understanding. General Crook told him if he wanted to go along as a prisoner, to come on; and if he did not, to go on back to the mountains and he would send more scouts there to find him.

He said: "Geronimo, you are so much of a liar that I do not want to trust you any more, and if you go with me you will have to go to the guardhouse till the authorities at Washington decide what to do with you."

He told Geronimo he would camp for the night up at the scout's camp on the San Bernardino Creek, and if he wanted to talk, to come up there. General Crook then pulled out, and as Crook had brought Micky Free down to me, I asked Micky if he wanted to stay back with me and talk to Geronimo and he said he would, so I told the outfit to go on to camp and that I would stay and talk to Geronimo a while.

Crook and his escort went on, and Micky and I sat down to have a talk with Geronimo. The chief had about twenty men, well armed and very well mounted. I asked him where he got his horses, and he said that the Mexicans were raising horses for him in Sonora, and he went and got them when he wanted or needed them. I told him that General Crook was very mad at him for leaving the Reservation, and he said he knew Crook was mad, but if he could talk to him he could explain a good many things. I told him to come on and go to camp with me and I would try and get the General to talk to him. He asked me how many scouts and soldiers there were in camp, and I said I would not tell him. He asked me if I would try to trap him, and I told him he could come and make his talk and if he and the General could not agree, that he could again go to the mountains. He said he would go with me.

Geronimo and I rode ahead of the rest of his men, and he

made a great complaint to me about a man like Chihuahua doing as he was doing, and said that Chihuahua was jealous because he could not be war chief. I then told Geronimo that Chihuahua would not talk that way of him, and he said, "Yes, he would," and added that Chihuahua told him that it was no more good to be on the war path and he only said so because some Mexican killed his favorite boy on their last raid before I struck them on the Arras.

Geronimo seemed to feel very bad about Chihuahua's giving up, and well he might, for it showed to me an open break in their camp.

That night Geronimo wanted to talk to General Crook, but Crook told him if he wanted to go to Bowie to the guardhouse, to come on, and if he did not, that his talk was no good and for him to go on back to the mountains and he would soon be after him with the scouts. Geronimo wanted to talk to the scouts, but I would not let any of the scouts see him except Micky, and I knew he was immune from the influence of Geronimo.

While I was giving the scouts orders to keep away from the camp of Geronimo, Chihuahua came up and said, in a low tone, to me, to put him and all the people with him under a close guard.

This I did, and, while Chihuahua would not tell me anything, I could plainly see that Geronimo was only with us to try and get some of the men belonging to Chihuahua's band to desert and go with him on the war path.

Geronimo saw me putting a guard over the prisoners who had before been entirely free, and he asked me why I was doing it. I told him I would take all of them to the guardhouse at Bowie, and that no more "good talk" was going to go; that if ever the Chiricahuas did go back to the Reservation, they would only go to the guardhouse, as they would never be turned loose again.

Geronimo said that was very hard, and no more of them would surrender under those conditions. I told him I could do no good talking to him, and that if he was there at sun-up next morning that he would be taken prisoner by force.

When morning come, there was no Geronimo. He and his band had gone, and, as long as I was not allowed to make a prisoner of him, I was glad to know he was gone, for he had a wonderful influence with all Indians. He was such a great talker that he could make right seem wrong.

We took all the prisoners we had up to Bowie and put them in a new guardhouse we had made especially for our Chiricahua prisoners. We had a couple of hundred by this time, and we were also informed (anyhow I was) that General Crook had been relieved, and that General Nelson A. Miles was to take command of the Department.

Things in an Indian way were at at a standstill for a couple of months, and then I was informed by the Quartermaster that there would be no more Chief of Scouts, and that I was to be sent to Camp Apache as interpreter.

This was quite a blow to my pride, but one of my best friends was a Captain Thompson, of the Fourth Cavalry; he was made adjutant general under Miles, and he told me to go to Apache and stay there till General Miles looked around and saw the lay of the land. He told me that Miles was going to try the renegades a lick with cavalry. The proposition was to enlist five Apaches in each troop of cavalry to do the trailing and scouting for the troops.

So things were arranged and started under the new administration.

Huachuca was now made headquarters of the Department. All the newspapers said that Miles was a brilliant officer, and was a great Indian fighter, and that the career of Geronimo and of Horn was about at an end. A San Francisco newspaper had come out with an article, saying that Horn was as much Apache as he was Mexican; that I had more influence with the hostiles than Geronimo himself; that I went to his camp whenever I wanted to without the least fear of being hurt, and that I was always the interpreter, and could say anything I wanted and no one could dispute what I said, as no other white man could talk their language, or was trusted by them.

When this article came out, I went to the Quartermaster, at Apache, where I was stationed, and told him that I would quit the government, as I was evidently very much in disgrace. I left at once and went over to a ranch in the Aravaipa Cañon, which I had always called home, and where I had always kept some extra saddle horses. I had some mines there that I had wanted to work for a long time, and I did not want to work for the government any more while things were going as they were. Again, the newspapers said that, as I had now left the government employ, General Miles would not have any traitors in his own command, and would soon put down the renegades or kill them all!

I knew the cavalry would never be able to do anything but get whipped, but had I told anyone so, I should have been laughed at for my pains; soldiers could easily whip the renegades if they could get at them, but the renegades could avoid them till they got the soldiers into a trap, and then give them both barrels. Had I told General Miles this, he would doubtless have called me a fool.

Well, two companies of the Tenth Cavalry, under Captain Leebo, ran onto a camp of renegades down towards Calabasas, and got whipped, and never saw one Indian.

Two days later the same thing happened to a troop of the Fourth Cavalry. About a month later a big bunch of renegades came up by Fort Bowie and across by the Dragoons. They killed a man in the Dragoons, and turned back on their route and killed two men and a boy in Piney Cañon, in the Chiricahua Mountains. They then went into Mexico and killed four Mexicans, just on the line, at a *vinataria,* or mescal still. These stills are scattered all over northern Mexico, and, previous to this, not a man connected with any of them had ever been killed.

Four or five squaws got lost from this bunch that came through last, or else they deserted and came into Fort Bowie, and they said that Ju, a Warm Spring chief, and a half-brother to Nana, had been killed by the Mexicans over in Janos, in Chihuahua. The way we afterwards got the story was that twenty-six bucks went into this town of Janos and got drunk; the Mexicans gave them all the mescal they could drink, and killed nearly all of them. Ju, in trying to get away, was running his pony at the top of its speed, and it fell down a bank and killed him. This was why Geronimo was killing the mescal men.

Things were looking bad for the Chiricahuas, and for the troops, also; and the newspapers that had expected so much from Miles now said that he was a failure!

The Apache scouts, with each troop of cavalry, would not work well, and they could not understand the troop commanders, and the troop commanders could not understand them.

In August, a detachment of troops came to the ranch where I was, and brought me a letter from the Quartermaster at Fort Huachuca. He wanted me to come over and go to work. I sent back word that I was all ready to go to mining, and did not care to go to work for the government again. Again came a detachment with a second letter, this time from General Miles himself, asking me to come to Huachuca and see him, and have a talk with him about the Indians.

I made arrangements with the boys who were in with me on the mine to do my share while I was gone, then I got on my horse and went to Huachuca to meet General Miles.

The General told me there that he wanted me to go to Mexico and find Captain Lawton (the General Lawton killed in the Philippines), and act as chief of scouts with him and see what we could do.

I went down and struck Lawton's camp at a place in Sonora, called Sierra Gordo. I crossed a trail of Indians in the Heiralitas Mountains as I went down, and, after I reported to Lawton, I told him what I had seen, and he asked me what to do. He had twenty-five Apache scouts and two troops of cavalry and four or five white scouts. I told him to leave all the outfit except the scouts and to go and take up the trail I had just left. This we did, and as we were all in light traveling order, we went at a good lively gait, and, as Dr. Wood (General Leonard Wood, of Cuban fame), said, "We will run them off the earth!"

For once the state troops of Sonora were out and trying to co-operate with us; but all that was necessary for anyone to do was to keep in the mountains and give us supplies and all the information they could, and we would make them run till they got tired of running. We had already captured a great many women. (The renegades told it that we killed seventy-five women and children on the Arras, where Captain Crawford was killed by the Mexicans.)

Geronimo was from ten hours to four days ahead of us for five weeks, and his rear guard saw us many times, so they afterwards said. It was a great race, and I knew the renegades could not stand it much longer. They had no time to raid and get fresh horses, except as they could pick them up, and when they would gain a few days on us we would hear of them by the helio, and we could drop the trail where we were and cut in ahead.

As we were coming up by Fronteras, as usual, we found a couple of women that had given out, and we put them on pack mules and took them on to Fronteras. There Captain Lawton had a helio dispatch to drop the chase, and for me to come to Huachuca. The dispatch had been there for two days.

Before I got ready to start, there came another to wait there, as Lieutenant Gatewood and a couple of Chiricahua bucks were coming to try to open up communications with Geronimo. These were two men who had come in with the Chief Chihuahua.

The Chiricahuas had been leaving signs for a couple of weeks that they wanted to talk, and these signs had all been reported by me to Captain Lawton, and by Lawton to General Miles.

We stopped close to Fronteras for four days to let Gatewood and his two men get ahead, so they could communicate with Geronimo, but at the end of that time Gatewood came back and reported to Captain Lawton that he could not get his two friendly Indians to approach the Chiricahuas.

Gatewood told Captain Lawton that he could not open communications in that way. Lawton asked me if I could do anything, and I told him frankly that I was the only one who could do anything! Gatewood said that General Miles did not want me to go into the camp alone, as he did not know if he could trust me. I had previously told Lawton that I could and would go alone, but would not go if anyone went with me, as I did not care for myself, but anyone else might get killed.

That was the way the thing stood. I would go alone or not at all; and Gatewood was ordered by Miles not to let me go alone. There we all stopped and waited till Lawton could send a heliograph to General Miles, explaining the situation to him.

While we were waiting for his answer, the soldiers brought in a squaw. Lawton told me to ask her where she came from, and she said she had come from the renegade camp of Geronimo, and that Geronimo wanted to see me and talk to me. I was very much put out at the way I was being treated, and would not tell Lawton, but told him to call George Wratton, a boy who was with Gatewood, and let him do the interpreting. This he did. The squaw said that Geronimo was in the mountains, forty or fifty miles from there, and wanted me to come to him, and wanted all the soldiers to stop chasing him till he saw me. Lawton still had not heard from Miles, and so he sent this word, also to him.

Next day Miles sent word to send Gatewood and myself to see what we could do. Then I could not go, because I did not know what I could tell Geronimo, and Lawton said, "Tell him anything you want to, but get him to come and talk to Miles." I said that was what I wanted to do, but could not unless Miles said he wanted to talk to him. I told Lawton that I could never tell Geronimo but one lie, for he would find it out, and the next time I went into his camp he would tell me I had lied to him, and then he would kill me. I refused to go unless General Miles promised me he would meet old Geronimo at a date Geronimo and I should fix.

This word was sent to Miles, and he said for me to fix

a date and he would keep it. Ten minutes after I got this dispatch I mounted my horse to start, and Gatewood said he would take his chances if I would let him go. I told him he would not be taking any chances, and to come on.

We struck the camp up on the Terras, as the squaw told me we would, but she would not tell me where it was until I was on my horse ready to go.

We did not have to go up to the mountain, as Geronimo met us down on the Bavispe River, and we had a long talk. I made arrangements to go with him to the Skeleton Cañon, in the United States, and meet Miles there in twelve days. That would give Miles time and to spare, and I was afraid he would not come, as he was the kind that wanted to make a renegade Indian think he was a big man, and Geronimo was just about as vain as Miles was, and thought that he, too, was a big man.

The only courier I had was Gatewood, and I sent him back to tell Captain Lawton the arrangements I had made with Geronimo, and for all the troops with him at Fronteras to come to the mouth of the Caballon Creek, and I would meet him there with the renegades. Geronimo had told me to have the American soldiers around close, as he did not want to get mixed up with the Mexicans. His idea and mine were one on that; and, anyhow, I calculated to stay with the renegades, as they had no grub, and I did not want them to kill cattle, of which there were plenty around there. I wanted to get rations from our command, which I did when I met them.

Captain Lawton was very much gratified to see how well I had done, and he said for me to stay with the renegades and he would do as I said. He told me he had sent a dispatch to Miles to meet us at the Skeleton Cañon, as I had directed.

I went over and told Geronimo, and he asked me if this dispatch had come to me direct, and I told him that it had come to Captain Lawton.

"You go," said he to me, "and send a dispatch yourself, and get an answer from him direct, saying he will meet me."

I went back to Lawton's camp and told him I must have a dispatch from Miles myself, saying he would meet Geronimo and me. Captain Lawton said he did not think Miles would send me a dispatch of that kind. Anyhow, I sent Miles the dispatch, and told him I wanted word from him direct, to say if he would meet Geronimo at Skeleton. The dispatch I received in reply was: "See Captain Lawton. He is in command in the field. I can't do any business with a civilian."

I told Lawton, after showing him the dispatch, that the stuff was all off, and that Geronimo would be on top of the Terras Mountains by morning. Captain Lawton did not know what to do. It was night by this time, and we could not send any more messages. I was thinking Miles was a monkey, as I rode back to Geronimo's camp.

It was dark when I reached there, as he was camped about four miles from our troops' camp. I told Geronimo how I had come out, and I translated the dispatch to him, and he, without answering, called to his people to get ready to pull out, and in less than five minutes all began to say, "We are ready."

Geronimo then said he could not do business with General Miles through an officer, and said time might change the big soldier, and rode off in the darkness, followed by his people. (There were only 136 of them left at this time.)

I rode back to Lawton's camp and told him that I was going home, and if General Miles ever needed me again, if ever he could condescend to do business with an Indian

208

through me when I had all the responsibility to shoulder, that I should be at his service. I told him Geronimo was gone, and before Lawton could understand the situation, I rode away and went up to John Slaughter's ranch.

It was daylight when I reached the ranch. I turned out my horse, and, as breakfast was soon ready, I ate, then lay down on Slaughter's bed and went to sleep.

There was a troop of cavalry camped at Slaughter's, and about noon a lieutenant came up and asked Slaughter if I ever stopped there as I came through the country. Slaughter said, "He never passes here without stopping."

"Well, then," the lieutenant said, "he may come by here today." He had heard by helio that I was coming north.

Slaughter said, "He is here now, asleep. He got here at daylight."

The lieutenant said, "Wake him up, for God's sake! I have a dispatch for him from General Miles."

John came in, gave me a kick, and told me that I was wanted. I went out, and the officer handed me the dispatch. It read: "Make any arrangements you want to for me to meet Geronimo. I will go where and when you say to meet him."

That was a stunner! Here Geronimo had been riding south all night, and I had ridden forty miles north, and both had started from the same point! There were easily seventy-five or eighty miles between us now.

I went to the helio station and sent a dispatch, saying Geronimo had gone back south, but to order the troops to lie still and I would try to see if I could find him.

In just one week I had Geronimo back in the same neighborhood and had communicated with Lawton. Everybody was afraid I could not get the renegade chief back the second time. I sent word to Miles to meet me in four days at Skeleton Cañon, and he was there on time.

Miles came up into the cañon, and I took Geronimo and Natchez and came down to meet him. Miles had three interpreters with him, and, after I brought him and Geronimo together, he said to one of his interpreters to tell Geronimo that he wanted to have a good, long talk with him, and that they had better get where they could sit down. Geronimo did not answer Miles, but said to the interpreter, "You are a Tonto, and I will have nothing to do with you. I will only talk through the chief. I will have nothing to do with any one but him."

General Miles said: "Oh, all right, but the chief is not a sworn government interpreter, and these other men are."

"I don't ask for him to be sworn," retorted Geronimo, "when he comes to my camp do you suppose I ask him if he is telling me the truth? No! That I never do. I am a liar," went on Geronimo, "when it suits my way of doing, but this boy and I speak only the truth to each other. You do not like him; I do not know why, and still when you do not like or trust him to do your business you must have a cause for it. What is the reason? Tell me what he has done, for there was a time when he was trusted, and he is a son of the old chief, Sibi; and Sibi, the man of iron, and my people have been fighting each other for thirty years and Sibi never lies. Nothing a man does is wrong if he tells the truth. Tell me what this boy has done that was wrong? You sent him word that you would have nothing to do with him, and I sent you word I would not have anything to do with anyone else."

Miles said: "Do not let us talk about that; let us talk of what you want to do."

Geronimo said, "I want to surrender with all my people. I will do as you say, and go where you tell me to go or send me. I am tired of the war path, and my people are all worn out."

General Miles then told him to come on in to Bowie and he would see what would be done with them. So, after all, the great talk was very small.

When we got to Fort Bowie, all the soldiers formed on the parade ground, and Geronimo and his outfit rode in and laid down their arms.

Then General Miles did do a fine act without any authority or orders from the War Department. He wired down to Bowie station, on the Southern Pacific railroad, got a special train, took all the Chiricahuas, the ones we had brought in and the ones in the guardhouse, marched them down, loaded them on the train, locked them in the cars, and put guards all over the train. Then they pulled out, and the dreaded Chiricahuas, the terror of Mexico and all the Southwest, were gone, never more to return, and Arizona was left in a more peaceful condition than it had ever enjoyed before.

The old Mexican captain, Jose Maria, did not come in, and I learned that he was still in Mexico with five other Indians. A Chiricahua named Wasse jumped off the train down in Texas while the train was running at full speed. He turned up in the Sierra Madres later, having made all the distance on foot, through the settlements of Texas, and the Texas marshals were after him all the time. He spoke Mexican like a native, and could pass for one anywhere in Texas. He was an outlaw for many years, living around in the mountains, and coming in to the Reservation once in a while to get a fresh squaw. Any kind was good enough for him. He would take a Yuma squaw as soon as any other kind, and he could not speak a word of the Yuma language.

I took all my scouts to the Reservation, discharged them and was then discharged myself. I went back to the Aravaipo to go to work on the mine. I stayed and worked at the mine all winter.

CHAPTER TWENTY-THREE

The Rustlers' War — Horn Called as Mediator — Becomes Deputy
Sheriff of Yavapai County — Outbreak of "Apache Kid" — Toga's
Heart Split in Two — Sieber, One Against Eleven — "Apache Kid's"
Surrender — He Kills Guards and Escapes — Roping Contests
Among Cow Boys — Horn Breaks Record — Horn Goes to Den-
ver to Work for Pinkerton National Detective Agency — A Train
Robbery Case — Horn Captures "Peg Leg" Watson — Horn and
Stewart Run Down Joe McCoy — Horn Quits the Pinkertons and
Goes to Work for the Swan Land & Cattle Company of Wyoming
— Life Story Continued in Yellow Journals

EARLY IN APRIL of 1887, some of the boys came down
from the Pleasant Valley, where there was a big rustler war
going on and the rustlers were getting the best of the game.
I was tired of the mine and willing to go, and so away we
went. Things were in a pretty bad condition. It was war
to the knife between cowboys and rustlers, and there was a
battle every time the two outfits ran together. A great many
men were killed in the war. Old man Blevins and his three
sons, three of the Grahams, a Bill Jacobs, Jim Payne, Al
Rose, John Tewkesbury, Stolt, Scott, and a man named
"Big Jeff" were hung on the Apache and Gila County line.
Others were killed, but I do not remember their names now.
I was the mediator, and was deputy sheriff under Bucky
O'Neil, of Yavapai County, under Commodore Owens, of
Apache County, and Glenn Reynolds, of Gila County. I
was still a deputy for Reynolds a year later when he was
killed by the Apache Kid, in 1888.

After this war in the Pleasant Valley I again went back
to my mine and went to work, but it was too slow, and I
could not stay at it. I was just getting ready to go to Mexico

and was going down to clean out the spring at the mine one evening. I turned my saddle horse loose and let him graze up the cañon. After I got the spring cleaned out, I went up the cañon to find my horse and I saw a moccasin track covering the trail made by the rope my horse was dragging. That meant to go back, but I did not go back. I cut up the side of the mountain and found the trail where my horse had gone out. It ran into the trail of several more horses, and they were all headed south. I went down to the ranch, got another horse and rode over to the Agency, about twenty miles, to get an Indian or two to go with me to see what I could learn about this bunch of Indians.

I got to the Agency about two o'clock in the morning and found that there had been an outbreak and mutiny among Sieber's police. It was like this: Sieber had raised a young Indian he always called "the Kid," and now known as the "Apache Kid." This kid was the son of old Chief Toga-de-chuz, a San Carlos Apache. At a big dance on the Gila at old Toga-de-chuz's camp everybody got drunk and when morning came old Toga was found dead from a knife thrust. An old hunter belonging to another tribe of Indians and called "Rip" was accused of doing the job, but from what Sieber could learn, as he afterwards told me, everybody was too drunk to know how the thing did happen. The wound was given in a very skillful manner and as it split open old Toga's heart it was supposed to be given by one who knew where the heart lay.

Toga and old Rip had had a row over a girl about forty years before (they were both about sixty at this time), and Toga had gotten the best of the row and the girl to boot. Some say that an Indian will forget and forgive the same as a white man. I say no. Here had elapsed forty years between the row and the time old Toga was killed.

214

Rip had not turned his horse loose in the evening before the killing, so it was supposed he had come there with the express intention of killing old Toga.

Anyway the Kid was the oldest son of Toga-de-chuz and he must revenge the death of his fatther. He must, according to all Indian laws and customs, kill old Rip. Sieber knew this and cautioned the Kid about doing anything to old Rip. The Kid never said a word to Sieber as to what he would do. The Kid was first sergeant of the Agency scouts. The Interior Department had given the Agency over to the military and there were no more police, but scouts instead.

Shortly after this killing, Sieber and Captain Pierce, the agent, went up to Camp Apache to see about the distribution of some annuities to the Indians there, and the Kid, as first sergeant of the scouts, was left in charge of the peace of the Agency.

No sooner did Sieber and Captain Pierce get started than the Kid took five of his men and went over on the Aravaipo, where old Rip lived, and shot him. That evened up their account, and the Kid went back to where his band was living up above the Agency. Sieber heard of this and he and Pierce immediately started to San Carlos.

When they got there, they found no one in command of the scouts. Sieber sent word up to the camp where the Kid's people lived to tell the Kid to come down. This he did, escorted by the whole band of bucks.

Sieber, when they drew up in front of his tent, went out and spoke to the Kid and told him to get off his horse, and this the Kid did. Sieber then told him to take the arms of the other four or five men who had government rifles. This also the Kid did. He took their guns and belts and then Sieber told him to take off his own belt and put down his gun and take the other deserters and go to the guardhouse.

Some of the bucks with the Kid (those who were not soldiers) said to the Kid to fight, and in a second they were at it—eleven bucks against Sieber alone. It did not make any particular difference to Sieber about being outnumbered. His rifle was in his tent. He jumped back and got it, and at the first shot he killed one Indian. All the others fired at him as he came to the door of his tent, but only one bullet struck him; that hit him on the shin and shattered his leg all to pieces. He fell, and the Indian ran away.

This was what Sieber told me when I got to the Agency. And then I knew it was the Kid who had my horse and outfit. Soldiers were already on his trail.

From where he had stolen my horse, he and his band crossed over the mountain to the Table Mountain district, and there stole a lot of Bill Atchley's saddle horses. A few miles further on they killed Bill Dihl, then headed on up through the San Pedro country, turned down the Sonoita River, and there they killed Mike Grace; then they were turned back north again by some of the cavalry that was after them.

They struck back north, and Lieutenant Johnson got after them about Pontaw, overtook them in the Rincon Mountains, and had a fight, killing a couple of them, and put all the rest of them afoot. My horse was captured unwounded, and as the soldiers knew him, he was taken to the San Pedro and left there; they sent word to me, and eventually I got him, though he was pretty badly used up.

That was the way the Kid came to break out. He went back to the Reservation, and later on he surrendered. He was tried for desertion, and given a long time by the federal courts, but was pardoned by President Cleveland, after having served a short term.

During the time the Kid and his associates were hiding

around on the Reservation, previous to his first arrest, he and his men had killed a freighter, or he may have been only a whisky peddler. Anyway, he was killed twelve miles above San Carlos, on the San Carlos River, by the Kid's outfit, and when the Kid returned to the Agency after he had done his short term and had been pardoned by the President, he was rearrested by the civil authorities of Gila County, Arizona, to be tried for the killing of this man at the Twelve Mile Pole.

This was in the fall of 1888. I was deputy sheriff of Gila County at that time, and as it was a new county, Reynolds was the first sheriff. I was to be the interpreter at the Kid's trial, but on July 4, 1888, I had won the prize at Globe for tying down a steer, and there was a county rivalry among the cowboys all over the Territory as to who was the quickest man at that business. One Charley Meadows (whose father and brother were before mentioned as being killed by the Cibicus on their raid) was making a big talk that he could beat me tying at the Territorial Fair, at Phoenix. Our boys concluded I must go to the fair and make a trial for the Territorial prize, and take it out of Meadows. I had known Meadows for years, and I thought I could beat him, and so did my friends.

The fair came off at the same time as did court in our new county, and since I could not very well be at both places, and, as they said, could not miss the fair, I was not at the trial.

While I was at Phoenix, the trial came off and several of the Indians told about the killing. There were six on trial, and they were all sentenced to the penitentiary at Yuma, Arizona, for life. Reynolds and "Hunky Dory" Holmes started to take them to Yuma. There were the six Indians and a Mexican sent up for one year, for horse stealing. The

Indians had their hands coupled together, so that there were three in each of the two bunches.

Where the stage road from Globe to Casa Grande (the railroad station on the Southern Pacific Railroad) crosses the Gila River there is a very steep sand wash, up which the stage road winds. Going up this, Reynolds took his prisoners out and they were all walking behind the stage. The Mexican was handcuffed and inside the stage. Holmes got ahead of Reynolds some little distance. Holmes had three Indians and Reynolds three.

Just as Holmes turned a short bend in the road and got behind a point of rocks and out of sight of Reynolds, at a given signal, each bunch of prisoners turned on their guard and grappled with him. Holmes was soon down and they killed him. The three that had tackled Reynolds were not doing so well, but the ones that had killed Holmes got his rifle and pistol and went to the aid of the ones grappling Reynolds. These three were holding his arms so he could not get his gun. The ones that came up killed him, took his keys, unlocked the cuffs, and they were free.

Gene Livingston was driving the stage, and he looked around the side of the stage to see what the shooting was about. One of the desperadoes took a shot at him, striking him over the eye, and down he came. The Kid and his men then took the stage horses and tried to ride them, but there was only one of the four that they could ride.

The Kid remained an outlaw after that, till he died a couple of years ago of consumption. The Mexican, after the Kid and his men left the stage (they had taken off his handcuffs), struck out for Florence and notified the authorities. The driver was only stunned by the shot over the eye and is today a resident and business man of Globe.

Had I not been urged to go to the fair at Phoenix, this

218

would never have happened, as the Kid and his comrades just walked along and put up the job in their own language, which no one there could understand but themselves. Had I not gone to the fair, I would have been with Reynolds, and could have understood what they said and it would never have happened. I won the prize roping at the fair, but it was at a very heavy cost.

* * *

[At this point in Horn's story, I wish to insert a clipping which I have been fortunate enough to secure. It is from the Philadelphia Times, of —— 27th 1895, and is timely just here.]

"In Arizona and New Mexico, roping contests used to be held as a kind of annual tournament, in August, to the fair, or else as a special entertainment, often comprising, among other features, horse racing, a bull fight, baile and fiesta. Roping contests are generally held in a large field or enclosure—such as the interior of a race course. Inside this compound is built a small corral, in which are confined wild beef cattle, usually three-year-old steers, just rounded up off the range.

"The contest is a time race, to see who can overtake, lasso, throw and tie hard and fast the feet of a steer in the shortest period. The record was made at Phoenix, Arizona, in 1891. The contestants were, Charlie Meadows, Bill Mc-Cann, George Iago, Ramon Barca and Tom Horn, all well-known vaqueros of the Mexican-Arizona border. Tom Horn won the contest. Time, 49½ seconds, which I do not think has since been lowered.

"Two parallel lines, about as far apart as the ends of a polo court, were marked by banderoles or guidons. A steer was let out of the corral and driven at a run in a direction at right angles to the lines marked. As the steer crossed the second line, a banderole was dropped, which was the signal for a vaquero to start from the first line, thus giving the beef a running start of 250 yards. The horses used were all large, fleet animals, wonderfully well trained, and swooped for their prey at full speed and by the shortest route, turning without a touch of the rein to follow the steer, often anticipating his turns by a shorter cut. When the vaquero got within fifty yards of his beef the loop of his riata was swinging in a sharp, crisp circle about his right arm, raised high to his right and rear, and when twenty yards closer, it shot forward, hovered for an instant, and then descended above the horns of its victim, which a moment later would land a somersault. Before the beef could recover his surprise or wind he would have a half hitch about his fore legs, a second about his hind legs, and a third found all four a snug little bunch, hard and fast.

"The rope, of course, is not taken from the head; it is all one rope, the slack being successively used. Sometimes the vaqueros used foot-roping instead of head. It requires more skill and is practiced more by the Mexicans, who think it is a good method with large-horned cattle while in herd, where heads are so little separated that a lasso would fall on horns not wanted. In foot-roping the noose is thrown lower and a bit in front of the beef, so that at his next step he will put his foot into the noose before it strikes the ground. If the noose falls too quickly for this, it is jerked sharply upward just as the foot is raised above it.

"I have seen men so skillful at this that they would bet even money on roping an animal on a single throw, naming the foot that they would secure, as right hind, left fore, and so forth. As regards the lash end of the riata, two methods in this contest were also used. In the 'Texas style,' the lash of the riata is made hard and fast to the horn of the saddle. The instant the rope 'holds,' a pony who understands his work plants his fore feet forward and checks suddenly, giving the steer a header. His rider dismounts quickly, runs to the beef, which the pony keeps down by holding the rope taut.

"As soon as the vaquero faces the pony and grasps the rope near the beef, the pony moves forward, and with the slack of the rope the beef is secured. While the beef is plunging or wheeling on the rope the pony is careful to keep his head toward the beef, or, as the sailor would say, he goes 'bow on.'

"The Texas method is best adapted to loose ground, where it is much easier on the vaquero, but it is utterly unsuited for mountain work or steep hillsides, as the pony would lose his footing and land up in the bottom of a cañon.

"For such country, the California style is used. Here the lash is not made fast; a few frapping turns are made about the horn, and the rider uses his weight and a checking of the pony to throw the beef. When he dismounts, he carries the lash end forward, keeping it taut, toward the beef, taking up the slack and coils it as he goes, and with it secures the beef. The pony is free after the steer is thrown. It is the more rapid method. Tom Horn used it in the contest won, when he made his record. With it the vaquero has free use of his riata for securing the beef. But it is a hard method, and plainsmen prefer letting Mr. Bronco take the brunt of it.

"Tom Horn is well known all along the border. He served as government guide, packer, scout and as chief of Indian scouts, which latter position he held with Captain Crawford at the time the Mexicans killed him in the Sierra Madre

Mountains. He is the hero referred to in the story of 'The Killing of the Captain,' by John Heard, Sr., published some months ago in the Cosmopolitan Magazine."

* * *

[Horn's narrative is now resumed.]

In the winter I again went home, and in the following spring I went to work on my mine. Worked along pretty steady on it for a year, and in 1890 we sold it to a party of New Yorkers. We got $8,000 for it.

We were negotiating for this sale, and at the same time the Pinkerton National Detective Agency at Denver, Colorado, was writing to me to get me to come to Denver and go to work for them. I thought it would be a good thing to do, and as soon as all the arrangements for the sale of the mine were made, I came to Denver and was initiated into the mysteries of the Pinkerton institution.

My work for them was not the kind that exactly suited my disposition; too tame for me. There were a good many instructions and a good deal of talk given the operative regarding the things to do and the things that had been done.

James McParland, the superintendent, asked me what I would do if I were put on a train robbery case. I told him if I had a good man with me I could catch up to them.

Well, on the last night of August, that year, at about midnight, a train was robbed on the Denver & Rio Grande Railway, between Cotopaxi and Texas Creek. I was sent out there, and was told that C. W. Shores would be along in a day or so. He came on time and asked me how I was getting on. I told him I had struck the trail, but there were so many men scouring the country that I, myself, was being held up all the time; that I had been arrested twice in two days and taken in to Salida to be identified!

222

Eventually all the sheriff's posses quit, and then Mr. W. A. Pinkerton and Mr. McParland told Shores and me to go at 'em. We took up the trail where I had left it several days before and we never left it till we got the robbers.

They had crossed the Sangre de Cristo range, come down by the Villa Grove iron mines, and crossed back to the east side of the Sangre de Cristos at Mosca Pass, then on down through the Huerfano Cañon, out by Cucharas, thence down east of Trinidad. They had dropped into Clayton, N. M., and got into a shooting scrape there in a gin mill. They then turned east again toward the "Neutral Strip" and close to Beaver City, then across into the "Pan Handle" by a place in Texas called Ochiltree, the county seat of Ochiltree County. They then headed toward the Indian Territory, and crossed into it below Canadian City. They then swung in on the head of the Washita River in the Territory, and kept down this river for a long distance.

We finally saw that we were getting close to them, as we got in the neighborhood of Paul's Valley. At Washita station we located one of them in the house of a man by the name of Wolfe. The robber's name was Burt Curtis. Shores took this one and came on back to Denver, leaving me to get the other one if ever he came back to Wolfe's.

After several days of waiting on my part, he did come back, and as he came riding up to the house I stepped out and told him someone had come! He was "Peg Leg" Watson, and considered by everyone in Colorado as a very desperate character. I had no trouble with him.

We had an idea that Joe McCoy, also, was in the robbery, but "Peg" said he was not, and gave me information enough so that I located him. He was wanted very badly by the sheriff of Fremont County, Colorado, for a murder scrape. He and his father had been tried previous to this for mur-

223

der, had been found guilty, and were remanded to jail to wait sentence, but before Joe was sentenced he had escaped. The old man McCoy got a new trial, and at the new trial was sentenced to eighteen years in the Cañon City, Colorado, penitentiary.

When I captured my man, got to a telegraph station and wired Mr. McParland that I had the notorious "Peg," the superintendent wired back: "Good! Old man McCoy got eighteen years today!" This train had been robbed in order to get money to carry McCoy's case up to the Supreme Court, or rather to pay the attorneys (Macons & Son), who had carried the case up.

Later on I told Mr. McParland that I could locate Joe McCoy, and he communicated with Stewart, the sheriff, who came to Denver and made arrangements for me to go with him and try to get McCoy.

We left Denver on Christmas Eve and went direct to Rifle, from there to Meeker, and on down White River. When we got to where McCoy had been, we learned that he had gone to Ashley, in Utah, for the Christmas festivities. We pushed on over there, reaching the town late at night, and could not locate our man. Next morning I learned where he got his meals, and as he went in to get his breakfast, I followed him in and arrested him. He had a big Colt's pistol, but did not shoot me. We took him out by Fort Duchesne, Utah, and caught the D. & R. G. train at Price station.

The judge under whom he had been tried had left the bench when McCoy finally was landed back in jail, and it would have required a new trial before he could be sentenced by another judge; he consented to plead guilty to involuntary manslaughter, and took six years in the Cañon City pen. He was pardoned out in three years, I believe.

Peg Leg Watson and Burt Curtis were tried in the United

States court for robbing the United States mails on the highway, and were sentenced for life in the Detroit federal prison. In robbing the train they had first made the fireman break into the mail compartment of the compartment car. They then saw their mistake, and did not even take the amount of a one-cent postage stamp, but went and made the fireman break into the rear compartment, where they found the express matter, and took it. But the authorities proved that it was mail robbery and their sentence was life.

While Pinkerton's is one of the greatest institutions of the kind in existence, I never did like the work, so I left them in 1894.

I then came to Wyoming and went to work for the Swan Land and Cattle Company, since which time everybody else has been more familiar with my life and business than I have been myself.

And I think that since my coming here the yellow journal reporters are better equipped to write my history than am I, myself!

Respectfully,

TOM HORN

A few letters from Horn, and to him, throwing additional light upon the character of the man; and furnishing some of the reasons for belief in his innocence — Also a summary of the "Horn Case" and estimates of the man by those who knew him best

LETTERS

NO. 1—OWNBEY TO HORN

DENVER, COLO., JANUARY 24, 1902

Mr. Tom Horn,
  County Jail,
    Cheyenne, Wyo.

DEAR TOM:

I see by the papers that you are in serious trouble. After reading an account of the charge preferred against you, I can not for the life of me believe it is true. Knowing you for so long and knowing you so intimately I can not comprehend how a man of your sense and ability could be guilty of so great a charge as is preferred against you.

Now, Tom, you will remember the Cotopaxi robbery, which was committed several years ago by "Peg-leg" and Curtis, and the long, hard chase we had after them, endeavoring to catch them. You will remember Ed Kelly, of Walsenburg, who first put me on the trail of Curtis and "Peg-leg," and you will again remember me wiring you and Doc Shores to meet me at Walsenburg—that I was on the trail of the robbers. Doc Shores, as you know, is with the Rio Grande Western as their special agent; he formerly was sheriff of Gunnison county, and his reputation is beyond reproach. We went down on the prairie between Trinidad and Walsenburg, and Kelly went back on all his first statements and endeavored to throw us off the trail. You will remember he would have been killed down there on the prairie and left for the coyotes to devour had it not been for your interference.

Now, Tom, I am at a loss to believe, after your protecting such a character as Kelly from being shot out on the plains, where mortal man would have never known anything about it, that you would be guilty of murdering a fourteen-year-old boy in cold blood. You know that scoundrel Kelly would have been shot for lying to the officers had it not been for your interference.

Tom, I do not believe you are guilty of the crime. I am writing this in all justice to you and the community at large; knowing you as I do, and knowing your ability and sense, I can not believe you would stoop so low as to murder a fourteen-year-old boy for the small sum of five hundred dollars, when you could in all probability have made that amount in a week, legitimately.

I live in Loveland, Colorado, and if there is anything I can do for you, or aid you in any manner as far as it is right, I am at your service. You can write me at Loveland, Colorado, box 271, and tell me what you think about it. I will give a copy of this letter to the press this afternoon, to be published in your behalf, as I do not believe you guilty of the crime. Write me and tell me if there is anything I can do to aid you.

As ever your friend,

F. M. OWNBEY

P. S.: I will write Doc Shores this afternoon (although I presume he has seen an account of your trouble), and see if there is anything he can do for you. My sympathies are with you, Tom, because I believe you innocent.

CHEYENNE, WYO., MARCH 1, 1902

John C. Coble, Esq.,
   Bosler, Wyo.

DEAR JOHN:

I have just made an elaborate investment in writing material, so I will drop you a line and will continue to do so every week from now on. I am still doing business at the same old number, but times are very dull just at present. I look for an increase in business in a few weeks.

If I had the machine here I would play a few lines something like "Go away back and sit up."

My girls have all left off writing to me and my heart is lonely now. If I had some place to work I would be as happy as a clam. Well, I guess I am happy anyhow.

If the boys are looking for a good place to go, tell them to go to Cheyenne to jail. About all the talk I hear is which are the best jails and how to get out of jails, and doing the hobo act, and good places to go to make a good stake, and where to get the biggest glass of beer for 5c, and who gives the best free lunch for nothing, and general information that is of a great deal of benefit to any one to remember.

Do you do any fishing nowadays, and if so, send me in one that weighs five or six pounds, for I am hungry for fish. Send it to me by express, care sheriff.

Where is Charley Irwin going to keep his family? How is the Michigan coming on? What made Jim Meade leave Montana?

I don't see how I am going to get out of the case with any money, but from what I can hear from the outside, I

228

will have notoriety enough to run a divorce mill. Well, money is but dross anyhow.

I have fully made up my mind that I will go way back to Missouri and sit down on a farm. This sporting life isn't what it is cracked up to be. I will be in jail anyhow four months, and I am too slow to ever catch up with myself again. Just think, four months that I don't even get to see a newspaper! Is that what you call life in the Far West?

You and Charley are the only ones who have been in to see me. I am going to write to a friend of mine here in town to send me some reading matter, as I have read everything here that I can find. By the way, that was a nice lot of literature you sent me before you left town.

Let me know if you hear anything from my saddle, bed and valise. Let me know, also, if you hear from the agents and they don't know anything of the stuff.

Tell Stone and Irwin to dry the beef hides good and straight, as I started to do, and not to put them one on top of the other when they are green.

I want to get out of here by the time greens get ripe, so I can walk back to Missouri and live on greens.

Well, Johnnie, I feel the same as I did when we were in that train wreck: You can't hurt a Christian.

Have you got the plumbago fence moved and let the contract for ploughing yet? I wanted to do that ploughing myself, but can't get around to it this spring.

Regards to Irwin, Stone and all the boys. Tell Stone to write.

With regrets, in jail,

Tom Horn

CHEYENNE, WYO., MARCH 5, 1903

C. B. Irwin, Esq.

Bosler, Wyo.

DEAR CHARLEY:

I received the $5.00 all O. K. Yes, send down your riata and I will splice it and glad of the chance. I am just getting the new hair work so I begin to understand it. I will keep on practicing for a few days yet before I start to do any work.

This winter does look to me like a corker. The backbone of it may soon break.

How did those ropes last? Was the big one any good? Shall I send it back when I get it done or will I leave it here till one of you come in? Send it to R. A. Proctor, for he is the only man here to tend to such things.

I have had a bad cold, but am getting over it.

Don't forget the hair, if you have any on hand when you send in the rope. I wrote to Sam Moore to send me in some white hair and Proctor saw him on the street here the same day I wrote, and he said he would send in some right away. Send in that hair bridle of Johnnie's, so I can take pattern from it. Send it with the rope. I will only want it a day or so; I can splice the rope in an hour.

Yours truly,
TOM HORN

CHEYENNE, WYO., OCTOBER 3, 1903

Chas. J. Ohnhaus, Esq.,
  Cheyenne, Wyo.

SIR:

I was informed by the sheriffs and my lawyers that the Supreme Court has refused to grant me a new trial, and that I am to be hanged November 20th.

Now, sir, I am going to make an appeal to you to act in my behalf, and it certainly is not much I ask—only that you make an affidavit to the facts in this supposed confession of mine.

You and I and Snow and La Fors and Stoll all know that you changed your stenographic notes, at the instigation of some one, from what was actually said, to what you wanted me to say. In speaking of this money that was paid to me on the train between Denver and Cheyenne, La Fors said it was paid to me by George Prentice and that Hi Kelly had given two one hundred dollar bills and a fifty dollar bill.

Why was that cut out of your notes?

On first entering the marshal's office La Fors showed me his rifle, and we had some conversation about the sights on the rifle, which he said were aperture sights, and he explained to me how they were used.

Why was that cut out of your notes?

You said in your notes that I said that I ran across there bare-footed, when, as a matter of fact, I told La Fors that if he ever wanted to cover his trail to go bare-footed. In speaking of the rock under the boy's head, he asked me if it was a sign, and I said I supposed it was. I never said

231

I put it there, nor did I intimate that I put it there. I did not say "That is the sign I put out to collect my money."

You put that in at the instigation of some one.

You put in your report that I said: "That was the best shot ever I made, and the dirtiest trick I ever did."

You and I, and the others I have mentioned, know that was made up by Stoll or La Fors, and put in the notes by you.

You said in your notes that I was paid a certain sum for killing three men and shooting another one, and every word of that also was manufactured.

There were other things of more or less importance put in your notes at the suggestion of some one.

Now, the people that know you say that you are a nice, model young man, and a Christian. Now, surely you would be doing a Christian act to come out and make an affidavit to the facts in this case of mine.

You are a young man not yet in the prime of life, and do you want to go through life knowing, as you do, that your perjured testimony took away my life? You may live to be an old man, and every day of your life you can not help but think of the terrible wrong you have done me by being made a tool of by men who would, if it would add to their notoriety, do the same by you that they have done by me. I suppose you got, or was promised, a certain sum of money for doing as you did. Did you enjoy spending it? No! every cent of it is red with the blood of a man who never harmed you in any way, shape or form.

You may live to be an old man, and every day of your life will, if I am hung, be a day that you can say to yourself: *"If I had only told the truth in Tom Horn's case, I could have saved his life.*

I am appealing to you for the *truth* only, and that should

be the first Christian principle of any one with a claim on Christian principles.

I ask only that you will go to my attorneys and tell them the whole truth as to where these notes were changed, at whose instigation they were changed, and what was done with the original notes. If they are not destroyed you can still produce them; and if they are destroyed, you can tell them at least the facts in the case, and forever clear your mind and conscience of a burden that you will certainly find hard to bear through life, no matter how stout-hearted you may feel.

Have I ever harmed you, that you should seek my life in this manner? If so, when and where?

There are too many men mixed up in this business that know the truth, and it will sooner or later come out, even if every one implicated does all in his power to conceal it; and then what will the public think of the one or more when they do know what must eventually leak out, hide it as you may?

You were made a tool of by some one, and now, for the last time, I ask you to tell only the truth.

Surely I am not asking much from any one when I ask you to tell only the truth.

This is the strongest appeal I can *write* to you, and now I am going to ask you, if you ignore this appeal, to come and see me in a few days, so I can talk to you personally.

Yours truly,
TOM HORN

CHEYENNE, WYO., OCTOBER 9, 1903

John C. Coble, Esq.,
  Bosler, Wyo.

DEAR JOHNNIE:

Proctor came to me last night and showed me your letter. How is everybody? Who is boss on the ranch? How is Dunk getting on since he got married? Where is Stone, the Savage?

Write me and tell me all the news of the country. What kind of prices are you going to get for beef? How is the feed on the range and did you have a good hay crop? Who put it up—and all the news you have.

I think you will have no trouble to get to see me next month.

I have been informed that it might do me some good to tell all I know, but I can't figure out who would believe anything I said, and what I know is next to nothing. Of course, I know of that man coming to see you to join some gang of men in the hills to do something to the sheep, and I know you refused to have anything to do with any of the outfit. That man never spoke to me at all about the sheep.

I know, also, that the man that I went after and made come to the ranch and burn his brand off of the E yearling, offered me five hundred dollars to kill off the whole bunch of sheep, so he could buy the ranch cheap.

I know the husband of the woman who said: "I just know that was our yearling that that man had in his wagon," and how, when she was told the sheriff was looking for the owner, she said, "No, it was not ours." Well, that man said he would give me a hundred dollars, and his neighbor below him said (with a big oath), "Tom you have got this to do, and I will put up $250 today for my share."

Those are the only ones that ever said anything to me about the row and, as I said before, no one would take my word or oath either, so I could not do myself any good by telling that.

Let me hear all the news. When will you be through shipping?

Yours truly,
TOM HORN

NO. 6—HORN TO COBLE

CHEYENNE, WYO., OCTOBER 12, 1903

John C. Coble, Esq.
  Bosler, Wyo.

DEAR JOHNNIE:

I have written you a couple of letters, and also several to Judge Burke, but so far have not heard a word from any one.

I think that if you would go to Denver and see Billy Loomis that he could get an affidavit from Frank W. Mulock and those other two men with him, showing that he came here hired to swear to anything that was put into his mouth, and that Stoll and La Fors hired him to do so. It is certainly worth while to make the attempt.

Try and find out from Burke and Lacey if such an affidavit would do any good. I have written Burke several times in the last week, asking him if such an affidavit would do any good, but so far have been unable to get a reply of any kind from him. He does not answer my letters, or even acknowledge the receipt of them. Of course, it is not worth

235

while to get them if they will do no good, but where there is absolute perjury shown, and it is also shown that these men were paid to swear falsely, it would certainly cut some figure with the governor.

I wrote Ohnhaus a letter and asked him to come up and tell the truth and save a life; this I did on the 4th of this month, and I have not heard from him yet. Last night Proctor brought me word that Burke said it would be a good idea to write a letter to Mulock and see if he would come out and tell the truth, but no word can I get saying what good it would do.

Of course, with Ohnhaus it is different; for he took down the conversation in shorthand and then changed it at the instigation of some one. He can tell the whole job, and that would get me a pardon, but he will probably refuse to do so.

Anyhow, everything should be tried. You know that there is no time to spare if this thing is to be brought around.

Burke has got too much to do to attend to this, and if you will give it your personal attention, I feel sure you can accomplish something.

I have today written to Billy Loomis at Denver, to see Mulock and see if anything can be done in the matter, and told him to communicate with you in regard to the matter; also told him to write Burke.

Johnnie, drop me a line as soon as you get this, so I can tell if you are getting my letters. How are everybody and everything? I hear beef prices are way down.

If you go to Denver and can get this affidavit from this man, get him to tell, also, who told him what to swear to.

Let me hear from you soon.

Yours truly,
TOM HORN

CHEYENNE, WYO., OCTOBER 31, 1903

John C. Coble,
Bosler, Wyo.

DEAR JOHNNIE:

I had a long talk to-day with Judge Burke, and he spoke as though it would help my case a good deal if it was proven that I was not present when Nickell was shot so many times.

The night before Nickell was shot I was at Alex Seller's ranch, and went away in the morning (the morning Nickell was shot), and came back to his ranch in the evening. When I got back in the evening to Seller's ranch, Jack Linscott was there and stayed all night and left the next morning, going somewhere up on the North Laramie River. I left the ranch also, the same day, and came back to Seller's ranch again in the evening, and Jack Linscott also came back to Seller's ranch, and as Linscott and I both got in about the same time, Sellers was telling both of us about Nickell being shot the day before, and Jack said he did not hear of it at R. R. before he left.

I then told both of them all about the sheep business, and the Nickell and Miller war, and about the Nickell boy being killed a short time before, which they had heard. There was a good deal of talk about it, so they will remember it well.

There were also several men there working at putting up hay. I don't know their names, but think one of them was a Newell.

Linscott was driving a buggy. I still stayed on at Seller's for a couple of nights more after Linscott left. I was at Seller's ranch for two nights before Nickell was shot, and two or three nights after. Now, Sellers has sold out and I don't know where he is. You might look him up and show him this letter, and he can not help but recall the whole circumstance.

I will write Linscott at Rock River and see if he will come in and see Judge Burke and make an affidavit to these facts.

Yours truly,

TOM HORN

P. S. I am writing Linscott to write Burke.

NO 8—HORN TO COBLE

CHEYENNE, WYO., NOVEMBER 17, 1903

John C. Coble,
  Bosler, Wyo.

DEAR JOHNNIE:

Proctor told me that it was all over with me except the applause part of the game.

You know they can't hurt a Christian, and as I am prepared, it is all right.

I thoroughly appreciate all you have done for me. No one could have done more. Kindly accept my thanks, for if ever a man had a true friend, you have proven yourself one to me.

Remember me kindly to all my friends, if I have any besides yourself.

Burke and Lacey have not shown up yet.

I want you to always understand that the stenographic notes taken in the United States marshal's office were all changed to suit the occasion. The notes read at the trial were not the original notes at all. Everything of an incriminating nature read in those notes was manufactured and put in. It won't do any good to kick at that now, so let 'er go.

238

If any one profits by my being hung, I would be sorry to see them disappointed.

It would, perhaps, be somewhat of a trying meeting for you to come to see me now. Do as you like. It might cause you a good deal of pain.

I am just the same as ever, and will remain so.

The governor's decision was no surprise to me, for I was tried, convicted and hung before I left the ranch. My famous confession was also made days before I came to town.

I told Burke to give you some writing I did; be sure and get it. You will not need anything to remember me by, but you will have that anyway. Anything else I may have around the ranch is yours.

I won't need anything where I am going. I have an appointment with some Christian ladies to-morrow, and will write you of their visit to-morrow night.

I will drop you a line every day now, till the Reaper comes along.

Kindest to all.

> Yours truly,
> TOM HORN

CHEYENNE, WYO., NOVEMBER 20, 1903

John C. Coble, Esq.,
Cheyenne, Wyo.

As you have just requested, I will tell you all my knowledge of everything I know in regard to the killing of the Nickell boy.

The day I laid over at Miller's ranch, he asked me to do so, so that I could meet Billy McDonald.

Billy McDonald came up and Miller and I met him up the creek, above Miller's house. Billy opened the conversasation by saying that he and Miller were going to kill off the Nickell outfit and wanted me to go in on it. They said that Underwood and Jordon would pay me.

Miller and McDonald said they would do the work. I refused to have anything to do with them, as I was not interested in any way. McDonald said that the sheep were then on Coble's land and I got my horse and went up to see, and they were not on Coble's land.

I promised to stay all night again at Miller's, as McDonald said he would come up again next morning.

He came back next morning and asked me if I still felt the same as I did the day before, and I told him I did.

"Well," he said, "we have made up our minds to wipe up the whole Nickell outfit."

I got on my horse and left, and went on about my business. I went on as John Brae and Otto Plaga said I did, and on to the ranch, where I got in on Saturday. I heard there of the boy being killed. I felt I was well out of the mix up.

I was over in that part of the country six weeks or two months later and saw both McDonald and Miller, and they were laughing and blowing to me about running and shooting the sheep of Nickell. I told them I did not want to hear of it at all, for I could see that McDonald wanted to tell me the whole scheme. They both gave me the laugh and said I was suspicioned of the whole thing.

I knew there was some suspicion against me, but did not pay the attention to it that I should.

That is all there is to it so far as I know.

Irwin, who swore I came into Laramie on the run on that Thursday, just simply lied.

All that supposed confession in the United States marshal's office was prearranged, and everything that was sworn to by those fellows was a lie, made up before I came to Cheyenne. Of course, there was talk of the killing of the boy, but La Fors did all of it. I did not even make an admission, but allowed La Fors to make some insinuations.

Ohnhaus, La Fors and Snow, and also Irwin, of Laramie, all swore to lies to fit the case.

Your name was not mentioned in the marshal's office.

This is the truth, as I am going to die in ten minutes.

Thanking you for your kindness and continued goodness to me, I am,

> Sincerely yours,
> TOM HORN

NO. 10—CHAS. HORN TO COBLE

BOULDER, COLO., NOVEMBER 27, 1903

Mr. John C. Coble,
Bosler, Wyo.

KIND FRIEND:

We buried Tom with all due respect that relatives and friends could show. We had the largest funeral that was ever in this town. Everybody showed due courtesy to the hearse as it went seven blocks. They stood on the street with their hats off as we passed along. When we arrived at the cemetery there was hardly standing room. There must have been anyhow 2,500 people at the funeral.

Tom told our sheriff that he had written me a letter. I have never received it. I expected this letter all of the time, and this is the reason that I never wrote.

I would like to know if he had any personal effects; if so, please let me know what and where they are. I received his hat, shoes and grip from Sheriff Smalley.

We appreciate, from the bottom of our hearts, all that you have done for him; that is, myself and family.

We have no picture of him, nor anything but what I have related in this letter.

I received a letter from Attorney Burke, of Cheyenne, requesting me to place a guard over the grave, which I had already made arrangements for, and did, and this guard still remains and will until I call him off. He is an old friend of ours and Tom's, and never falls down on anything.

I see by the papers that you are seriously ill, which I am exceedingly sorry to hear.

Hoping to hear from you soon, and that you will be in better health when this reaches you, I remain,

Yours friend,

CHARLES HORN

P. S. Give the Irwin boys my regards.

CHAS. HORN

MISS KIMMELL'S STATEMENT

BORN AND REARED midst the comforts and refinements of civilization, I have, nevertheless, been most strongly attracted by the frontier type; so, when, in July of 1901, I went to take the Miller-Nickell school in the Iron Mountain country, I was happy in the belief that I would meet with the embodiment of that type in its natural environment. I was doomed to disappointment, for all the cattle men and cow boys I saw were like the hired hands "back East."

I was beginning to regret that I had not been born some twenty years earlier, when, on the night of July 15th, there stopped at the Miller ranch a man who embodied the characteristics, the experiences and the code of the old frontiersman. It was Tom Horn.

Horn went to Wyoming in 1892 and for the following five years worked as cow boy for several cattle companies.

At the beginning of the Spanish-American War General Maus received instructions to look up Tom Horn and secure his services in the organization of the pack train for the army going to Cuba. In the fall of 1898, Horn was ordered by Miles to Tampa, Florida, as chief pack master for Shafter's army, with the rank and pay of colonel. Shortly after this, he was made master of transportation.

At St. Louis, where the pack train of 520 mules and 133 packers was organized, a delay occurred which necessitated the shipping of the train from Tampa just one day behind Colonel Wood and Lieutenant Colonel Roosevelt and their Rough Riders.

When the train arrived at harbor, Horn found that the transports could not approach the landing near enough to disembark the mules. Nervous and anxious, he consulted the officers in charge of the transports, and together they decided to visit the flag ship and get orders from headquarters. Being personally acquainted with General Shafter, Horn approached him with the earnest request that permission be given to attempt the landing of the pack train, so that supplies and ammunition might be hurried after the Rough Riders, already twenty-four hours in advance. Shafter remonstrated: "But Colonel, you can not get your transports to the wharf." "Only give me an order to land my mules and they will be landed," was the reply. "You have the order," came the brief but welcome answer. Disembarking the train began without delay, the manner being original with Horn. A mule would be taken to the gangway, where four men were stationed with ropes. There was a "push all together," and—the mule was in the water.

The 520 were thus unloaded and headed for shore, perhaps a mile distant. Only two of the animals were lost. One was trampled underneath and drowned, while another, a big Missouri mule, swam in the wrong direction. Two seamen were sent after him to head him back, but the faster the sailors rowed, the swifter swam the mule; and the last seen of him he was far out in the ocean headed for old "Mizzoury." By daylight those 518 mules were packed and on the trail.

Too great emphasis can not be given to the fact that but for the energy and ingenuity of Tom Horn, there would have been no supplies nor ammuniation at the front when that notable engagement at San Juan Hill took place. Let any thoughtful, fair-minded person reflect upon the possible consequences if the chief of the train had not insisted upon immediate landing, and then with tireless zeal, kept his hundred and more packers at work through the long, tropical night.

A few hours before the battle of San Juan Hill, Leonard Wood and Theodore Roosevelt met with Horn while they were journeying afoot toward the front. Their horses were worn out, so they asked Horn for fresh ones. Now, Horn had received his orders to supply no one mules; but, having served with Wood in Arizona and esteeming him highly, he made an exception, and gave mounts to both of them.

Incidentally, Horn's description of the San Juan fight is the best in detail ever given. According to this eye witness, a degree of injustice has been done the Seventy-first New York in branding the entire regiment as cowards, whereas, there was only a deplorable lack of discipline and training. Horn saw one officer use every means to stop the retreat— stampede rather—of his men, pleading, commanding, threatening, even striking at them with his sword; and finally, seeing that his efforts were unavailing, he broke his sword and stamped upon the pieces. But his men streamed past him and his few staunch followers, dodged among and under the feet of the pack mules whence the disgusted packers, with oaths and lashes, strove to dislodge them. The officer—he of the broken sword—seeing that the packers' efforts were also in vain, joined a colored regiment just then charging up the Hill.

Having contracted the Cuban fever, Horn was compelled to return home before the close of the war. After a trying hospital experience, he went to the ranch of John C. Coble, which he thenceforth made his headquarters.

By this time the rustlers in the Iron Mountain country had grown so bold that the leading cattlemen in those regions combined and hired Horn as a stock detective. His duty was to ride the range in the open season to discover offenders and prevent stealing. The Iron Mountain country is settled principally by small ranchmen, but is bordered by many large ranches. It is only about fifty miles square, but it probably contains more rustlers to the square inch than any other place twice its size. These rustlers, like most of their kind, are ignorant, shiftless and vicious. True, there are a few respectable families, but they are decidedly in the minority.

The most talked-of families in the district were the Millers and the Nickells, whose quarrels had long been public property. They had taken homesteads about twenty years before, and for the past ten years a feud had existed between them. The quarrel had extended even down to the younger children, and fights between them were not uncommon. The feeling grew so bitter that in February, 1901, Jim Miller, the father, stabbed Kels P., the head of the Nickell family, seriously, but not fatally. The latter had long been at the outs, not only with the Millers, but with nearly all of his other neighbors The climax came in the early summer of the same year, when Nickell brought sheep into the district—an unpardonable sin in cattle country.

This was the situation with which Tom Horn had to deal. So well did he succeed that the stealing almost ceased. Horn's big, muscular body and keenness in understanding a situation had much to do with his success; but his main weapon was his reputation as a killer. He himself carefully fostered this reputation, for as he would say to his friends: "That is my stock-in-trade." Nothing but powerful fear could restrain the rustlers; so Horn, when he "just hanpened" to drop in upon a cattle-thief, would entertain the family by accounts of his experiences as a government scout, deputy sheriff and as a Pinkerton detective. These bloody tales would leave his auditors open-mouthed, and for days after his departure not a calf would be stolen in the neighborhood.

247

Of course, there were killings. There always are when cattlemen and rustlers are neighbors. Naturally, the rustlers blamed Horn for these deaths, for they hated him in proportion as they feared. Then, Horn himself boasted of the killing of certain cattle thieves—that was additional stock-in-trade. So it came to pass that many people believed Horn responsible for all the killings. They forgot that other stock detectives were riding, that cattlemen as well as their detectives can handle guns, and that the rustlers quarrel among themselves! The authorities could never fathom the mysterious killings, and the trouble went on.

On the morning of July 19, 1901, William Nickell, the fourteen-year-old son of Kels Nickell, was found dead about three-quarters of a mile from his home, shot through the heart. There was no clue, but the Millers were immediately suspected. One theory was that Jim Miller, lying in wait for "Ole Nick," as he called his arch-enemy, had shot the boy by mistake; but at the first session of the coroner's inquest, July 22d, strong evidence tended to show that Victor Miller was the guilty one, he having had many personal quarrels and fights with William Nickell. But the evidence was not strong enough to warrant an arrest, and it looked as though this tragedy would also remain unsolved.

August 3d the excitement, barely subsiding, was given an impetus by the tresspassing of Nickell's sheep upon Miller's deeded land. Several hundred sheep taken from their owner's homestead, driven across the public range and down into a meadow of a neighbor's deeded land, was certainly provocation from a cattleman's standpoint. Bloodshed was narrowly averted by the withdrawal of the sheep; but no one was surprised when the next day Kels Nickell was shot. He at once declared he recognized his assailants as Jim Miller and one of his grown sons.

This declaration is intensified by the statements of Nickell and his wife to Mr. and Mrs. Joe Reid, neighbors: "They will try to lay this on Tom Horn, but he never done it! It was the Millers."

At the second session of the coroner's inquest, August 9th, some of the younger Nickell children testified that they had seen the men ride away in the direction of the Millers', one on a bay and the other on a gray horse. This was serious evidence against the Millers, for of Miller's three riding horses, one was a bay and one a gray. Thirteen shots had been fired at Nickell, two taking effect, but his wounds were not serious.

Soon after the shooting, while he still lay in the hospital at Cheyenne, four masked men descended upon Nickell's sheep, sent off the herder and clubbed a large number of the flock. Accustomed to strife though he was, this was too much for Nickell; he sent for his family to come to Cheyenne, and his ranch was put up for sale. The remainder of the flock was withdrawn from the country by their owners, Nickell having simply pastured the sheep on shares.

All these stirring events had not taken place without some suspicion being directed toward Horn. The Millers strove adroitly to throw suspicion upon him; in fact, both Gus and Victor Miller repeatedly said to me: "It's all right to let suspicion fall on Tom Horn! He doesn't care, and it might help us." Then there were many rustlers interested in having Horn out of the way, whether he was innocent or guilty.

There were only two points which could possibly be construed against Horn—his cherished reputation as a killer, and the fact that two days prior to the killing he had stopped at Miller's. Horn's friends claimed this latter fact was evidence in his favor, as it was well known he could enter a neighborhood, gather his information and depart, with no one the wiser; so, had he been on a murderous errand, he would not have shown himself. Horn himself always explained his presence there by claiming that he had heard Nickell's sheep were out on Coble's land; but finding that such was not the case, was homeward bound when he stopped at Miller's.

Horn's movements are best shown by a quotation from a letter he wrote to his attorney. He says:

The morning K. P. Nickell was shot, I left Sellers' ranch, which is more than one hundred miles from the Nickell neighborhood, and went down into Dave Cochran's pasture and ran across Dave and talked the news of the country over with him. We talked of the killing of the Nickell boy. I told Dave all I knew, of my leaving there the day before the boy was killed, sheep trouble, and so on. I went on back to Seller's ranch that night. I met Cochran on the round-up, some six weeks later, and he told me that the day after he talked to me in his pasture he got the news of K. P. Nickell being shot on the day before—which was the day I was talking to him in his pasture."

On the other hand, is it improbable that the Millers took advantage of the stock detective's presence in the neighborhood to score against their old enemies the Nickells? Certain it is Nickell's sheep had never bothered any of the cattle outfits for which Horn was working; equally certain it is that the Millers had the provocation!

The second night of his stay at Miller's, Horn made a remark which can not be harmonized with the theory that he was mixed up in the Nickell affairs. Jim Miller had been telling about Nickell's threat to drive his sheep upon Miller's property, and he ended with a hard chuckle: "If Old Nick turns his sheep in on my land, I'll turn my cattle in on him." Horn quickly and seriously replied: "Oh, don't do anything wrong!"

The summer waned, and with its passing, Horn was thrown out of employment. The sheep were out of the country and the rustlers had been intimidated, so Horn's employers decided to dispense with his services.

Among the officers who had been working on the Nickell case was one Joe La Fors, a deputy U. S. marshal. This man had always posed as a friend of Horn's; so when, in the latter part of December, he told Mr. Coble that he knew of an opening in Montana for a stock detective, and that he would help Horn get the position, neither Horn nor Coble were surprised.

The position was secured and Horn went as far as Omaha, where he got drunk and lost his outfit. Having returned to Coble's ranch for a new outfit, he received a letter from La Fors, saying that a representative of the Montana people was in Cheyenne and wished to meet him. La Fors also had a letter from Montana, which he wished to show him.

On his way to Cheyenne Horn stopped at Laramie and again got drunk, and the morning he reached Cheyenne continued drinking, so that he was too drunk to talk to La Fors, who made another appointment for the afternoon. Horn missed this appointment also, and La Fors went out to look for him. He found him asleep on a chair in the back room of a saloon. Waking him, he *led* him to the marshal's office, and there occurred that famous "confession." As to what was really said in the marshal's office, there are two accounts—one is Horn's and the other is Joe La Fors and his confederates'.

The next day, January 13, 1902, Tom Horn was arrested, charged with the murder of William Nickell.

What evidence the authorities held was not made public until the preliminary hearing, on May 10th, when it was disclosed that at this interview with La Fors, the district court stenographer, one Charles Ohnhaus, and a deputy sheriff, one Leslie Snow, had been secreted by La Fors behind the door, between the marshal's two offices. These three testified that during the interview Horn was perfectly sober; that he had confessed to the murder of William Nickell, and of two rustlers, Lewis and Powell, who several years before had lived in the Iron Mountain country; that he had confessed to shooting at Kels Nickell with intent to kill; that he had said killing was a business proposition with him.

Horn's trial came up on October 13th. In addition to these statements, there was a great showing of testimony against him; but when sifted, it left the "confession" the main dependence of the prosecution. The attorneys for the defense considered Horn's chances better than even, as the only thing against him of importance was the so-called "confession"—and he was drunk when this talk occurred. The so-called confession was not in the language of Horn, filled as it was with profanity and vulgarity, and it is a well known fact that Horn, drunk or sober, was never vulgar and seldom profane. The language sounds more like Leslie Snow than Tom Horn. Even the unfriendly newspapers predicted either an acquittal or a hung jury.

Great was the surprise, then, when, at 5 P.M. on October 26th, the jury brought in a verdict of guilty. This jury was composed principally of small ranchmen, most of whom were from the districts adjacent to the Iron Mountain regions. After the trial it was discovered that Horn and his friends, Duncan Clark and Sam Moore, had recovered stolen stock from some of the jurymen. So the stock detective had been tried by a jury, the majority of whom were

252

cattle rustlers! It is no mystery to a cowman why the case was lost. During the trial a prominent ranchman publicly said: "Show me a cattleman who's against Tom Horn, and I'll show you a rustler!"

An appeal was taken, first to the district judge and then to the Supreme Court. As was anticipated, the district judge refused a new trial. The rulings during the trial were such that the defense could not hope for much from this judge. They did, however, have some faith in the Supreme Court, for the attorneys for defense cited seventy-nine errors.

While the matter was in the hands of this Court things were quiet, except that certain newspapers kept loading the public with sensational stories that plots had been laid for the escape of the prisoner. August 9, 1903, Horn did break jail, and was at large for about fifteen minutes. The alarm had been quickly given, so he was captured but a little distance from the jail.

While effecting his escape he secured an automatic Browning pistol, and his enemies have always claimed that he would have killed the jailer if it had not been that he did not understand the mechanism of the gun. It is hard for his friends to believe that he could not operate so simple an arrangement, when they consider that he had handled firearms all his life.

Murder was evidently not in his heart, for he could easily have killed the jailer by striking him with the stock of the gun after he was tied.

After Horn had surrendered, and, surrounded by officers and others, was returning to jail, Deputy Sheriff Leslie Snow rode up, and with the butt of his gun aimed a murderous blow at the prisoner's head. It was only due to the quickness of a policeman in throwing up his arm that the stroke missed the temple, for which it was intended, and its power may be judged from the fact that the policeman's wrist was broken. Certain of the Wyoming and Denver newspapers had much to say about Horn's "murderous attack" upon the jailer, but they said nothing about Snow's murderous attack upon Horn.

September 5th came the Supreme Court's adverse decision. Then, on the 31st of October, the last appeal was taken—to the governor.

Boarding, as I did, with the Miller's, I not only passed through the occurrences which were made public, but I obtained a thorough view behind the scenes. After the second session of the coroner's inquest, I overheard three conversations between Jim and Victor Miller, in each of which conversation statements were made by both, incriminating Victor Miller as the murderer of William Nickell. Twice afterwards Jim Miller acknowledged to me that Victor had confessed to him the killing of the Nickell boy; and on the 10th of October, 1901, Victor Miller himself confessed to me that he was the murderer. I agreed to say nothing about Victor's criminality, provided they would make no attempt to sidetrack the crime on Horn, or any other innocent person. I felt it would be unfair to punish Victor and leave untouched his father and Kels Nickell, the original cause of all the trouble. Moreover, I took into consideration the youth of the self-confessed murderer (Victor was but eighteen) and that he had grown up in the midst of quarrelling and strife. So I held my peace.

When Horn had been brought to trial, I seriously contemplated laying my knowledge of Victor's guilt before the authorities; but as the attorneys for the defense repeatedly wrote me that they were confident of winning their case, I thought that by my continued silence I could save Victor Miller, and yet not jeopardize Horn. After the jury brought in their verdict I was ready to reveal my knowledge of Victor's guilt, for I had no intention of shielding a guilty man at the expense of an innocent one. However, owing to legal technicality, the lawyers could not use this evidence until the case was placed in the governor's hands. When that time arrived I made an affidavit, setting forth in detail my knowledge of Victor Miller's criminality, and then I went to Cheyenne from a distant place in order to appear in person before the governor.

The newspapers had much to say about the frequent interviews the governor held with the "school-ma'am," and how he painstakingly questioned her concerning the situation in the Iron Mountain country, etc. In this they drew entirely upon their imaginations. I held but one interview, worthy of the name, with the governor, and in this his questions were very evidently prompted more by a curiosity concerning my personal, private affairs than by any anxiety to inform himself upon the true situation.

I did, however, hold a long, comprehensive interview with Judge Corn, chief justice of the Wyoming Supreme Court, in which he made the following statement: "You understand the Supreme Court did not determine Tom Horn's guilt or innocence; they simply passed upon whether or not there had been evidence enough before the jury upon which a verdict could be passed. As for myself, I have not yet made up my mind whether he is innocent or guilty. In fact, I would be perfectly eligible as a juror to try the case."

I also held a short interview with Judge Jesse Knight, of the Supreme Court, in which he said he did not read all of the testimony placed before the Supreme Court, and made this further statement: "I have taken no part in this case since it left the hands of the Supreme Court. I might have if they hadn't attacked Joe La Fors." It is a question how

Horn's friends could assert his innocence without attacking Joe La Fors.

In addition to my testimony, a great deal of other evidence strongly in support of the defendant was presented to the governor.

Among the things submitted were two letters from Frank W. Mulock, of Denver. It will be remembered by those who followed the case, that this man and Robert G. Cousley testified at the trial that they had heard Horn in a Denver saloon boast of the killing of the Nickell boy. Mulock's letter to Lacey came as a complete surprise; and a careful reading of these letters leads us to but one inference—his conscience was hurting him!

"DENVER, OCT. 5, 1903

"Hon. J. W. Lacey, Cheyenne, Wyoming

"DEAR SIR: I was sorry to hear that the Supreme Court had refused Tom Horn a new trial, after the very able defense you rendered him. I am one of the Denver witnesses that testified against him.

"Last April, in Pueblo, and twice here in Denver last week I have seen a man who is a double for Horn. One Geo. S. Roberts, was to have been a witness against Horn, but failed to show up at the last minute. This Roberts was bartender at saloon here where the fellow *claiming* to be Horn made the alleged confession. From what Roberts has told me since Horn's conviction, I am inclined to think Horn was the subject of a base conspiracy. I met Roberts in Kansas City last October, and he told me he could procure evidence to acquit Horn, besides what he himself knew. I think Roberts is in New Orleans, La., at present and I am satisfied I could induce him to procure anything favorable to Horn that he knows. I think if the showing is made to Governor Chatterton, that without a doubt, the governor would grant a pardon or commutation of sentence.

"I am willing to do all I can towards the reparation of the wrong done Horn, if any wrong has been committed. I will go to New Orleans and see Roberts, and I am fully satisfied I can induce him to go before the governor or make proper affidavits. I do not ask any compensation for my services, even if it is developed that Horn is pardoned or commuted.

"If you will furnish transportation to New Orleans and return to Denver, with accompanying legitimate expenses, I am ready to go at once. If I do not hear from you in two or three days, I am going to Idaho for the winter. If I could see you personally, or one of your representatives here in Denver, I could go more into details in reference to Roberts' position in the case. You can address me by wire, 1134—Fifteenth street, care Jno. D. Ross, Denver. I will expect an answer from you Tuesday or Wednesday.

"Yours in confidence,
"Frank W. Mulock"

"Denver, Colo., October 13, 1903

"R. G. Couseley, Esq.,
  "1412 Olive St.,
    "St. Louis, Mo.
"Friend Bob:

"I sent you a copy of an affidavit last week about the Horn case. You remember when we were in Kansas City last fall what Roberts told us about that fellow we met in the Scandivanian saloon not being Tom Horn. I have since found out things that lead me to believe that Roberts was telling the truth. I don't think we ought to let this matter drop now and let Horn be hung without our doing the square

257

thing. As I told you in the letter before, I wrote to Mr. Burke, one of Horn's lawyers, and yesterday I met him again, and he urges me to do everything we can.

"Please attend to this at once, and write me or T. F. Burke, of Cheyenne, Wyo., and tell him the circumstances and what Roberts told us in Kansas City.

"Hoping to hear from you at once, I am,
        "Yours truly,
            "FRANK W. MULOCK"

It seemed as though this evidence must at least save Horn's life.

On the 14th of November, at half past three, the governor made known his decision—he would not interfere. On the afternoon of this day a singular incident came under my notice. At exactly 4 o'clock a man called at my room in the hotel and presented a note from the governor. The note read as follows:

"Miss Kimmell: Will you please let me take those letters again? I read them so hurriedly yesterday I would like to see them again at my leisure. The bearer is my deputy secretary of state. Yours truly, F. Chatterton."

The governor had reference to the correspondence between Attorney Burke and myself in relation to the Horn case. The strange thing is that the governor's written decision had been lying on Judge Lacey's desk for half an hour!

I have been accused of presenting theories as evidence. Would it be too far-fetched a theory to advance that the governor had now found time to consider the evidence, although his decision had already been made; or did he have the deputy take those letters across the street to the prosecuting attorney, so that the latter might make copies of them? It is a fact that after Horn was dead the prosecuting attorney had copies made of his farewell letters to his mother and his sisters. I learn upon unimpeachable authority that while Stoll's stenographer was typewriting these farewell letters, her eyes filled with tears, so that she could hardly write. Stoll, coming into the room, took in the situation and jeered at her. The state's case was ended, so it is evident that his sole purpose was to acquire souvenirs— of what? Of work well done! The hanging of an innocent man!

So it was that on November 20, 1903, at about 11 A.M., Tom Horn was hanged. There are those who can tell the grewsome details. It is enough for his friends to know that he smiled to the last.

After all has been said and done, why was he hung? The answer is: "Because of a drunken talk." It was clearly demonstrated that upon the Sunday morning of his interview with La Fors Horn had forty drinks within him; yet his maudlin words were called a "confession." If his confession was bona fide, it is strange he should so soon afterwards have vigorously denied it and continued to deny it even to his death; and if he had a guilty soul, it is singular he should choose to unburden himself to a mere acquaintance and give no sign to his friends.

It was characteristic of Horn that when he was sober he was quiet in manner and modest, but that when he was drunk he was loquacious and boastful. His own account of his interview with La Fors was that they were trying to out-lie each other, and, as La Fors had turned the subject upon killings, each boasted of killings he had done. The role was an easy one for Horn—it was his stock in trade in the Iron Mountain country. Cow boys on the lone prairie and scouts, far from civilization, when sitting around the campfire, habitually spin yarns; and Horn had been both cow boy and scout. It needed not this training, however, to make him a romancer. He was born one. He had an active imagination, a keen perception and a genius for language. He was truthful in the ordinary affairs of life, but if the spinning of a yarn would give pleasure, he was not one to let facts stand in the way. He always maintained that his statements to La Fors were changed to suit the requirements. The alleged confession is undoubtedly characterized by striking peculiarities.

Aside from the fact that the language used was not that of Horn, it has never been explained why, out of the multitude of his friends, he should have selected John C. Coble and me to speak disparagingly about. Could it be that the authors of the "confession" calculated that nothing but a strong resentment would turn us against him!

Many things conspired to send him to his death, chief among which was the attitude of a number of the newspapers of Wyoming and Denver. These were controlled by parties who would stop at nothing and stoop to anything to ruin the defense. Accordingly they printed great masses of damaging lies, and would not admit the smallest favorable point.

It is said that one of the newspaper reporters of the case being remonstrated with for inaccuracy of statement in the report given gave this excuse: that the best authority upon this class of news laid down the rule for the guidance of reporters as follows: "In case a crime has been committed which incenses the public mind, if the accused is able to divide the publc sentiment, then take the sympathetic side of the case; but if the accused has few or no friends, then jump onto him with both feet and stamp him out of existence, for by so doing you will satisfy the mind of the public and close the incident."

They habitually pictured the prisoner viler than the vilest, and as much a degenerate physically and mentally as spiritually. In addition to this calumny, there was much perjured evidence, and the truth was twisted until it became a lie. Then there were political ambitions in the way.

This was evidenced by a conversation between the governor and the prosecuting attorney of Douglas county, Wyoming. A few hours after the governor had made known his decision, the prosecuting attorney telephoned to him in reference to the Indian outbreak that had recently occurred. While he was making his report the governor interrupted him by asking: "How do the people up there take my decision in the Horn case?" It seems that the governor had taken steps to learn at first hand how the people of Natrona county felt, for during the proceedings before him, he absented himself to attend a dance at Casper.

As a prominent lady aptly put it: "The governor of Wyoming does not believe in capital punishment personally, but he does politically!"

Why Tom Horn should have been convicted will always be an open question, with an ever-increasing number believing in his innocence.

That such a result should have been reached upon the evidence produced, and especially that executive clemency should have been refused in face of the showing made in support of the application therefor, is indeed difficult of explanation.

Tom Horn has been called a murderer of children, but read the following incidences, a few of his many kindnesses to the young and to the suffering:

In the Arizona days the little son of an army officer conceived a great liking for him, and used to follow him around. One day when he, the boy, and other scouts were out riding they were surprised by Indians. A sharp encounter ensued, in which the scouts, being outnumbered, were forced to retreat. As they were dashing off, Horn noticed the boy had slipped from his horse. At the risk of his own life he went back, lifted the child onto the saddle in front of him, and succeeded in escaping.

Sam Moore, former foreman for the Swan Land and Cattle Company, writes:

"Sheriff Cook, of Albany County, Wyoming, told me in the waiting room of the Cheyenne depot at the time of Horn's trial, that Tom and himself (Cook) were in Greeley, Colorado, together, and while standing around the depot, a passenger train came in.

"Among the passengers who got off the train were two or three little, ragged, hungry-looking children, who singled Tom from among the crowd and came up to him, asking for help. Tom instantly acted, and took them to a restaurant and filled them up with a hearty meal. After which he took them to a clothing store, and dressed them up with new clothes and bought each a pair of shoes—as they were bare-footed. Cook said: "Don't tell me a man like him is around killing children."

"Tom once saved my life by a good throw with his lariat at the right time. I shall never forget it."

A family in the Laramie Peak country tell of an altercation between two of their cow boys, in which one was fatally wounded; and how Horn sat for hours by the dying man, nursing him as tenderly as a woman could have done.

Horn hated a thief, and most of all a cow thief; but it was his habit to give a rustler every possible chance for re-

262

form before reporting him. It has frequently been said that in his duties as a stock detective he learned dark secrets of his employers, Ora Haley, Whittaker Brothers and Al Bowie; and it was predicted that if he had to die, he would reveal his knowledge, for these men did not lift a little finger to help him in his trouble; but if he knew of any shady transactions of these men, he kept them to himself.

When his last hour had come and ministers talked to him about his soul's salvation, he listened carefully, but made no hypocritical pretension to a feeling he did not possess. He said he had never thought much about such things, but he realized that one ought to prepare for the future life. Notwithstanding statements to the contrary, he always believed in the life to come, and in redress for human wrongs.

He was the representative of a type not common. He was a man of action, and in times of strenuousness could out-do and out-endure all others; but in his hours of leisure he could be as indolent as a Mexican grandee, and would tell his romances with the ease of a *literateur*.

It would be hard to find Tom Horn's match physically. Standing six feet two, he was built in perfect proportion to his height—broad-shouldered, deep-chested, full-hipped. Without an ounce of superfluous flesh upon him and with muscles of steel, he could perform feats of strength which were the admiration and despair of other men. He was as straight as an Indian; but had the swinging carriage of the old-time frontiersman, with just the suggestion of a swagger in it. With strong jaws, and chin, and nose, he would have been hard-featured but for the full lips which could so easily curve into a smile.

The unflinching stare of his keen eyes which one sometimes encountered, was the signal-light of a sublime nerve— a nerve which enabled him to look a horrible death in the face and smile. This was one reason why his enemies so hated him. They could imprison him, they could kill him— they might even torture him—but they could never make his soul cringe, his nerve falter.

Strong in feeling as he was, he was unfailingly good-natured and polite; and with his German blood, he had inherited the Teutonic sense of humor. Enjoying a good time himself, he liked to see everyone else have one, and many tales can be told illustrative of his big-heartedness. His enemies can call him a desperado, but his whole life was spent in keeping the desperate in check. His experiences were broad and deep, and he rendered much gallant service to his country. Riding hard, drinking hard, fighting hard— so passed his days, until he was crushed between the grind-stones of two civilizations.

The mortal part of him lies in the cemetery at Boulder, Colorado, beneath the western breezes and the western sun-shine which he loved so well; but in the hearts of his friends, Tom Horn will live forever as the nerviest and the biggest-hearted man they have ever known!

GLENDOLENE MYRTLE KIMMELL
Denver, Colo., April 12, 1904

"LIFE'S RAILWAY TO HEAVEN"

[Tom Horn counted among his most valued friends the Irwin brothers, Charles and Frank, and rightly so; for when his last moments had come (moments from which the most devoted shrank), theirs were the last friendly faces he beheld—these two, who were there to sustain him, singing, at the scaffold's foot, with brave tear-choked voices, a song to cheer their former comrade in his extremity.]

Life is like a mountain railroad, with an engineer
    that's brave;
We must make the run successful, from the cradle
    to the grave;
Watch the curves, the fills, the tunnels; never falter;
    never quail;
Keep your hand upon the throttle, and your eye
    upon the rail.

Chorus:
Blessed Savior, Thou wilt guide us till we reach that
    blissful shore,
Where the angels wait to join us, in Thy praise forever more.

You will roll up grades of trial; you will cross the bridge
    of strife;
See that Christ is your conductor, on this lightning
    train of life;
Always mindful of obstructions, do your duty, never fail,
Keep your hand upon the throttle, and your eye upon
    the rail.

You will often find obstructions; look for storms of wind
    and rain;
On a fill, or curve, or trestle, they will almost ditch
    your train;

265

LIFE OF TOM HORN

Put your trust alone in Jesus; and your eye upon the rail.

As you roll across the trestle, spanning Jordan's
swelling tide,
You behold the Union Depot, into which your train
will glide;
There you'll meet the Superintendent, God the Father,
God the Son,
With the hearty, joyous plaudit, "Weary pilgrim,
welcome home."

266

STATEMENT FROM AL SIEBER

TOM WENT TO WORK for me in the government pack train in 1882; he was with me and worked steady with me for three years. A more faithful or better worker or a more honorable man I never met in my life.

During the period of three years, I made numbers of scouting expeditions, and oftentimes needed the help of a man I could rely on, and I always placed Horn in charge; for it required a man of bravery, judgment and skill, and I ever found Tom true to the last letter of the law to any and every trust confided to his care.

In '83 Horn was with me when I went into Mexico with General Crook, and we brought back the Chiricahua Apaches to the White Mountain Reservation here in Arizona. During that trip Horn proved himself a very valuable man to me on many occasions.

In making my side-scouts alone, I would always place Horn in charge of all Indian scouts left behind in camp. This required a man who was cool and had judgment to control and handle these scouts. Also, on other side-trips, when I took a few pack animals, I ever made it a point to take Tom with me, as it very often required me to have a man that I could rely on in every way, as I oftentimes had to split my crowd after being out. At these times I would always put Horn in charge of one set of scouts, tell him where and the time to meet me, and what to do; and I never had him fail to obey my orders to perfection. No matter what came up—rain or snow, clouds or sunshine— Tom was there to meet me, and true to the trust.

This gave me such confidence in him that in 1885, when the Chiricahuas broke away from their White Mountain Reservation here (which caused the Indian War of 1885), and I followed them into Mexico with Captain Crawford, I took Tom Horn along with me. While I was out on the campaign, the balance of the Apaches on the Reservation became very unruly, which caused General Crook to call me from Mexico back to the Indian Reservation here in Arizona Territory. When I left to obey the orders, I placed Horn in charge of my scouts with Captain Crawford, and he stayed in Mexico.

Captain Crawford finally overtook the Indians and had a fight with them. This is the time Captain Crawford lost his life by the Mexican troops who ran onto Crawford's outfit, mistook the camp for hostiles, and opened fire on them. Crawford and Horn yelled to the Mexicans that they were friendly; but before the firing ceased, Crawford lost his life, and Tom Horn was shot through the arm.

Notwithstanding all this, Lieutenant Maus and Tom Horn brought the hostiles, or at least the biggest part of them, back across the line, and would have brought them safe to the Reservation had it not been for some white men camped near the old San Bernardino ranch, who sold the Indians whiskey and mescal. This caused the Indians to become drunk and unruly, and about one-half of them broke away from the Maus command and went back into Mexico. The rest were brought to Camp Bowie, and shipped from there to Florida. This break was the cause of prolonging the Indian War at least one year longer.

Horn's part in the war deserves the greatest praise for his services and the handling of his Indian scouts.

Shortly after this, General Crook was relieved of the command of the department of the southwest, by General Miles, and Horn quit the government service, although I saw him frequently afterwards. He went to work in Pleasant Valley as a ranch hand. After this, there was a fierce war in this section known as the Pleasant Valley war, between the cow men and the sheep men. There were between twenty and thirty men killed during the fight. Tom took no part with either side, although every inducement was offered him to take sides.

Tom remained in that vicinity until he went to Denver, as he told me, to go to work for the Pinkerton outfit. Since that I know nothing of him, only what I read in newspapers.

Now, I wish to state that during the time of three or four years he was around me, and with me, I never once saw him under the influence of liquor. The most he ever drank was a glass of beer when out with a gang of the boys. And knowing him, as I do, and taking all into consideration, I can not, and will not, ever believe that Tom Horn was the man the papers tried to make the world believe he was. These words and sentiments can not be put too strong, for I can never believe that the jolly, jovial, honorable and whole-souled Tom Horn I knew was a low-down miserable murderer.

In regard to my picture, I have none here, and have no show at present to have one taken, and as for my scouting costume, it was ever the same as that of any roving man; for, during my twenty-one years of fighting and hunting hostile Indians, I never wore long hair or buckskin clothes.

Now, sir, if this will be of any benefit, use it to suit yourself. It is all facts to a letter.

Your friend,

AL SIEBER

ROOSEVELT, A. T., APRIL 7, 1904

CLOSING WORD

I HAVE NEVER MADE A STATEMENT for publication. All alleged statements and interviews published, whenever and wherever they may have appeared, were without authority and without any foundation in fact.

Throughout the recent trial, despite argument of friend and abuse of foe, I have invariably refused to be interviewed, realizing the misrepresentation which might await me. Condemned if I spoke, condemned if I did not speak, I found myself driven to the position of a private citizen protecting his individual interests and the interests of others entrusted to his charge from the rapacity of maudlin and not over-scrupulous newsmongers. The marked unfairness of the Colorado-Wyoming press in handling the trial has been unaccountable to the uninformed, but to those who know, this prejudiced attitude may be clear.

Given: a "bunch" of reporters, inferior, unscrupulous space-fillers, of whichever sex, whose instructions have been

"Get copy, copy still,
And then let Justice follow—if she will,"

and then the prisoner at the bar becomes, so far as the news reports are concerned, a "black-hearted, bloody-handed, inhuman monster," and spite, retaliation and baffled scheme for gain combine to hatch brood after brood of lies, harmless or harmful as they may be, and with or without consequences, but lies just the same, deliberately manufactured and circulated. For example, weigh such press statements as these: that Horn at any time lost his nerve; that the defense paid for evidence; that Horn was unruly as a boy; that Duncan Clark resigned his foremanship of the Iron Mountain ranch because of trouble over his testimony;

that Horn tried to kill his jailer the day he attempted to gain his liberty; that Horn was informed of the governor's decision before the 17th day of November, 1903; that Horn's last letter to me was handed over by Proctor, deputy sheriff, to Charles Irwin, *unopened* and in the presence of witnesses at the scaffold; and that I declined to pay any part of the funeral expenses of Horn after his execution.

On the contrary, Horn was never known to lose his nerve; not one cent was paid or offered for evidence; Horn was not incorrigible in his youth; there was not the slightest connection between Duncan Clark's resignation and his testimony at the Horn trial; had Horn desired to shed blood in his attempt to regain his liberty, he could easily have done so, as the jailer was wholly at his mercy; the prisoner was informed of his approaching execution exactly three days before his death, as his letter given on preceding pages of this book shows; his last letter to me (certainly a sacred trust) was desecrated by unfriendly newspaper reporters, passed from hand to hand, and was given Charlie Irwin in the sheriff's office *after* the execution; and I certainly paid, and wished to pay, every item of the funeral expenses—a fact quite easily proven.

Yet it is through these equivocations, and other products of reportorial imagination, that the great and all-fair press, alive (?) to its grave responsibility where a human life is at stake, proves its trustworthiness! It is thus that the all-powerful moulders of public opinion proceed to mould!

And it has not been the press alone, but there have been men in positions of trust, puffed up with their "little brief authority," who have besmirched their trust and stooped to odious means for their selfish ends. If it be true that "kings play chess with nations for pawns," then it is as true that Wyoming politicians play the game of justice with human souls for pawns, and, I may add, with Cowardice as referee.

The story is done. Close the pages that tell of fighting our country's foes, of secret service, of Cuban campaigning, of zeal, of faithfulness, of fearlessness. Unwritten always must remain the record of Tom Horn's bravery, loyalty, generosity, and the countless kindly acts which marked his pathway through life. I am proud to say that he was my friend, always faithful and just. When can I hope to see such another! And no man ever walked more bravely to his death.

I am convinced, and I re-assert it to be true, that Tom Horn was guiltless of the crime for which he died. Nor am I alone in this belief. He suffered the death, but there is a Great and Final Referee in all matters of Justice. To Him— the last and final decision.

JOHN C. COBLE

Iron Mountain Ranch, Bosler, Wyoming,
March 1, 1904